# THE ILLUSTRATED
# ENCYCLOPEDIA OF
# DRESSAGE

# THE ILLUSTRATED
# ENCYCLOPEDIA OF
# DRESSAGE

## COMPILED BY MARTIN DIGGLE

Trafalgar Square Publishing

First published in the United States of America in 2005 by
Trafalgar Square Publishing, North Pomfret, Vermont 05053

**Printed in China**

ISBN-13: 978-1-57076-331-1
ISBN-10: 1-57076-331-3

Library of Congress Catalog Control Number: 2005909243

The sources of photographs and other illustrations used within the text are acknowledged, as
appropriate, within the captions.
Jacket photographs top left, top centre, bottom left (front), top left (back), bottom left (back) and
those on the spine by Elizabeth Furth; bottom right (front) and top right (back) by Bob Langrish;
bottom right (back) by Karl Leck; bottom centre (front) courtesy of Hilda Nelson; other images
(front) postcard from the Spanish Riding School of Vienna and engraving from *A General System of
Horsemanship*.
Designed by Judy Linard
Edited by Jane Lake
Colour separation by Tenon & Polert Colour Scanning Limited, Hong Kong
Printed in China by New Era Printing Co. Ltd, Hong Kong

# ACKNOWLEDGEMENTS

I am grateful to a number of people who have helped in various ways with the compilation of this encyclopaedia. Max Gahwyler, who has done so much to promote dressage in the USA, offered great support to this project, and material he supplied formed the basis for some of the biographical notes on American and American-based riders and trainers. This information was supplemented by details provided by John Bloomer of The Dressage Foundation, and Beth Rasin, of *The Chronicle of the Horse*, supplied a most interesting copy of that journal and generously gave permission to use information extracted from it. Leeta Bobart, former editor of the Australian publication *The Public Arena*, helped enormously in researching the personal details and competition successes of international riders and trainers. Jo Bowns, of British Dressage, kindly provided information on contemporary British riders and answered queries on various points of detail relating to competition rules. Professor Hilda Nelson assisted in matters pertaining to French equestrian history. Penny Hillsdon provided details of the late Franz Rochowansky, and suggested various lines of inquiry; Herbie Rijndorp helped with research on riders and trainers from The Netherlands and Carola Clüver provided invaluable assistance with respect to German personalities and equitation. The TTT, an educational trust who have their own entry in this encyclopaedia, kindly provided biographical information on trainers who give clinics at their establishment.

Thanks are also due to all who checked, amended and added to biographical notes sent for their approval, and to all who supplied photographs and other illustrative material, or gave permission for its use.

Finally, thanks to my friend and colleague, Jane Lake, who undertook the considerable task of editing this work.

# COMPILER'S NOTE

It is the aim of this Encyclopaedia to offer general guidance to the development and practice of dressage, both in its pure sense as 'training' and in its newer role as a competitive sport. Accordingly, it contains biographical entries of eminent trainers, authors and competitors, past and present, explanations of dressage terms and references to the rules of competition.

Any compiler of any sort of Encyclopaedia should be prepared to make the (rather obvious) point that, despite their best efforts, a work of this nature can never be truly finished. There is always more information out there, time moves on and things change. There are various corollaries to this, specific to this book. In the first place, the selection of the personalities included is, inevitably, somewhat arbitrary and reliant upon a variety of factors. Rather than seeking to list them, I would just say that there are doubtless people eminently deserving of inclusion, whose names will not be found in the pages of this edition. However, any relevant details made available to the publisher will gladly be considered for inclusion in future editions.

Ignacio Rambla riding Spanish walk. Photograph by Elizabeth Furth.

Also on the subject of individuals, it will be evident that specific competition successes can only (at best) be up to date at the time of publication and it is intended that further successes by those mentioned will be updated in future editions.

I am most grateful to all those who have helped in supplying information for this Encyclopaedia and I know that all concerned have done their best to ensure accuracy in respect of individuals' biographical details. However, it is sometimes difficult to check such matters in every respect and, if any anomaly is drawn to the publisher's attention, it will be rectified in subsequent editions.

With regard to competition rules, these are subject to minor changes on a regular basis, and points of detail relating to the same issue may also vary between the various organizing bodies. This point is made in many of the entries relating to rules, and readers wishing to ascertain what is, and is not permitted, are advised to check the *current* rules of the organizing body concerned.

So far as the use of this Encyclopaedia for general reference is concerned, the following notes may assist the reader:

Sven Rothenberger on *Jonggor's Weyden*. Photograph by Elizabeth Furth.

**Names of people** These are given surname first: **Steinbrecht, Gustav**. A few older, non-English names may have alternative spellings; in such cases, the form used for the entry is that which appears to be the most commonly used; where known, alternatives are mentioned after this in parentheses, e.g. **Grisone, Federico** (Also rendered as **Federigo** or **Frederic**, and **Grisoni**). Since these alternative forms generally have little impact on the overall spelling (and thus location) of the surname, they have not been given separate entries.

**Sequence of entries** To assist readers in sourcing material, this Encyclopaedia uses a strict letter-by-letter sequence of entries, as opposed to the word-by-word sequence. This has been done to avoid the seeming anomalies that can arise from the latter format (for example, in a word-by-word sequence, **de Pluvinel** would appear before **Decarpentry**). Further to this, names such as de Pluvinel and de la Guérinière are given in these forms, not as Pluvinel, de and Guérinière, de la.

In the German and Dutch languages, names such as Egon von Neindorff and Anky van Grunsven, when listed alphabetically, surname first, will appear in the forms **Neindorff, Egon von; Grunsven, Anky van**. However, since this convention may be unfamiliar to English readers, in this dictionary such names are rendered 'von' and 'van' first, and thus appear under the letter 'V'. This is in accord with the convention, mentioned above, of French names incorporating d' and de appearing under the letter 'D'.

**Sourcing entries** In order to avoid a great deal of repetition and unnecessary cross-referencing, this Encyclopaedia does not detail individually all the words or phrases that might be associated with an entry. Where appropriate, the most obvious noun is used as the basis for the definition. For example, there is an entry **canter**, but no 'cantering'; an entry **anticipation**, but no 'anticipates'. Where this process cannot be readily applied, a form considered especially common in dressage parlance is used, e.g. **lacking bend/impulsion**, rather than 'lacks...'

**Cross-referencing** Where a particular term does not appear within the body of a definition, but it is thought that cross-referencing might be useful to the reader, this is signified by the forms: See/See also **on the aids**.

**Breeds** Since dressage, both as a sport and a training process, is not limited to specific breeds, the very many breeds involved are not given their own entries. There is, however, a brief analysis (under **breed**) of how both dressage itself, and the different types of horses used, have interacted and influenced each other down the centuries.

# THE ILLUSTRATED
# ENCYCLOPEDIA OF
# DRESSAGE

# A

**a la brida**  Describes the style of riding developed in the Renaissance period. The rider sat in a saddle with a very high pommel and cantle, with legs very straight and pushed somewhat forward; the bit used was a very severe curb with a high port and long cheekpieces. This posture and equipment were modified by the influence of leading innovative horsemen over a period of several centuries.

**a la gineta**  A style of riding developed in the Iberian peninsula during the Renaissance period, where the a la brida style was modified under Moorish influence; usually entailed the use of a ring bit, rather than a curb. See also **Duarte, King of Portugal.**

**abduction**  The movement of a limb away from the median plane of the body, i.e. outward, as seen in certain phases of various lateral movements; the opposite of adduction.

**above the bit**  Faulty equine posture, in which the horse's head is carried higher than is desirable for the work being performed, and with a lack of flexion at the poll, which results in some degree of 'poking the nose' and compromises the communication between rider's hand and horse's mouth. A horse's head carriage has a biomechanical relationship to the curvature of the spine and the action of the hindquarters, and this type of head carriage is associated with a hollow back, muscular stiffness and lack of engagement of the hind limbs, the relative degrees of cause and effect being to some

Horse above the bit. Drawing by Maggie Raynor.

extent a product of circumstances. Where the overall training programme is at fault, where the rider's posture and aid applications are seriously flawed, or where the horse is suffering pain arising from faulty tack, all of these problems may be part and parcel of the same root cause. However, a horse may occasionally come momentarily above the bit because he is distracted (perhaps by a strange sight or sound), because he is surprised by a single ill-prepared or misapplied aid, or in response to a brief loss of balance.

A rule of thumb sometimes applied to produce a basic assessment of whether a horse doing straightforward work is above the bit entails drawing an imaginary horizontal line from nose to tail, at the level of his back where the saddle sits. If his nose is evidently higher than this line, it is likely that he is above the bit.

**abrupt**  An essentially self-explanatory judge's remark applied most commonly to downward transitions which are hurried or rough, because the aids were applied too late and/or with too much restraint. See also **restraining aids**.

**accepting the bit**  In the initial stages of training, this refers to the fact that the horse is unconcerned about the presence of the bit in his mouth; he does not play with it excessively, fight against its presence or seek to eject it. At a later stage, it refers to the fact that the horse responds willingly to the action and signals of the bit, flexing his jaw and poll as required by these signals and acknowledging the bit as a 'point of reference' for the purposes of turning, balancing and changing speed and gait.

**accuracy**  In a test, implies that the movements are performed as designated in terms of correct gait/gait variant, that they start and finish at the required points or markers, that transitions are smooth, that lateral work is performed with correct bend and inclination and, where relevant, is symmetrical on both reins, and that the figures are geometrically correct.

Accuracy is a key feature in the performance of a dressage test, not least since its presence or absence is likely to be closely related to the presence or absence of other major criteria; for example, it is very hard for a rider to produce an accurate test if the gaits are irregular, there is insufficient impulsion, the horse is resistant or the rider's own seat and aids are incorrect. However, especially in the lower-level tests, judges may prefer a slight loss of accuracy (in respect of a transition being a little early or late) to a transition that is accurately sited but rough or abrupt. (That is to say, the former is likely to be marked down less than the latter.)

**acting hand**   A hand that is sending a positive signal to the horse via the rein contact, as opposed to a passive hand. See also **yielding hand; taking hand; restraining aids.**

**action**   The manner in which a horse moves, the term usually being applied in the first instance to natural movement. This natural action is chiefly a consequence of the horse's conformation, especially the length of key bones and the angulation of joints between them, although the elasticity or otherwise of tendons and ligaments, and the condition of the muscles, will either heighten or impede this. The horse's temperament and energy level will also have some impact; the natural action of a keen, energetic horse will be more pronounced than that of a dull, lethargic one.

The action of any horse can be influenced positively by appropriate feeding, encouraging active forward movement, and by the progressive development in tandem of both suppleness and strength. Correct training may also serve to reduce faulty limb movement such as dishing or plaiting. However, since the actual skeletal structure of the horse cannot be altered for the better by training, it will inevitably have a major influence on the action of any horse, and this fact should always be taken into account by the rider/trainer. See also **conformation.**

**active**   A general term implying a willingness on the horse's part to move forward in response to relatively little encouragement from the rider. It would normally be understood that the term would not encompass undue hurrying; on the other hand, it would not necessarily imply the presence of powerful impulsion. The term 'pleasantly active' is sometimes used by judges to describe a novice horse whose way of going is generally proceeding along the right lines.

**active elevation**  See **direct elevation.**

Lateral movements such as a half-pass require both abduction and adduction of the limbs (see text). Photograph from Wilhelm Müseler's *Riding Logic*.

**adduction**  The movement of a limb towards the median plane of the body, i.e. inward beneath the body, as seen in certain phases of various lateral movements ; the opposite of abduction.

**Advanced**  Under British Dressage rules, the highest level of tests; includes FEI tests used in national and international competitions.

**Advanced Medium**  Under British Dressage rules, the fifth level of tests; coming between Medium and Advanced.

**affiliated**  Describes a competition connected to, and run under, the rules of an official national or regional organization.

**age, of horse**  The youngest age at which horses can compete under the rules of most dressage organizations is four; very few horses are mature enough, mentally or physically, to benefit from anything other than the most basic training much earlier than this. Training horses to perform the advanced movements correctly is inevitably a fairly protracted process, taking place over a period of years, to allow for the requisite development of strength, suppleness and understanding. Correctly performed dressage movements and exercises will help to keep older horses in good condition, provided that allowance is made for any unavoidable physical degeneration that may compromise the performance of particularly demanding work.

**age, of rider**  National dressage organizing bodies generally divide membership into junior and adult (or senior) sections, the maximum age for juniors usually being eighteen, and the minimum age for adults, twenty-one.

The gap between theses ages is often spanned by a 'young rider' membership, which may, in fact, be open to riders aged 16–21. Many, but not all, competitions are limited to a particular age sector.

**AHSA**   See **American Horse Shows Association.**

**aids, artificial**   Aids other than the rider's own physical attributes (see **aids, natural**) that are intended to support the natural aids, the most common being the spurs and whip. Subject to constraints of design, these two aids are allowed in many dressage competitions – indeed, the wearing of spurs is *compulsory* in many higher-level tests. There are, however, certain variations in the rules governing the use of artificial aids, for example, while a whip is permitted in most 'pure' dressage competitions, it is prohibited in all international events under FEI rules and is generally not permitted in a test that forms part of a horse trial. It is therefore sensible to check the rules that relate to a specific competition with respect to whip and spurs. Other devices that might fit the general definition of artificial aids are more commonly described as auxiliary reins.

**aids, natural**   The rider's own natural physical attributes – seat, weight, legs, hands and voice – that are employed to communicate with the horse. Despite the fact that the voice is indisputably a natural aid, and can play a useful role in training, its use during official dressage competitions is penalized. See **voice, use of.**

**airs above the ground**   Specific movements which entail some form of jumping on the horse's part, some to the extent that, for a while, all four feet are off the ground. These airs have sometimes been performed in slightly differing ways, and described in different words and forms, by different riders and schools of equitation. The eighteenth century French master, de la Guérinère wrote 'We have said that all jumps higher than the terre-à-terre are called airs above the ground. They are seven in number, viz. pesade, mézair, courbette, croupade, ballotade, capriole and the step and the leap [le pas et le saut]'. (For the last, see **un pas un saut.**) Writers nowadays might tend to include the terre-à-terre (an archaic kind of rocking, jumping, two-beat 'canter' on 'two tracks'), in the family of airs above the ground, and also the levade, a lowered form of pesade.

There has long been a debate about the degree to which the airs above the ground were first introduced as battle manoeuvres; some could be seen to have a practical application in this context, with others this seems unlikely. The latter may have been introduced for artistic rather than military reasons, and it is certainly the case that many riders who have developed and performed the airs have been concerned whilst doing so with equestrian aesthetics rather than combat. It is of interest that Thomas Blundeville, translator of Grisone and writing in the reign of Elizabeth I, commented of the airs: '…it is quite sufficient if in the entire royal stables there should be two or three horses capable of these movements' which makes it less likely that they were a requisite for a warhorse. A century of so later, the Duke of Newcastle, who had battlefield experience, dealt with the suggestion that high-school training would be detrimental to a warhorse because the horse would be 'playing tricks' by remarking: 'Even the best horsemen find it difficult to make a horse do "airs" at any time, and

Various airs above the ground being performed at a pillar, from the Duke of Newcastle's *A General System of Horsemanship*.

after three days campaigning they will not go in "airs", even if you would have them.'

While the airs above the ground are still performed by various bodies for display purposes, and by individuals who practise the traditional style of classical equitation, they are not currently required in mainline competition dressage.

**Albrecht, Kurt**   Born in Austria in 1920, Albrecht chose a military career and saw active service as an Artillery Commander in the Second World War, before becoming a prisoner of war in Russia. After the war, he joined the Austrian Constabulary and taught equitation at the Constabulary Central School. Albrecht was a great friend of Hans Handler and, when Handler succeeded Alois Podhajsky as Director of the Spanish Riding School, Albrecht joined the School to assist with administration, being appointed Substitute Director in 1965. In 1974 he succeeded Handler as Director, a post he held until 1985. From 1973 until 1987 Albrecht was in charge of judges' affairs for the Austrian Equestrian Federation, subsequently playing a leading role in equestrian educational advancement. His book *Principles of Dressage* is one of the most thoughtful and thought-provoking books of its genre.

**allures**   An old term from the French, meaning essentially, mode or form of movement. The natural allures were the basic gaits: walk, trot, canter and gallop. The term 'artificial allures' referred not to artificial gaits as such, but to the high and low airs.

**amble**   A lateral gait in which the two feet on one side are lifted more or less as a pair, followed by the two feet on the other side. It is different from a hurried walk that tends towards two-time in that its execution is leisurely, or even lazy. Some breeds and individuals have an inherent tendency to move in this way, rather than to walk correctly, and there have been times when the trait was encouraged by selective breeding, the movement being comfortable for inexpert riders. Amblers were, for example, popular in medieval Europe. Horses with an inborn tendency to move in this way do not make prime candidates for competition dressage since the walk (or approximations to it) is a difficult gait to improve. Where not inherent, ambling can be engendered, especially in lazy horses, both by insufficient use of the forward-driving aids and by crude attempts to 'collect' the walk with overactive hands.

**American Horse Shows Association (AHSA)** The national equestrian federation of the United States of America; produces and upholds rules for national competitions in accordance with FEI directives; devises national-level dressage tests, licenses judges and officials nationally.

**anticipation** The characteristic of a horse who performs a movement, transition, etc. before the rider has given the aids to do so. It can cause inaccuracy and thus loss of marks in a dressage test. Sometimes portrayed as disobedience, it in fact signifies a degree of willingness, intelligence and enthusiasm on the horse's part. Horses with a tendency to anticipate require judicious training, with minimal repetition; repeated schooling of a movement, especially in the same place, or repeated run-throughs of a particular test, will tend to engender anticipation in most horses.

**appui** Also spelt, appuy; an old French term meaning, essentially, contact.

**appuy** Alternative spelling of appui.

**arena** The area in which a dressage test is performed. Nowadays, there are two sizes of arena, 40 m x 20 m, in which most, but not all, of the basic-level tests are performed and 60 m x 20 m, in which all other tests, up to and including Grand Prix level are performed. There is an increasing tendency for some national organizations to devise basic-level tests which are designed to be, or can be, performed in the large arena.

The dressage arena in its modern form is comparatively new. The arena used for the inaugural Olympic Dressage competition (1912) was 40 m x 20 m, but the location of the marker letters would be unrecognizable nowadays. Of the current markers, only A, B, C, D and X were in use, and none of them was in their current position. The 60 m x 20 m arena, used in the 1924 dressage phase of the Olympic three-day event, employed all of the key markers which are still used for the 40 m x 20 m arena, and which form the basis of the modern 60 m x 20 m arena, but the supplementary markers, V, S, R, P, L and I were not added to the Olympic arena until 1932.

The current layout of arenas is shown in the accompanying diagrams.

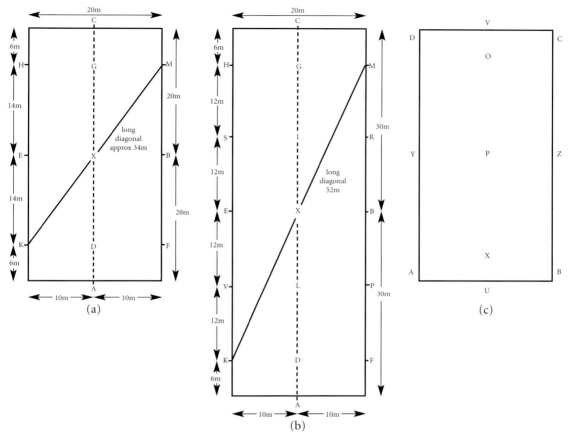

Current layouts of (a) 40 m x 20 m and (b) 60 m x 20 m arenas; (c) shows the layout and markers of the 40 m x 20 m arena used at the 1912 Olympic Games.

**arrest**   See **arret.**

**arret**   Also known as arrest; taken from the French term. A sharp action performed simultaneously with hand and spur (at the girth) to cause a resistant or inattentive horse to flex his haunches.

**artificial aids**   See **aids, artificial.**

**artificial airs**   An old term that was often used to describe any forms of equine movement other than the natural gaits of walk, trot, canter and gallop, these artificial airs being divided into the low airs, such as the pirouette, and the airs above the ground; the word thus had a wider meaning than artificial gaits.

**artificial gaits**   Modes of locomotion not normally demonstrated by horses in their natural state, i.e. those that have been taught for effect rather than to develop the horse's natural way of going; not required in mainline dressage competitions.

**Aubert, P-A**   A nineteenth-century French professor of equitation and author of several works on equitation, the best known of which is *Quelques Observations sur le system de M. Baucher pour dresser les chevaux* (1842). This book, which considers the question of whether Baucher's methods should be adopted by the French cavalry is, essentially, a criticism of those methods.

**auxiliary reins**   Devices based upon, or related to, reins, but with actions supplementary to the normal connection between hand and bit, intended to heighten or augment the influences of the rider's natural aids, especially the hands; available in many forms, some of the most common being

An assortment of auxiliary reins. Illustrations from Ulrik Schramm's *The Undisciplined Horse*. (*Reading anti-clockwise from top left*): running martingale; running rein; Chambon; side-reins; standing martingale; pulley martingale; the commanded de Gogue; the independant de Gogue.

martingales, draw or running reins, the Chambon and the de Gogue. Of these, the last two (named for their inventors) are widely employed, especially in continental Europe, more or less as integral features of work on the lunge (the de Gogue can also be used with the horse under saddle). While most authorities accept the occasional necessity for the informed, refined and targeted use of the appropriate auxiliary rein to correct specific problems in training, their habitual use is generally proscribed and may suggest deficiencies in the rider rather than the horse. The use of auxiliary reins is prohibited during dressage tests and also, under most rules, during the warm-up period prior to the test – the chief exception being that standard side reins are usually permitted when lungeing. Under some rules, certain other minor exceptions exist, for example the AHSA permits the use of a running martingale (only in conjunction with a snaffle) whilst warming up. Under British Dressage rules, however, using auxiliary equipment other than side reins during the warm-up results in elimination of rider, owner (if different) and horse from *all classes on the day of the transgression*. See also **forbidden equipment**.

# B

**backing**   The process of acclimatizing a previously unridden horse to having a rider on his back, from the stage of first accepting the rider's presence and weight, up to the stage at which the horse can be directed quietly around an enclosed area without sustained assistance from the ground.

**balance**   Fundamentally, the quality that permits a horse to remain upright; derived from an interaction between the nervous system and the musculature. The presence of a rider on a horse's back necessarily has an influence on the horse's balance, and poor rider posture and ill-applied aids can adversely affect this balance. In order to achieve optimum balance, and thus optimum efficiency of movement, it would be ideal for the burden of the rider's weight to be vertically above the horse's centre of gravity but, because of the horse's physique (long, relatively heavy head and neck) and the location of the saddle on the lowest part of the back, this positioning does not occur naturally – instead, the rider is positioned somewhat behind the horse's 'natural' centre of gravity. One object of training is, therefore, to strengthen and supple the horse and to encourage him to engage his hindquarters further under his body, thus moving his centre of gravity back towards that of the rider. This will occur to a certain extent in correctly performed collected movements, and the classical movements which demonstrate that it has been achieved to an advanced extent are the levade and the courbette. If strengthening, suppling and engagement of the hindquarters are not pursued, and the horse is allowed or encouraged to move with hindquarters trailing, the effect will be to move his centre of gravity further away from that of the rider, placing him on the forehand. In fast and free movement (especially gallop, but also extended trot and canter) the biomechanics of the movement are such that the mean (average) location of the horse's centre of gravity is further forward than in the collected gaits.

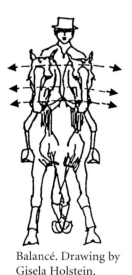

Balancé. Drawing by Gisela Holstein.

**balancé** A term that describes faulty movement in piaffe and passage. The root cause is insufficient true collection; because of this, the hind limbs are not carrying enough weight or generating enough upward thrust so the horse attempts to elevate his forehand via his forelegs. He pushes off with one foreleg and, while this provides some degree of lift, it also drives the shoulders to the side, so that the other foreleg is obliged to step away from the body to counteract the unbalancing push; it then initiates a push of its own. The consequence is a widened stance of the forelimbs, with the weight of the forehand oscillating from one forelimb to the other. The fault is often seen in horses who are somewhat lacking in strength of the hindquarters and/or are being asked for more limb elevation than they are currently capable of delivering.

**Balkenhol, Klaus** Born in 1939 in Westphalia, Germany, Balkenhol grew up on his father's farm, where he displayed an enormous enthusiasm for riding everything available, including the family goat! As a young adult, he chose to join the Dusseldorf Police Force rather than doing national service, and after six years, he became a mounted policeman. During this period, he developed

24

his interest in both the old classical masters and modern competition dressage, and tried to put theory into practice whilst riding on patrol. He also participated in National Mounted Police Competitions. When the horse he had been riding was retired, he was allowed to select a replacement with the idea of competing at a higher level. Balkenhol's choice was *Goldstern*, with whom he won the individual bronze medal at the 1992 Olympics, and team gold both that year and at Atlanta in 1996. Balkenhol's other successes included team gold medals at the European Championships in 1991, 1993 and 1995 and a silver medal at the 1994 World Equestrian Games at The Hague. He subsequently became coach to the German dressage team that won team gold and individual silver and bronze medals at the Sydney Olympics in 2000. In 2001 he resigned from his position as German coach and became coach to the USA dressage team but continues to live in Germany, to where the American riders travel to train.

**ballotade**   One of the airs above the ground. The horse makes a single leap into the air, so that all of his legs attain the same height; he then 'shows his heels' as though about to kick out with his hind legs, but does not actually do so.

Ballotade from the time of the Duke of Newcastle.

**balloting**   A procedure used by competition organizers if a particular class is over-subscribed. Competitors who are initially balloted out of the class are usually put in sequence on a waiting list and notified of the fact. If other entries then withdraw, the appropriate number from the waiting list have the opportunity to take their places. Competitors should refer to the rules of the organizing body concerned for the precise procedure involved.

**bandages**   Sometimes applied to horses' legs for support or protection when schooling, bandages are not normally permitted during a test, although they may generally be worn whilst warming up. They are, however, allowed in some specialized classes under certain rules, for example the AHSA rules allow them in quadrilles and pas de deux.

**baroque**   A term originally applied to the ornate architectural and musical styles of seventeenth- and eighteenth-century Europe, it is applied by extension to the classical high-school equitation of that period, and to the close-coupled, naturally high-stepping horses favoured in that era.

**Bartels, Tineke**   Born Tineke De Vries in Eindhoven, The Netherlands, in 1951, she began her competitive riding career as a showjumper, and then switched to eventing. Following her marriage to Joep Bartels, and the birth of her two children, she turned to pure dressage. She has competed in four Olympic Games since1984, winning team silver both in 1992 at Barcelona and in 1996 at Atlanta. She has also represented her country at two World Championships, winning team silver in 1986, and at five European Championships (winning one team silver and two team bronze medals). She also rode at the World Equestrian Games in 2002 and has competed in the World Cup on nine occasions. It was, in fact, her husband Joep's idea to create the World Cup, incorporating the Kür, and it was as a consequence of this that the Kür was incorporated into the Olympic Games.

She has also been involved in various activities to promote dressage, including writing on the subject, giving seminars, teaching and training. In recognition of these contributions to Dutch dressage, she has received an honour from the Queen of The Netherlands.

**Bartle, Christopher**   Born in 1952 in Yorkshire, England, the son of a former Major in the Royal Artillery and a mother (Nicole), who ran a riding centre. While he had ample opportunity to ride as a child, it was not until young adulthood that this developed into a passion. Then, between school and university, he spent some time in France, studying under Commandant de Parisot, former chief écuyer at the Cadre Noir. On returning to England, he trained with the Olympic medallist, Hans von Blixen-Finecke and attended Bristol University, where he gained an honours degree in economics and, whilst studying, hunted and competed on horses owned by Mary and Peter Fry. After completing his degree, he spent some time riding as an amateur jump jockey, before returning to the family riding centre. It was then that he acquired the former point-to-point horse *Wily Trout*, as a mount to take three-day eventing. Following a highly successful career in that discipline, this partnership began to specialize in pure dressage, winning a major class at Aachen and being placed 6th individually at the 1984 Los Angeles Olympics – the highest placing yet achieved by a British rider. They were also second in the World Cup in 1985.

After *Wily Trout's* retirement, Bartle concentrated again on eventing, being a member of the British team that won gold at the 1997 European Championships and also winning the Badminton Horse Trials on *Word Perfect* in 1998. In addition to his successes as a competitor, he has trained a number of top event riders and was appointed dressage trainer to the British three-day event teams at the 1996 and 2000 Olympics. In 2004, he was trainer to the German Olympic three-day event team; he is also Managing Director of the family's Yorkshire Riding Centre.

Christopher is not the only member of the Bartle family to have made a mark on the equestrian world. In addition to her abilities as an instructor, his mother, Nicole, applied her linguistic skills to translating into English such equestrian classics as Decarpentry's *Academic Equitation*, Üdo Burger's *The Way to Perfect Horsemanship* and Ulrik Schramm's *The Undisciplined Horse*. His sister, Jane Bartle-Wilson, a very successful dressage rider, represented Britain internationally and, along with her brother, was a member of the British Olympic team in 1984.

**base of support**   Effectively, the mean distance between a horse's hind feet and forefeet, both at halt and in movement, with particular reference to the gait variants. For example, in collected canter, when the horse is moving in a rounded outline, with his hind legs engaged well beneath his body, his base of support will be much shorter than when he is performing extended canter.

**Baucher, François** (1796–1873) A highly controversial figure, who rode entirely in the manège, Baucher began his career under the tutelage of his uncle, director of stables to the Governor of Milan. Whilst in Italy, he would have witnessed the practices of the old Neapolitan School, which were still dominant in that country.

In 1816, political upheaval saw Baucher's return to France, where he managed and taught in several private manèges. In 1834, he moved to Paris and established a relationship with the fashionable Franconi circus. Riding

François Baucher, as depicted in General Decarpentry's *Academic Equitation.*

haute école in the circus gave Baucher the prestige he yearned for, and in 1842 he published his 'new method' (*Méthode d'Equitation basée sur de nouveaux principes*).

In 1855, Baucher was badly injured when the chandelier of an indoor school fell on him. Thereafter, he never performed in public again, although he remained able to do some riding and teaching. In later life, he became very reflective and appears to have modified some of his earlier ideas.

The controversy that surrounded Baucher's writing and teaching is well documented in Hilda Nelson's *François Baucher the Man and his Method*, in which the author writes: 'The goal of Baucher's method is the total disposition of the horse's strength and the total submission of the horse to the will of the horseman.' Eminent figures of the time who disagreed strongly with his methods included the Comte d'Aure, Louis Seeger and Gustav Steinbrecht. What is beyond question is that Baucher trained a number of dangerous horses to perform advanced movements in a remarkably short time, and James Fillis said of him: 'He had the great merit of not describing anything which he could not do.'

Baucher remains respected, in whole or in part, by many eminent authorities and his reputation is believed by some to have been compromised by equestrian politics, the limitations of his own powers of expression, and the insensitivity of his translators.

**behind the bit**   A term used to describe the attitude of a horse who is not willing to take a regular, light contact with the bit and thus tucks or cramps his head and neck behind the position he would adopt were he willing to do so. The reason for this attitude may be simple disobedience or nappiness but it is more commonly rooted in ineffective use of the rider's driving aids and/or discomfort caused by heavy rein aids, misdirected attempts to impose a certain head carriage, or inappropriate bitting.

Horse behind the bit. Drawing by Maggie Raynor.

**behind the leg**  An idiomatic phrase used to describe a horse who is not properly attentive to the rider's leg aids; there is no immediate forward impulse in response to the rider's forward-driving leg aids; the horse is not fully between leg and hand or on the aids; the opposite of in front of the leg.

**behind the movement**  Said of a rider whose posture is out of balance and harmony with the horse's movement in such a way as to compromise and retard the free forward movement of the horse; typically, the rider's seat may be too far back in the saddle, with the weight distributed in such a way so to prevent the horse's back muscles from operating properly; the horse may even 'hollow' away from seat. As corollaries to such a posture, there may be a restrictive rein contact and the rider's legs may not in be in the optimum position for applying the aids.

**behind the vertical**  Describes the angle of the horse's face when it drops behind a line perpendicular to the ground. When the horse is being ridden in a collected, working, medium or extended gait, this is always considered to be a fault and is often a sign that the horse is overbent, behind the bit or working with a 'broken neck'. However, if a horse is being ridden correctly in a low and round outline as a stretching and suppling exercise, his head may be a little behind the vertical simply as a consequence of the low angle of his neck.

Faulty head position of a horse who is behind the vertical. Drawing by Gisela Holstein.

29

Paul Belasik. Photograph by Karl Leck from *Dressage for the 21st Century.*

**Belasik, Paul**  Born in Buffalo, New York in 1950, Belasik showed a strong affinity with animals from childhood, his early interests including monkey breeding and falconry, as well as horses. After entering Cornell University as part of the pre-veterinary programme, he graduated with a science degree and had, in the meantime, won prizes for his painting and become a published poet.

By the time of his graduation in 1971, Belasik's career as a horseman had already begun; he taught college courses, evented and competed in dressage at all levels. However, never really excited by competition, he began to focus more on an in-depth study of equitation for its own sake. Initially involved in breeding and training German horses, he focused first upon the German system, broadening and deepening his studies to encompass the different schools of riding. He cites as major influences H.L.M. van Schaik, who instilled in him a love of the classicists and Nuno Oliveira, with whom he spent some time in Portugal. His interest in the philosophical aspects of equitation has been augmented by studies of Zen Buddhism and the martial arts, and these influences are evident in his equestrian writings, which include *Riding Towards the Light, Exploring Dressage Technique, The Songs of Horses* and *Dressage for the 21st Century.*

As a trainer, Belasik holds clinics and lectures on a national and international basis. His broad-based clientele includes international competitors and riders of all levels who do not necessarily compete.

**bend**  A term generally used to signify the lateral flexion throughout a horse's body; can sometimes be qualified, for example as 'bend only in the neck', to signify a faulty attempt at shoulder-in.

**bending**  The process of acquiring or exhibiting bend, as in 'bending round the rider's inside leg', or 'bending through a corner'.

**Berenger, Richard**   Master of the Horse to King George III; translator into English of Claude Bourgelat's *Le Nouveau Newcastle*...In 1771 Berenger also published his own work *History and Art of Horsemanship*. The book, which included a translation of Xenophon's *Hippike*, was described by W.S. Felton as '...the last significant English book which sought to present a scientific approach to classical horsemanship (prior to the twentieth century)...'

**better**   A remark sometimes used by a judge to indicate that a way of going continued from one test movement into another has improved in the latter movement.

**between leg and hand**   Describes the state of a horse who is responding to the rider's leg aids (going readily forward from the leg) and accepting the contact of the bit; the necessary basis for the rider to exercise any real, regular control. See also **on the aids**.

**bilateral**   On both of two sides.

**biomechanics**   The relationship between the physiology of living creatures and the laws and principles of physics and mechanics. For example, the bones of a horse's hind legs are, in mechanical terms, a series of levers that articulate at the joints by the motivating actions of the muscles and tendons. Some understanding of how the horse 'works' in these terms is essential if training is to be effective. The precise biomechanical functions of an individual horse will be influenced by his specific conformation, which is why certain aspects of conformation are favoured, or not, depending upon the use for which a horse is intended.

**bit**   Strictly speaking, the main (curb) mouthpiece of a double bridle; historically, there was a distinction made between the bit (curb) and bradoon. However, the term is now used in common parlance to signify any mouthpiece (including the various forms of snaffles) to which the reins are attached.
   In dressage tests, it is compulsory to use a bit (or bits, in the case of a double bridle); bitless bridles are not permitted. National bodies have rules relating to the types of bit permitted, which are generally based on the FEI rules. The details of the rules are quite complex and are subject to periodic

modification to take account of innovations in bit design, and riders wishing to use anything other than long-established basic patterns of snaffles, bradoons or curb bits would be wise to consult the up-to-date rules of the organizing body concerned to check validity. This remark also applies to the use of snaffles or double bridles. Generally, it is the case that the former are compulsory at the lowest levels of competition (under British Dressage rules, Preliminary and Novice) and the latter compulsory at the highest levels (Advanced and International competitions), with either being permitted at the intermediate levels, but specific checks should be made as necessary.

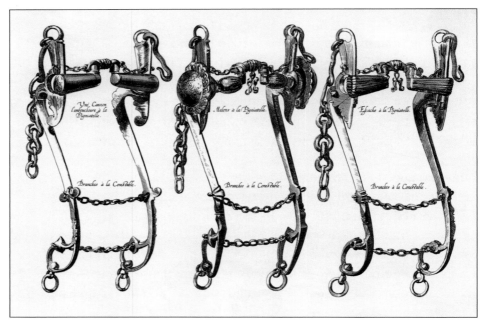

Examples of antique bits, from the Duke of Newcastle's *A General System of Horsemanship*.

**bit guards**   Devices, usually in the form of rubber disks, sometimes fitted to a snaffle just inside the bit rings, intended to protect the outer edges of the horse's lips from pinching or rubbing. Not normally necessary if the bit is appropriate to the horse's mouth, and not permitted during competition.

**blocking**   Impairment of the communication between horse and rider as a result of sustained muscular contraction. Blocking can be instigated by either horse or rider, and may sometimes be sustained by both. However, it inevitably impairs the quality of the work or movement being performed, and the wise rider will always try to seek a solution. Depending on the nature of the blocking and the rider's skill, this may take various forms, but a basic remedy is to reduce the demands being made upon the horse and to encourage restoration of free forward movement.

**body armouring**   A term sometimes used to describe a horse's response to fear or confusion that takes the form of tension in all the main muscle groups. Humans and other animals show the same instinctive response in certain circumstances. Although, in horses, body armouring may at one level involve resistance or apparent disobedience to the aids, it is rarely the aids *as such* that the horse is reacting to; it is more likely the case that obeying the aids will involve the horse in something he perceives to be dangerous or painful, or that he does not understand what is required and is fearful of the consequences of misinterpreting the signals. As prey animals, it is probable that most horses will exhibit this response on some occasion, but where it is seen on a regular basis it is usually an indication that the rider/trainer is making demands that the horse is not psychologically equipped to cope with.

**Boldt, Harry**   Born in Insterburg, East Germany, in 1930, the son of the highly regarded equestrian Heinrich Boldt, supervisor of a competition yard in Essen. With his father as his first instructor, Boldt became a successful showjumper then, trained by Käthe Franke, his main focus switched to dressage. In 1964, riding *Remus* at the Tokyo Olympics, he won team gold and individual silver medals, a feat he repeated twelve years later in Montreal, riding *Woycek*. During the 1970s Boldt won the German National Championship three times; he also won seven individual and eight team medals at various European and World Championships and was awarded the German Riders' Gold Medal of Honour for his perform-ances. From 1981 to 1996 he was coach to the German dressage team, during which period the team won a total of fifty medals at Olympic, European and World Championships, thirty-one

Harry Boldt. Photograph by Elizabeth Furth.

33

of them being gold. He was also the individual trainer of German team member Nicole Uphoff from 1988 to 1995.

The author, in 1978, of the highly regarded book *Das Dressur Pferd*, Boldt married Australian dressage rider Margo Lippa in 1990 and now resides in Perth, Australia, where he is involved in training the national team.

**Bonde, Count Carl** The Swedish rider who won the first Olympic gold medal for dressage, at the 1912 Stockholm Olympics, riding *Emperor*. In its inaugural year, the dressage competition was called Individual Prize Riding and included various elements not seen nowadays. Bonde subsequently judged at the Olympic Games in 1928, 1932 and 1948.

Ellen Bontje. Photograph by Elizabeth Furth.

**Bontje, Ellen** Born in The Netherlands in 1958, Bontje rode as a child and then went to work in a racing stable. At the age of twenty-one, she went to Germany to work with Josef Neckermann, initially as a groom. In 1982, she started to train with Conrad Schumacher, while continuing to work with Neckermann until his death. Having achieved considerable success at Grand Prix level, her first appearance in the Dutch Olympic team came at Seoul in 1998, where she scored the highest marks of the team, then at both the 1992 and 2000 Olympics she was a member of the team that won silver medals. She was also a member of the Dutch teams that won silver at the 1994 and 1998 World Championships and has represented her country at five European Championships, at which the teams have won three silver medals and one bronze.

**Borg, Major Robert** Born in 1913, the son of an American army officer and a Spanish mother, Borg spent his latter childhood on the family farm in Oregon, surrounded by horses. After graduating, he spent some time at Warm Springs Reservation, helping to round up wild horses and subsequently breaking and training them.

Borg first became interested in dressage when he attended the Los Angeles Olympics in 1932, being enthralled by the schooling sessions. In

1940, Hiram Tuttle, who had ridden in those Games, visited Oregon to give a Grand Prix exhibition. Afterwards, Borg approached Tuttle, who was much impressed by his enthusiasm, and invited him to his farm to evaluate his skills. Surprised and impressed by Borg's ability, Tuttle continued to help him and the pair became great friends.

Shortly after their meeting, war broke out and Borg enlisted, becoming the very last enlisted man to be assigned to the cavalry. In 1943, he became an instructor in the Department of Horsemanship at Fort Riley, and in 1947, he outscored Tuttle in the Army Olympic Trials.

Prior to the 1948 Olympics in London, Borg went with the American equestrian team to train in Munich, where he met, worked with and befriended the eminent German trainer, Otto Lörke. Borg personally trained four horses for these Olympics and worked with two of the team members, and America won team silver, with Borg fourth individually. In 1952, he trained the American three-day event team that won an Olympic bronze medal and in the 1955 Pan-American Games, Borg won individual silver.

In 1959, a freak accident left Borg's legs paralysed but, after being told he could never ride again, he personally devised a platform from which he could mount. However, since he could no longer ride as he used to, he gave up judging, another activity he had been involved in for many years. One of his rare qualities as a judge was that he always issued an open invitation to any competitor to discuss their performance at the end of a competition – a practice that led to him giving many impromptu lessons.

**boring on the bit**   The action of a horse who deliberately bears down on the bit with his head and neck, in an attempt to wrest control from the rider's hands; this may be a response to undue constraint on the rider's part, or simply an act of insubordination – discerning the difference between the two is crucial to effecting a cure. A similar action may also be seen in generally submissive horses who are suffering from the effects of an upper respiratory tract infection (i.e. discomfort or congestion). It differs from leaning on the bit and on the forehand in that boring is an overt activity as distinct from simply poor balance. See also **nose-diving**.

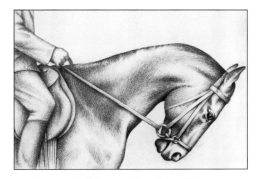

Boring on the bit. Drawing from Üdo Burger's *The Way to Perfect Horsemanship*.

**Bourgelat, Claude** (1712–1779) Born in Lyons, France, Bourgelat managed the Riding Academy in that city for some twenty-five years from 1740. In 1744 he published his highly influential book *Le Nouveau Newcastle, ou Nouveau Traité de cavalerie géometrique, théorique et pratique*, which was translated into English by Richard Berenger, Master of the Horse to King George III. While this was Bourgelat's only book on equitation, he produced many publications on veterinary matters. In 1762 he founded, and became Principal of, the first Veterinary School in Lyon and, at the request of King Louis XV, subsequently founded the second Veterinary School at Alfort, near Paris.

**bracing the back** An action in which the rider increases the tonicity of the lumbar muscles and pushes the lumbar vertebrae forwards a little; this being achieved largely through accentuating the stretch in the body, rather than by leaning back. The effect is not achieved by overtly hollowing the back, which just creates stiffness and compromises the ability of the seat to perform its shock-absorbing role. The correct adjustment of posture reinforces the relationship between the rein contact and the effect of the rider's seat bones and the action is usually a component element of the half-halt. As with all aids, the effect should not be prolonged unnecessarily.

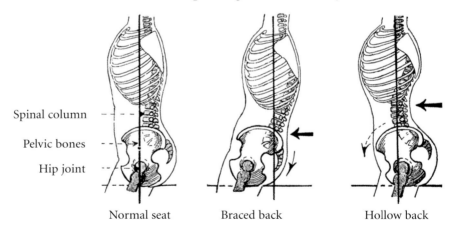

Spinal column

Pelvic bones

Hip joint

Normal seat        Braced back        Hollow back

Drawings of actions of the back, from Wilhelm Müseler's *Riding Logic*.

**bradoon** Also called bridoon; the upper of the two bits of a double bridle; generally formed as a lighter and somewhat thinner than standard snaffle; essentially performs the same function as a snaffle, this being augmented as required by the action of the curb.

36

**bradoon rein**   The rein which attaches to the rings of the bradoon on a double bridle.

**break gait**   To change from the intended or prescribed gait into another gait; an action on the horse's part that does not involve a conscious or intended signal from the rider. The gait may be broken upward (e.g. from trot to canter) as a result of excitement or anticipation on the horse's part, or because of inappropriately applied driving aids from the rider; or downward (e.g. from canter to trot) as a result of inactivity, loss of balance or unwittingly constraining aids from the rider. When occurring in a dressage test, is often signified by the judge with the term 'broke'.

**breed**   A particular, distinct race or stock of horses, the genealogy of which is normally recorded by the associated breed society. There are not usually any restrictions concerning breed in competitive dressage, except when a particular competition, perhaps run by a breed society or association, is open only to horses of that breed. However, as a consequence of typical breed characteristics of conformation, horses of particular breeds may be more or less readily disposed to perform certain movements, and typical breed temperament may also influence tractability and other factors pertaining to training.

Through the centuries, and throughout the equestrian world, the types and breeds of horses popular for various reasons (especially military, aesthetic and sporting considerations) have influenced the development of dressage and the types of movements performed. Also – and perhaps to an increasing degree in more recent times – the requirements of dressage (and other equestrian sports) have had an influence on breeding.

From the Renaissance period and through the seventeenth and eighteenth centuries, close-coupled, high-actioned horses, whose conformation lent itself readily to high degrees of collection, were favoured, and much emphasis was placed upon lateral work, high-school movements and the airs above the ground, performed in a manège that would be considered  small today. Extension, in the modern sense of the word, was not performed – when de la Guérinière writes of 'the extended, brisk trot on a circle' he is clearly referring to some degree of lengthening of a relatively collected gait, rather than the extended trot performed today.

Perhaps the most famous of the breeds to provide the 'type' favoured in this era was the Lipizzaner, still used today in the Spanish Riding School. However, it is noteworthy that this breed was itself derived from an admixture of Andalusian, Neapolitan and native Northern Italian stock, successively crossed with various other breeds. Thus it is evident, even in that era, that dressage practitioners were keen to refine the raw material with which they were working.

The eighteenth century saw the emergence of the Thoroughbred as a new breed, initially in England. Developed with an emphasis on racing, it became more influential in the hunting field and in the breeding of officers' chargers and, by the early nineteenth century, the Thoroughbred and its way of going across country were attracting attention in continental Europe. While this interest had both military and sporting aspects, these were closely combined, since many of the leading equestrian figures of the era were serving cavalry officers. One consequence of this interest was that a number of breeders began to add Thoroughbred blood to breeds that had been fundamentally of light draught type, producing finer, relatively long-bodied, but still powerful horses, the precursors of the modern Warmblood 'sport horses'. Much debate was stimulated as to whether, and how, the traditional, highly collected riding style of the manège should be adapted to riding this new type of horse, in particular across country, but also in the school. The more astute figures of the period, whilst retaining the classical principles of riding, modified their technique to take account of the different conformation, developing, for example, a degree of extension which had not been achievable with the smaller, shorter-coupled horses of earlier times.

It was towards the end of the nineteenth century that competitive dressage began to emerge as an embryonic sport and it is noteworthy that, the first time dressage appeared in the Olympic Games (1912), the arena used was 40 m x 20 m, significantly bigger than the average manège of earlier times. By the time of the next Olympics (1920), the arena had expanded to 60 m x 20 m, and extended trot and canter were designated movements. As competitive dressage continued to develop through the twentieth century more emphasis, in terms of the movements and how they were judged, was placed on work that suited the 'modern' type of horse rather than the older baroque type. Interesting observations about this process have been made by authorities such as Alois Podhajsky (*My Horses, My Teachers*, etc.), who competed at the highest level on both Lipizzaners and the 'newer' breeds; during this era. The increasing emphasis on extended work did not, however, preclude the need for collected movements such as piaffe, passage, pirouettes, etc., and these dual requirements heightened demands for horses who could do both with, as nearly as possible, equal facility. In many cases, these demands were met by Warmbloods specifically bred to achieve a conformation which allowed for flamboyant extension but also provided the power and elevation necessary for collected work. While horses of this type have been prevalent in top competition in the modern era, it is perhaps true to say that the current trend is towards a slightly lighter, more refined stamp. It should also be added that some individual horses who do not conform to this modern type have been highly successful, by virtue of excellent rider/horse rapport, and the fact that the horses perform the movements to which they are best suited extremely well, and those to which they are not best suited, to the very best of their ability. Further to this, there has also been something of a revival of interest in the 'old' types, with breeds such as the Lusitano and Andalusian performing creditably in major competitions. Enthusiasts for such horses (and others who see beyond the boundaries of competition) make the valid point that dressage, ultimately, is not concerned with meeting arbitrary criteria (achieving a specific length of stride, etc.) but with perfecting the training of the individual horse.

**bridle** The horse's headgear to which the reins and bit(s) are attached. The organizing bodies of competition dressage have various rules relating to the type of bridle permitted for different competitions, the most fundamental of which relates to the use of the snaffle (single) bridle and the double bridle at the various levels. Additionally, there are rules relating to other parts of, or adjuncts to, the bridle, including patterns of noseband, bit guards, tongue straps, anti-fly impregnated browbands, fly fringes and nose gauze. Such rules are subject to minor variation, and it is advisable to check the current rules of the relevant organizing body before attempting to use any bridle or associated equipment that varies from the most common patterns. See also **bit; tack**.

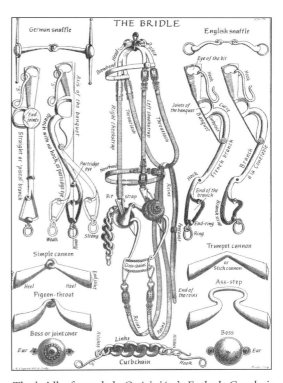

The bridle, from de la Guériniére's *Ecole de Cavalerie*.

**bridle hand**   Through the Renaissance period and for some time onward, it was customary for riders to hold the reins in one hand – usually the left – the other thus being free, either in practice or principle, to hold a weapon. The hand in which the reins were held was thus known as the bridle hand.

**bridle lameness**   A gait irregularity which may mimic that occasioned by physical injury, but for which actual physical injury is not the cause. Usually manifested by the ridden (or sometimes simply bitted) horse taking a short step with one leg, this movement disappearing when the horse is led in a headcollar or turned loose. At its most basic level, bridle lameness is associated with restrictive (and especially uneven) rein contact, particularly if the leg and hand aids are not employed in appropriate combination. At a more complex level, it is associated with making demands of the horse that do not accord with his current level of training, for example asking too much collection of a horse who has not yet been sufficiently straightened, especially when the residual crookedness is related to one hind leg being stronger than the other.

**bridling**   An old term, used to convey the idea that the horse is accepting the bit to the extent of willingly flexing the poll and jaw; the term 'fully bridled' had much the same meaning as ramener.

**bridoon**   See **bradoon**.

**Brink, Jan**   Born in Hoor, Sweden in 1960, Brink initially competed as an eventer; he was also a top-class ice-hockey player and a member of the Swedish national team. After attending Bereiter Schule in Warendorf, Germany, and training with Kyra Kyrklund, he became a regular member of the Swedish dressage team, winning team bronze at the 1998 World Championships in Rome. He has also taken part in four European Championships and two Olympic Games (2000 and 2004) and competed at the World Equestrian Games in Jerez in 2002. He now runs his own training centre in Sweden.

**British Dressage**   The national organizing body for dressage in Great Britain; promotes and regulates the sport in Britain, manages the representation of Great Britain in international dressage competitions and advises the British Equestrian Federation on dressage matters.

**broke**   See **break gait**.

**broken neck**   A term used to describe an incorrect or 'false' flexion of the neck; instead of a correct flexion at the poll and a graceful arching of the neck, there is marked flexion of the neck behind the second vertebra. This faulty outline is usually the consequence of a rider trying to pull the horse into an outline, instead of riding him forwards onto the bit. If a horse becomes confirmed in this outline, he may learn to use it as an evasion and 'run away with his head in his chest'.

'Broken neck'. Drawing from Ulrik Schramm's *The Undisciplined Horse.*

**brushing**   Known as interfering in the USA; the striking of the inside of the fetlock area of one foot by the opposite foot. This may be the result of serious flaws in conformation, in which case it will seriously affect the level to which the horse can be trained, or minor flaws exacerbated by lack of muscular development, in which case it should be minimized as the horse gains in strength, or of transitory conditions such as fatigue and/or lack of balance. If a horse has a tendency to brush, this should be alleviated through simple work designed to improve musculature, straight movement and good balance before any greater demands are made.

**brushing boots**   Boots designed to protect the horse's limbs from the effects of brushing; most organizing bodies allow the wearing of protective boots whilst warming up for competition, but they are not allowed during the test itself.

**bucking**   A jump, or series of jumps by the horse, in which the back is arched and the head and neck lowered to a marked extent as a continuation of the arching of the back; the horse may also kick out with the hind legs and twist the body laterally to a greater or lesser extent. Horses at liberty may sometimes buck through sheer exuberance and fresh horses under saddle may perform mild bucks as a form of 'jumping for joy' during the first minutes of being ridden, an action typically accompanied by pricked ears. This latter action is markedly different from violent bucking, carried out with the obvious intention of dislodging the rider – an activity that signifies serious rebellion on the horse's part. Bucking that is contrary to a horse's usual character may signify pain, and a physical investigation of the horse, and possibly the saddle and girth, is advisable. Bucking (for any reason) during a dressage test will always be viewed as disobedience and any movements in which it occurs will be marked down by the judge.

**Burger, Üdo** (1914–1980) One of Germany's most respected veterinary surgeons and animal psychologists, Burger was an accomplished horseman and a highly respected judge. Involved with horses from an early age, he was reputed to become fretful if unable to spend some time each day in their company. Very obviously a horse lover, he wrote (without giving specific detail) that a horse had actually saved his life in wartime. His professional skills gave him a profound understanding of both the horse's movement and motivation, and he could be blunt in his criticism of rough riding, and of those who made insufficient effort to understand the horse's nature. His thorough understanding of the horse, both in biomechanical and psychological terms, and his intolerance of what he termed 'bogus horsemanship', are evident in his book *The Way to Perfect Horsemanship.*

**Bürkner, Felix** Born in Göttingen, Germany in 1883, Bürkner had his first riding lesson at the university riding school of that town at the age of twelve.

He subsequently became an artilleryman and attended the military riding academy in Hanover, during which time his equestrian exploits included hunting and racing. Within two years, he won six imperial prizes, among them a form of eventing competition for German officers. In 1912, he participated at

Felix Bürkner riding the Thoroughbred *Caracalla*. Photograph from Waldemar Seunig's *Horsemanship.*

the first Olympic Games in Stockholm, finishing 7th, and subsequently worked as a riding instructor at the Hanover military academy. After the First World War, he founded both a show stable in Berlin and the German Riding School in Düppel (in the south-west of Berlin) and went on to become one of the most successful German riding instructors of the 1920s and 30s. In 1937, when the army built a new cavalry school in Krampnitz, Bürkner became its Director. During this time, he created the German school quadrille, which was later revived by Walter Gunther and Georg Theodorescu for the 1972 Olympics. In 1950, he was the first German rider to win an international dressage competition post-Second World War and, with this performance, he started to revive the reputation of German equitation worldwide. He died in 1957, leaving as a legacy his motto: 'Life is too short to ride in walk and to smoke bad cigars.'

**bute**   The common abbreviation for the anti-inflammatory analgesic drug phenylbutazone, a drug widely used in the treatment of minor injuries and to keep in abeyance the effect of more serious, ongoing conditions. A forbidden substance under British Dressage rules, but permitted in 'restricted levels' (i.e. subject to a maximum acceptable plasma level) by some other organizations.

**BYRDS**   Acronym for British Young Riders Dressage Scheme; those riders affiliated to British Dressage who are under twenty-one years of age.

C

**cadence**   The root of this word is the Latin *cado*, meaning fall; it is primarily a musical term and, even in this context, is subject to various dictionary definitions, many of which have no relevance to equitation. It has, however, been used in equestrian circles for centuries, sometimes by those who have applied their own definitions and sometimes by those whose usage is so vague as to have no discernible meaning. One of the musical definitions is: 'The concluding notes of a musical composition or of any well-defined section of it.' And it is perhaps the phrase 'well-defined' that has most relevance in an equestrian context. This phrase – or 'well-marked', or 'accenuated' – used in the context of the footfalls, implies that the movement is animated, regular and performed in good balance.

Cadre Noir rider Pierre de Bastard in courbette. Photograph by Elizabeth Furth.

**Cadre Noir** Originally those officers of the cavalry school at Saumur (distinguished by their black uniforms) charged with providing instruction in both military and academic equitation, which thus encompassed cross-country riding in different forms as well as high-school work. Separated from Saumur (which was, by that time, known formally as the Ecole d'Application de l'Arme Blindée       et de la Cavalerie) in 1968          and subsequently (1972) became part of France's Ecole Nationale d'Equitation, a body whose aims include        instruction       and preparation for state qualifica-tions, preparation for national and international competition, study and research and the preser-vation and diffusion of the equestrian art. Along with the Ecole Nationale, the Cadre Noir relocated to Terrefort, a few kilometres from Saumur. Now with a mixture of military and civilian instructors, the Cadre Noir continues its tradition of working in all the equestrian disciplines, but perhaps remains best-known for its reprises, or displays of high-school equitation which feature many of the high and low airs.

**caller**   See **commander**.

**campagne school**   An old term, originally with military (campaign) connotations that referred to a broad level of the horse's training; the horse was obedient, well balanced and a safe and reliable conveyance both in the manège, in open country and, where necessary, in battle. By extension, the term was used to signify the period and processes necessary to attain this level – which were also necessary for the basic preparation of horses destined to progress to high-school work.

**canter**   A three-beat gait in which the horse's hooves strike the ground in the order: one hind foot, the other hind foot and the diagonally opposite forefoot together, the remaining forefoot, this sequence being followed by a brief period of suspension during which all four feet are momentarily off the ground. The horse is said to be on either the left or right lead, depending upon which single forefoot strikes the ground at the end of the three-beat sequence. See also **counter-canter** and, for faulty forms, **disunited** and **four-time**.

**canter on a long rein**   A movement incorporated into some British Dressage tests: the horse is allowed to lower and stretch his head and neck while the rider retains a light rein contact; the horse should continue to canter in the same rhythm and tempo and retain his balance.

**Cappellmann, Nadine**   Born in 1965 in Aachen, Germany, the daughter of a successful rider who was heavily involved with CHIO Aachen, one of the biggest horse shows in Europe. Trained by Klaus Balkenhol, she finished 4th individually at the 2000 Olympics and was a member of the German team that won gold. At the 1998 World Championships in Rome she won a team gold medal and at the 2002 World Equestrian Games in Jerez she won both individual gold and a team gold. She has competed at three European Championships, winning three team gold medals and one individual bronze, and in two World Cups.

**capriole**   One of the airs above the ground, which is produced from a single courbette. The horse, having jumped more or less straight up, as high as possible and nearly parallel to the ground, finishes the leap with a strong

Capriole from the time of the Duke of Newcastle

backward kick with both hind legs. The horse then lands with the forefeet in advance of the hind feet.

**Carmona, Major Hector** (1925–1987) A Chilean cavalry officer, Carmona was a leading pentathlete who represented his country at Olympic and international level in that sport. In 1959, whilst on military manoeuvres, he was involved in a vehicle accident that damaged his right hand so badly that the injury led to a medical discharge from the army. Having subsequently taught himself to fence and shoot left-handed, he remarkably remained a force to be reckoned with in the pentathlon but, looking for a new means of earning a living, he focused his attention on riding. In the aftermath of his injury, when he had been treated in the USA, he had made some contacts there and learnt that dressage was very much a growing sport, and so he moved to that country in 1964, taking some Chilean horses with him.

Besides his own Grand Prix successes on these horses, Carmona attracted great attention through the successes of his young pupil, Martha Knocke, and he was asked to coach the American dressage team in preparation for the Pan-American Games. The team achieved a silver medal but, ironically, two Carmona horses loaned to the Chilean team helped that country to secure the gold. However, the American three-day eventing team, which Carmona also helped, achieved the gold medal in their discipline, and Carmona was to go to the 1968 Olympics as USET coach.

In the same year, Carmona founded the Los Alamos Equestrian Center in New Jersey, one of the first schools in the country dedicated to dressage. After ten highly productive years, he combined this operation with Blue List Arabians, owned by Dr Gail Hoff, whom he had married. Subsequently, the partnership concentrated for some time on schooling Arabs for dressage with great success, especially with the Arab Stallion *Serr Maariner*. However, Carmona became increasingly interested in breeding horses of the type ideally suited to top-level competition, and began to import young Hanoverian and Swedish Warmblood stallions to cross with domestic stock. In the aftermath of his death, his work is continued by his wife.

**carousel**  An orchestrated ride to music performed by a group of riders, usually greater in number than those performing a quadrille; performed at the French Cavalry School, Saumur, at least since the early part of the nineteenth century and still performed by the Cadre Noir and, on occasion, by other equestrian institutions – the Spanish Riding School mounts a display known as the *grosse schulquadrille*.

**carriage**  The manner in which a horse deports himself; influenced by his conformation, balance, animation, and mental state. See also **self-carriage**.

**carted**  Said of a rider whose horse, ignoring or defying the usual controls, has taken charge, usually at speed. Although not an essential ingredient of the ideals of dressage, this can still happen, either as an act of outright rebellion on the horse's part, or if the horse is seriously alarmed by some occurrence in or around the arena. In a test, there may be various ramifications. See **disobedience; error of course; leaving the arena**.

**cavalletti**  From the Italian, meaning 'little horses'; wooden rails fastened asymmetrically at both ends to small cross- or block-shaped ends, so that their height can be adjusted. Normally used in a series to help regulate stride length and rhythm and to work the horse's limbs and back; used judiciously they can be a valuable training aid, but injudicious or untutored use can be counter-productive. A tool much valued by the late Reiner Klimke, who wrote a book, *Cavalletti*, describing their use.

Working over cavalletti in rising trot. Photograph from Reiner Klimke's *Basic Training of the Young Horse*.

**Cavendish, William**  See **Duke of Newcastle**.

**centre line**   The line AC that bisects a dressage arena; X is the centre point along this line; other markers on this line are D and G (6 m from A and C respectively) and, in a 60 m x 20 m arena, L and I (18 m from A and C respectively). Dressage tests invariably start and finish along the centre line and many movements are ridden to, from or around it. The centre line is usually imaginary, but in some minor competitions on grass arenas, it may be marked by a mown strip.

**centre of gravity**   The point of a body through which the entire weight of that body seems to act by the force of gravity. In a static, symmetrical body of constant mass, the centre of gravity will be at the geometrical centre. In a body of varying mass, capable of independent movement and changes of balance (as in a horse and/or rider), the centre of gravity is not a fixed point. In a ridden horse, at a normal halt or in movement at the standard basic gaits, the rider's own centre of gravity will be naturally somewhat behind (further to the rear than) the horse's. In the interests of maximum efficiency of locomotion, there are circumstances in which it is desirable to reduce this discrepancy to a practical minimum; in the case of fast galloping, the rider may attempt to move his own centre of gravity forward over the horse's, by shortening his stirrup leathers and folding his upper body forwards and down. In classical dressage, where speed is not a key requisite, but strength, precision, manoeuvrability and lightness of the forehand are, the aim is to align the horse's centre of gravity beneath the rider's by moving the horse's backward – which is achieved through training the horse to lower his haunches and step powerfully forward beneath his own body with his hind legs. See also **collection**.

**chair seat**   A postural fault: the rider sits towards the back of the saddle, with thighs sloping forwards and heels in front of a vertical line through the shoulders and hips. The weight is thus more or less anchored on the back of the seat, impeding the more subtle uses of the seat aids, and the lower legs are too far forward, similarly impeding the effective use of the leg aids.

The chair seat. Drawing by Brian Tutlo from Paul Belasik's *Dressage for the 21st Century*.

48

**Chambon**   See **auxiliary reins.**

**chambrière**   A form of whip used particularly in the sixteenth and seventeenth centuries when working a horse at the pillars.

**Chammartin, Henri**   Swiss winner of the individual gold medal at the 1964 Olympic Games in Tokyo, riding *Woermann*, and a member of the Swiss team that won silver that year. In 1956, riding *Wöhler*, he had been a member of the team that won Olympic bronze and in 1968, riding *Wolfdietrich*, he repeated that feat.

Henri Chammartin on *Wolfdietrich*. Photograph from Wilhelm Müseler's *Riding Logic.*

**change in the air**   Another term for flying change.

**change of direction**   In dressage, this is deemed to mean any manoeuvre that results in a change of rein and thus includes, for example, a counter-change of hand about the centre line. Thus a canter zigzag would be deemed to include changes of direction, even though the overall progression of the movement as a whole is in one direction (e.g. A–C).

**change of hand**   A traditional term that, in most contexts, has the same meaning as changing the rein, that is, to change the basic direction of travel around the arena. When this is done, there is a change in which hand/rein becomes the outside and the inside. However, in some circumstances, change of hand may be used to signify a short-term change in which hand represents the 'inside' and 'outside', within the context of a larger movement. For example, cantering around the arena to the right, the rider performs half-pass right to the centre line, where he asks for a flying change, then performs half-pass left back to the track, asks for another flying change and proceeds around the arena to the right (counter-change of hand). The changes of 'inside' and 'outside' that follow the flying changes would normally be referred to as changes of hand, rather than rein; the movement, as a whole, starts and finishes on the same rein.

49

**change of lead**    In canter a change from leading the gait with one foreleg to leading with the other. While the most basic way of doing this is via a few steps of trot, it is the form via a few steps of walk that is known as a simple change. The change that takes place within a single canter stride is known as a flying change. Although the movement is not required in dressage tests, horses can also change lead within the four-beat gait of gallop.

**change of leg**    Generally, this term is synonymous with change of lead. However (usually outside the bounds of pure dressage) it is sometimes used to signify an action purely on the horse's part, as seen in tired horses on uneven ground, or when a horse is trying to protect a weakened or injured limb.

**change of rhythm**    An unwarranted alteration from one discernible rhythm to another; against the rider's wishes, the rhythm becomes faster or slower.

**change the rein**    Generally, to change the basic direction of travel around the arena. See also **change of hand**.

**Charles I of Spain**    (1516–1556) Also monarch of an empire that included Austria and thus Emperor Charles V of that region. He was a ruler who had immense influence on the development of equitation in the countries under his dominion, and reputedly one of the best riders of his age. (Although not a contemporary, the Duke of Newcastle described him as having been the best rider in the world.) During his reign, the influence of the Neapolitan School was spreading throughout many European countries and, in Iberia, equitation was continuing to be influenced by the riding style of the Moors – a process that had begun in the reign of Duarte. Under Charles, the developing Spanish style of riding became influential in Austria, and there was a considerable importation of Spanish horses, factors which laid the foundations for the development of the Lipizzaner breed and the concept of a Spanish Riding School in Vienna.

**Chef d'equipe**    An individual with overall responsibility for a team of competitors.

**chewing the bit**    A term used to describe the quiet mouthing of the bit by a horse who is accepting its presence and signals; tends to promote the production of saliva through the activation of the parotid glands. Should not be confused with the strenuous actions of a horse who is attempting to evade the actions of the bit, the latter usually being accompanied by a markedly unsteady head carriage.

**circles**  Geometrical figures which, in whole or in part, form the basis for many movements and exercises. Correctly ridden, circles help to improve the horse's suppleness, balance and engagement. Incorrect circle work produces none of these advantages and may encourage or provoke faulty movement.

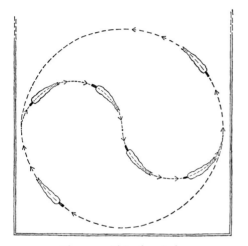 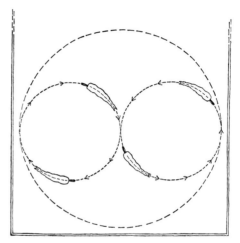

Change within the circle                    Figure of eight within the circle

Figures based on circles, from Alois Podhajsky's *The Complete Training of Horse and Rider.*

**Clarke, Stephen**  Born in England in 1953, Clarke showjumped and evented before turning to pure dressage in 1979. The winner of five National Championship titles, all with different home-trained horses, he has represented Great Britain internationally on numerous occasions and was reserve rider for the 1988 Olympic Games. In recent years, he has concentrated more on training and judging, travelling worldwide in these capacities. As an international dressage judge, he has officiated at many major events, including European Championships, World Equestrian Games, World Cup Finals and Olympic Games. A long-time Chairman of British Dressage's Judges' Committee, he has made a major

Stephen Clarke in his role as a judge. Photograph by Elizabeth Furth.

51

contribution to improving systems and procedures and encouraging the recruitment and training of judges. He is also a member of the FEI Dressage Committee.

**classical**   A term which does not have a definitive meaning, but which is widely used to signify equestrian practice that adheres to the principles laid down by acknowledged masters of the equestrian art. These might be summarized as the progressive education of the horse with a view to the ongoing enhancement of suppleness, strength, impulsion, balance, lightness and obedience, i.e. those qualities evident in the horse performing haute école work.

**Classical Riding Club**   A club founded in 1995 by Sylvia Loch, with the aim of promoting the true principles and ethics of classical equitation, which are enshrined in its charter. While based at the founder's home in Scotland, the club is essentially an international networking organization, with members in a number of countries including the USA. Although not primarily a competitive body, the club does produce some dressage tests of its own, the criteria of which comply with its underlying ethos. It also publishes a quarterly newsletter which, amongst other issues, emphasizes the desirability of a humane approach in all the riding disciplines; it has campaigned for the end of the use of draw reins in training dressage horses and, in 1998, published a booklet *Making a Difference*, aimed at influencing the judging of dressage. Some of the ideas mooted in this booklet have been adopted in whole or in part in both Britain and the USA. Contact details for the club are: The Classical Riding Club, Eden Hall, Kelso, Roxburghshire, TD5 7QD, UK; e-mail crc@classicalriding.co.uk; website:www.classicalriding.co.uk.

**clean**   Said of a flying change, or a sequence of flying changes, when executed correctly, i.e. with the correct sequence of legs and with rhythm maintained.

**collection**   This term implies something very similar to the French term rassembler ('to gather together') and reference to the latter may assist in avoiding the too narrow and 'mechanical' definitions sometimes ascribed to collection. This applies especially to the concept of collection as 'a state of preparedness'; many authorities have mentioned the link between the alert mental state and the biomechanical pose of the horse ridden in the collected gaits and the physical and mental attitude of a horse in his natural state responding to various demanding stimuli. However, a major difference between these two is that, while an untrained, relatively unfit horse can adopt a collected pose momentarily, sustained collection – especially in the ridden horse – is physically

The power and lightness of collection. Photograph of Carlos Couneiro by Elizabeth Furth.

demanding. Working towards collection must, therefore, be a gradual process, allowing time for the horse to increase in strength and suppleness and also for him to develop the levels of understanding and obedience necessary in order that he can comply with the rider's collecting aids.

In mechanical terms, it might be said that collection describes a state in which the horse, having developed strength in the hindquarters, uses the strength in this area to carry a greater proportion of his and the rider's weight, thereby improving his balance and overall poise. Consequent upon the altered balance is lightness in hand, and the lowered hindquarters, increasing the ratio of lift to thrust in the action of the hind legs, produce the characteristically elevated, animated steps. When this form of movement is specifically required, it is achieved by the rider, having generated energy from the horse's hindquarters, literally collecting the energy in lightly 'holding' hands so that the horse's resources are subtly gathered together. (A similar degree of energy, if channelled by the rider to increase the ratio of thrust to lift, produces the lengthened strides in their various forms.)

National organizations, along with many judges and trainers, are continually at pains to point out that collection is a state that applies to the whole horse, and that superficial similarities to certain characteristics of collection should not be misconstrued as evidence of it. Common examples include short strides that lack animation, a head and neck carriage imposed by force and a 'lightness' that is simply lack of contact.

**collective marks**   Those marks awarded by the judge after completion of the individual movements of a test, applied with reference to an overall assessment of various qualities.

**combined training**   An American term for horse trials. Also used formerly in some quarters to describe the competition now referred to as dressage with jumping.

**commanded test**   A test in which the elements of the movements are called out to the rider by a commander *(also known as a caller)*. A rider may choose to have a test commanded because of lack of time in which to learn it, having several different tests to ride in one day, etc. However, the practice is generally permitted only at the lower levels of competition, and may be subject to the individual organizer's preference. In many cases, it is not permitted when the test forms part of a horse trial. Riders wishing to have a test commanded should ensure that this is permitted well in advance of their performance. Where commanding is permitted, it is subject to various constraints, the flouting of which may incur penalties or, especially where it is deemed to constitute outside assistance, elimination. Commonly, these constraints include the following: the commander must only read out verbatim extracts of the test, with no special emphasis on any part of the instruction (e.g. 'At C *CANTER!!*'); if an instruction is repeated with the intention of redirecting a competitor who is about to make an error of course, such error may be penalized as having occurred; commanders cannot be introduced partway through a test; commanders may not stand inside the arena. In cases where a commander uses an electronic headset to communicate to a partially deaf or blind competitor, an independent third party must stand beside the commander to verify that only the words of the test are spoken.

Commanding a test effectively requires skill, experience, good timing, familiarity with arena layout (and preferably a working knowledge of the test in question) and, in windy weather, a strong voice. Therefore, competitors who wish to have a test commanded would be prudent in their choice of commander.

**commander**   Also known as caller. One who calls out the elements of the test movements on behalf of the competitor; may be used in some competitions and circumstances, subject to various constraints. See **commanded test**.

**comments, judge's**   The remarks made by a judge during the performance of the test movements, and in respect of the collective marks. These are necessarily brief and are intended to support or augment the actual marks given.

**compulsory movements**    Those elements of a freestyle test that the rider is obliged to include.

**concave**    Curved in a hollow outline; the opposite of convex. The inside of a horse correctly bent on a circle is curved in this fashion; however, the term is more often used in an equestrian context to indicate the 'hollow' side of a horse who exhibits crookedness.

**conformation**    The make and shape of a horse, based mainly on his skeletal structure, but also influenced by the type and quality of muscle fibre. While skeletal conformation cannot be altered (for the better) by training, correct, progressive training methods can enhance the quality and function of the

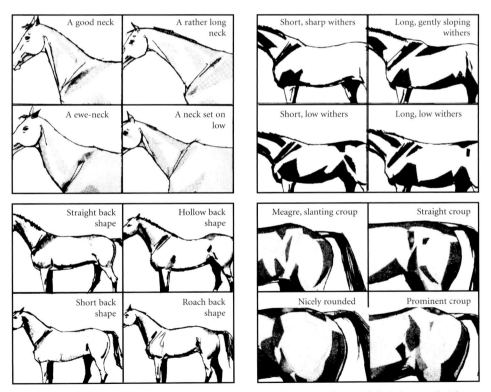

Drawings and comments on various features of conformation from Ulrik Schramm's *The Undisciplined Horse*.

associated muscles, tendons and ligaments, thus maximizing the horse's potential for powerful, free and balanced movement.

Whilst perfect conformation would represent the ideal in terms of the horse's potential for training, this is a rare quality and, in practice, the conformation of an individual horse is likely to be such that he will find some movements relatively easy and others relatively difficult – a reality of which all riders and trainers should be aware. Since dressage means training, the idea that any horse of less than perfect conformation is 'unsuitable for dressage' *per se* is erroneous; however, it is a fact that horses of distinctly poor conformation are unlikely to succeed at the higher levels of competition. See also **size**.

**connection**   A term used to describe the concept that there is harmonious communication between rider and horse; that neither is blocking the other and that the horse is able to move efficiently.

**constant angle**   Applied to lateral work; means that the inclination of the horse's body in relation to the direction of movement remains the same throughout the movement.

**contact**   Essentially, the existence of a discernible connection between the rider's hands and the horse's mouth, via bit and reins. The sort of contact desired in dressage, and indicative of correct training, is a soft, steady and elastic connection, fully accepted by the horse, who is willing to work forward readily into the rider's hands.

**convex**   Curved outward, in a 'bulging' outline. The outside of a horse correctly bent on a circle is curved in this fashion; however, the term is more often used in an equestrian context to indicate the opposite of the concave side of a horse who exhibits crookedness.

**corners**   All rules of dressage require that the corners of the arena should be ridden in the form of a quarter circle; British Dressage and FEI rules stipulate that, at collected and working gaits, the corners should be quarters of approximately 6 m circles; at medium and lengthened gaits, they should be quarters of approximately 10 m circles. Under AHSA rules, at Training Level, the quarter circles should be at least as small as the smallest full circle required in the test; at First Level, they should be no bigger than quarters of 10 m circles when ridden in trot or 15 m when ridden in canter. The AHSA rules thus recognize the fact that, in the early stages of training, horses may not have attained sufficient suppleness and balance to maintain correct movement on small circles.

A change of direction at right angles should be ridden in the same manner as a corner.

**correction** The putting right of an error made by the horse through misunderstanding or misinterpretation of the aids; the correction of a genuine error should not involve any action of overt punishment.

**counter-canter** On a circle or part thereof, or around an arena, intentionally cantering with the leading leg being that on the opposite side to the direction of movement. When schooling, counter-canter has a role in enhancing suppleness, straightness and obedience; it also appears as an element of some test movements, for example in canter serpentines.

**counter-change of hand** A movement based upon half-pass and involving a change of direction, i.e. a prescribed number of strides in half-pass are ridden in one direction, there is a change of hand and this is followed immediately by a prescribed number of strides in half-pass in the new direction. In its finished form, the movement should be completely symmetrical; the same number of strides in each direction, in which the same distance is travelled both forwards and laterally. These latter aims generally require judicious riding since most horses, even those advanced in their training, will have some vestige of one-sidedness and will perform any lateral work with greater facility to one side than the other. During the early stages of training, in trot, it is usually necessary to straighten the horse during the last stride or two of the first half-pass to facilitate a smooth change of hand; when ridden in canter, the change of hand is preceded by a flying change and it is always necessary to straighten the horse immediately prior to this in order to ensure that it is clean and balanced. See also **zigzag**.

**counter-position** The mirror image of position, applied when the rider requires the horse to adopt a subtle lateral flexion towards the outside (of the arena).

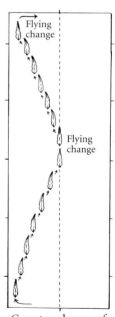

Counter-change of
hand in canter

Diagram of counter-change of hand in canter, from John Winnett's *Dressage as Art in Competition*.

The courbette as performed by a rider of the Spanish Riding School.

**courbette** One of the airs above the ground, executed from a levade-like stance. As described by de la Guérinière, it consisted of a single jump off the haunches, after which the forehand touched down – effectively, a more elevated and less ground-covering jump than the mézair; as developed by the Spanish Riding School, a consecutive series of jumps (two to five in a row), performed without the forelegs touching down. The latter form required enormous strength and great balance.

**cramped** Said of a horse who does not move freely; most commonly associated with constraining actions by the rider (especially overuse of the rein aids), but can also relate to aspects of conformation that place biomechanical restrictions on movement.

**crookedness** Failure on the horse's part to move truly straight. Although this may be a manifestation of resistance, sometimes provoked by the rider, the main root cause is literally inherent – horses, like people, are not born either truly symmetrical or straight, most have a natural degree of lateral incurvation. Working to minimize this and the consequential crooked movement is one of the trainer's main, longstanding tasks – marked crookedness will impair true collection (and thus all collected movements) and will cause asymmetry in lateral movements and tempi changes.

**cross canter** See **disunited**.

**crotch seat** Also known as the fork seat. A faulty posture adopted by some riders, often as a consequence of exaggerating what they consider to be good postural points. Essentially, the forward curve of the lumbar region is exaggerated, the rear of the seat is raised and the seat rocks forward, the pubis going down towards the pommel of the saddle. This posture is often accompanied by the chest being thrust forward and the shoulders being pushed back. In addition to lessening both the security and potential for effectiveness of the seat itself, this posture has the biomechanical effect of pushing the legs backwards. Physically strong riders may be able to resist this effect to some extent, but only at the expense of clamping their legs onto the horse's sides, producing a crude driving effect of the legs in tandem with a weak seat; in most cases, however, the rider's legs swing back too far and both legs and seat are rendered relatively ineffective.

**croupade**   One of the airs above the ground, a development of the courbette; effectively a single, high jump in which, at the apex, the forelegs are folded symmetrically towards the chest, and the hind legs are also flexed beneath the body.

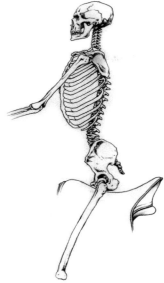

Skeletal arrangement of the crotch (fork) seat. Drawing by Brian Tutlo from Paul Belasik's *Dressage for the 21st Century.*

**croup-high**   In terms of conformation, describes a horse whose croup is higher than his withers; conformation that makes it difficult for the horse to really engage his hind limbs (see **engagement**) and tends to put him onto his forehand, giving a 'downhill' ride. The term is also used to describe a flying change in which the horse lifts his croup: this may occur because the horse has a faulty canter and/or is not fully in control of his own balance, or because the rider's outside leg swings too far back and irritates the horse (especially if the spur is involved), or because the rider's rein contact is too restrictive.

**croup to the wall**   See **renvers**.

**curb bit**   A bit, the action of which is based on a degree of leverage supplied by the cheekpieces, augmented by the action of the curb chain. Historically, such bits were commonly used in isolation; nowadays they are more commonly used in conjunction with a bradoon, as an integral part of a double bridle (such an arrangement being prescribed for the higher levels of competition dressage). As with other forms of equipment, the organizing bodies have rules relating to the design of curb bits permitted in competition.

**curb rein**   The rein which attaches to the rings on the curb bit of a double bridle.

**cut corners**   Said of a horse who, instead of travelling through the corners of the arena correctly bent on a quarter of a circle, steps towards the inside of the arena with a lack of true lateral bend; normally a consequence of inappropriate aiding, lateral stiffness, loss of balance or some combination of these factors.

# D

**daisy cutting**   A term more common in the showring than the dressage arena; signifies a very low action, in which much of the limb movement derives from the shoulders and hips, rather than from marked flexion of all the leg joints; horses who show this action are not readily disposed to move correctly in collection. A horse who moves in this way as a direct consequence of his conformation is not a shankmover in the induced sense of that term, but may become so if his trot in particular is developed incorrectly.

**Dallos, Gyula**   Born in Hungary in 1951, at a time when riding was not popular under the Communist regime, Dallos was nevertheless inspired by his grandfather, who had been a hussar. Largely self-taught, he was initially a showjumper and eventer but, after an injury received while playing soccer, he turned to dressage.  With the stallion *Aktion*, who went on to become very influential at stud, Dallos appeared at a number of World Cups throughout the 1990s, achieving consistently high placings. He has also been placed 4th in the World Equestrian Games and is a leading contender in the World Cup Freestyle. He is a physical training instructor and also coaches at the Budapest Equestrian Club. Dallos has been National Champion of Hungary thirteen times.

Comte D'Aure on his stallion *Le Cerf*. Drawing from Hilda Nelson's *Alexis-François L'Hotte The Quest for Lightness in Equitation.*

Gyula Dallos riding *Aktion*. Photograph from Charles de Kunffy's *Dressage Principles Illuminated.*

**D'Aure, Comte Antoine Cartier** (1799–1863) Master of the Horse to Louis XVIII and Charles X of France and, from 1848–1855, civilian chief instructor at Saumur. D'Aure was a staunch advocate of the need to approach outdoor riding rather differently from classical manège equitation; a matter of some debate during that era. In 1834 he wrote *Traité d'Equitation* to try to combat the influence of Baucher, of whose methods he was a stern critic. Despite their entrenched differences, even Baucher acknowledged that D'Aure was an excellent rider.

**Davison, Richard** Born in England in 1955, and living in Staffordshire, Davison started competing at an early age, his main trainer being Conrad Schumacher. A Company Director by profession he has, for some years, been one of Britain's most successful riders; for seven consecutive years (1996--2002) he was leading British International Dressage Rider (Puffa Rankings). He has represented Britain at three Olympic Games (1996, 2000 and 2004) two World Championships (1998 and 2002) and four World Cup Finals (1996, 1999, 2000 and 2003). He has also been a member of two medal-winning teams at the European Championships, achieving team silver in 1993 and team bronze in 2003 – in the latter year he was British Dressage National Champion and was also awarded the FEI Gold Badge of Honour.

Out of the saddle, Davison has long been heavily involved in the organizational and administrative side of dressage. Formerly Chairman of the British Horse Society Training & Examinations Committee and a committee member of British Dressage, he is currently a member of the FEI Dressage Committee and Vice President of the International Dressage Riders' Club, a member of the International and British Dressage Trainer Clubs and a member of the Guild of Sports Internationalists. He has also worked within the media, as a commentator and columnist.

**dead to the leg**   Describes a horse who does not respond readily to the rider's leg aids. Although this condition may, in part, be rooted in the horse's temperament, it will always be worsened by inappropriate training (ever heavier use of the legs, unsupported by judicious use of the whip). Similarly, a basically responsive horse may become 'deadened' by prolonged use of unnecessarily heavy or indecipherable leg 'aids'.

**Decarpentry, Gen. Albert**   (1878–1956) Born in Lambres, France, the son and grandson of enthusiastic pupils of François Baucher, Decarpentry soon decided upon a career in the cavalry. Wounded in action in the First World War at Verdun, he dismissed the permanent damage to his left elbow, saying that it kept his arm bent in the correct position for riding. The injury had no adverse affect on his career, since he was to become commander of cavalry at

Photograph of General Decarpentry by Blanchaud, from Decapentry's *Piaffer and Passage*.

Saint-Cyr and second in command of the Cadre Noir (1925–1931).

From 1939 onward, Decarpentry acted as judge at many international dressage competitions. He also presided over the FEI jury and became President of the FEI Dressage Committee, in which role he was highly influential in developing an international consensus on the aims and judging of competition dressage.

As a rider and equestrian thinker, Decarpentry was by no means confined by the Baucherist influences of his childhood, as both the references cited in his book *Academic Equitation* and the text itself show. It is also evident that he took innovative advantage of the then-young techniques of cinematography to help analyse equine movement.

Decarpentry was a modest man and, although held in great esteem as a rider, he had no desire to participate in competition, his legacy being the skill of his instruction, his work in developing the FEI and the integrity and scholarship he applied to his equestrian writing.

**deep and round**   A form of deep work reminiscent of certain Renaissance-period equestrian statues that has re-emerged in some quarters in recent times. In this position, rather than being stretched forwards and down, the neck is curled round so that the nose reaches back towards the horse's chest. Trainers who oppose this practice make the point that, in this posture, the benefits of the influence of the head and neck on the whole topline, as seen in low and round work are lost and claim that it has more to do with psychological domination of the horse than producing gymnastic benefit. Some equine physiotherapists have warned that prolonged maintenance of this posture may cause physical damage.

**deep work**   A term used to describe the horse being worked with his head low to the ground. This work is carried out by different individuals in different ways, depending upon their aims and intentions. See **long and low**; **low and round**; **deep and round**.

**de Gogue**   See **auxiliary reins**.

**de Jurenak, Kalman**   A native of Hungary, where he was trained in the cavalry, de Jurenak moved to Australia, where he worked as assistant to Franz Mairinger, before moving on to New Zealand. During his time as Olympic coach to both the dressage and three-day event squads of Australia and New Zealand, he emphasized the need for correct basics and the establishment of a rapport with horses, centred on getting them to understand and enjoy their work. From New Zealand he moved to Verden in Germany, and became Director of the Hanoverian Verbrand. The author of *Classical Schooling* (Vols. I and II) – with videotapes of the same name – and a number of magazine articles, his motto is 'Simplicity is an art'.

**de Kerbrech, Baron François de Faverot** (1837–1905) A French general, friend and disciple of François Baucher and editor of Baucher's latest precepts concerning his 'Second Manner', which Baucher had expressed to him orally. (Baucher had been constantly revising his many precepts throughout his life and continued to do so even when he was blind and ill.) In 1889, after Baucher's death, de Kerbrech edited Baucher's latest precepts and published them as *Dressage méthodique du cheval de selle d'après les derniers enseignements de François Baucher*. According to General Decarpentry, one should bear in mind that, after a period of twenty years, de Kerbrech may have unwittingly introduced into this work 'some refinements to Baucher's last thoughts'. However, this is not surprising since the two men had such a long relationship and thought very much along the same lines. Some commentators believe that de Kerbrech's 'refinements' may have included references to 'lateral suppling effects' that are, in effect, shoulder-in – an exercise that Baucher used, but never referred to by name. Some of Baucher's last procedures are also to be found in de Kerbrech's short work *Dressage du cheval de dehors*.

De Kerbrech was also an admirer of General L'Hotte and acted as intermediary between him and Captain Jacques de Saint-Phalle of the Cadre Noir, two horsemen whose equestrian skills he greatly admired, after the former had been angered by the latter's criticism of some of Baucher's concepts.

In common with many European horsemen of the nineteenth century (including Baucher), de Kerbrech was involved in the tradition of practising haute école in the circus. In that era, a number of notable female écuyères were performing in that genre, including the highly regarded Diane Dupont, for whom de Kerbrech was coach and trainer of her horses.

**de Kunffy, Charles** Born in Hungary to parents who were eminent horse breeders, de Kunffy started riding as a child, receiving expert instruction from riding masters who adhered to classical training traditions based on scholarship and a profound respect for the horse. Cross-country riding, jumping and dressage were viewed as complementary aspects of comprehensive methodology and de Kunffy competed successfully at all three.

After moving to America, he graduated from the University of California and taught philosophy and psychology prior to devoting himself to the equestrian arts, using his academic abilities to promote the classical equestrian ethos. Widely travelled, he has judged at FEI levels in America, Europe, Africa and Australia and conducts clinics, seminars and courses for judges and instructors on all these continents. He is the author of six books on equitation and numerous articles and videos.

Charles de Kunffy. Photograph from *Dressage Principles Illuminated.*

**de la Broue, Salomon** Born early in the sixteenth century and living throughout most of that century (precise dates uncertain), de la Broue was one of the most influential pupils of Pignatelli; he brought the latter's teachings to his native France and his book *Le Cavalerice François* (1594) was the first book on equitation written by a Frenchman. Contrary to the then accepted practice of always using a curb bit, de la Broue insisted that the horse's early training should be in a bradoon. He also continued to develop the idea, instigated by Grisone and passed on by Fiaschi and Pignatelli, of bringing the horse into the hand in response to the leg aids, and he is credited with being perhaps the first to use direct flexions. His work is referred to and acknowledged by de la Guérinière in the latter's famous book *Ecole de Cavalerie.*

**de la Guérinière, François Robichon**   (c.1688–1751) Widely regarded as the most influential figure in equestrian history, de la Guérinière was born in Essay, the son of a lawyer. A pupil of Antoine de Vendeuil, he also had a brother who ran a riding academy in Caen. In 1715, de la Guérinière was granted the title of écuyer de roi, and opened a riding academy in Paris, apparently under licence from the Duc d'Anjou.

At his Parisian academy, de la Guérinière taught not only riding, but what was described as 'the complete science of the horse'. By 1730 his reputation was such that he was given the Directorship of the Académie des Tuileries, which had been founded by Antoine de Pluvinel some one hundred years earlier. De la Guérinière's legacy was to develop, from the older style of

Engraving of François Robichon de la Guérinière, from *Ecole de Cavalerie.*

classical riding, a freedom of movement which characterizes modern classical equitation – an achievement which has led him to be described as the 'first of the modern classical riders' (W.S. Felton) and 'undoubtedly the father of modern equitation' (Henry Wynmalen). His lucid work *Ecole de Cavalerie* (translated into English as *School of Horsemanship*) is quite remarkable for its timeless relevance and wisdom, and continues to be a source of reference for many present-day authorities.

**demi-pirouette**   The French term for half-pirouette.

**de Miranda, Joaquin Gonçalves**   (1870–1940) In his early years, de Miranda was an écuyer in the Portuguese royal household, during which period he experienced the influence of Baucher, through a pupil of Baucher's named Brunot, and of Saumur, through a General Vito Moreira, who had spent three years at that establishment. Having been, for some time, Master of the Horse to the Portuguese royal family, at the start of the twentieth century de Miranda founded a school of equitation at Rua do Borja in Lisbon. This quickly became both fashionable and successful. A pupil, Jaime Celestino da Costa, reported that, in addition to requiring pupils to ride without stirrups for a year (to establish a good seat), de Miranda introduced a number of mounted games, including vaulting and bareback jumping. It was only the pupils who proved most adept at these exercises, and attuned to the horses, who were encouraged to pursue the 'upper level course' of dressage.

The most eminent of de Miranda's pupils was Nuno Oliveira, who started to ride with him at the age of eleven. Although Oliveira was still in his teens when his mentor died, de Miranda's enormous skill in the saddle and his dedication to his art had a profound influence on his pupil. Oliveira wrote of him: 'Mr. Miranda demanded great discipline and perfect calm from his riders...He insisted on absolutely correct movements, so that all his pupils knew how to do every act of high school dressage.'

**demi-volte**   The French term for a half-volte.

**depart**   The initial phase of an upward transition into a new gait, especially canter.

**de Pluvinel, Antoine**   (1555–1620) A French nobleman, whose wider roles included those of chamberlain and ambassador to The Netherlands, de Pluvinel was, from a young age, a pupil of Pignatelli in Italy. Shortly after his return to Paris, he opened an academy for the broad-based education of young gentlemen of noble birth, at which equitation was just one of a number of subjects taught. His most famous equestrian pupil was the young Louis XIII, and de Pluvinel's second book (his first being *L'Exercice de Monter à Cheval*) largely takes the form of a 'conversation' between the teacher and the royal pupil. This second book, commonly referred to as *L'Instruction de Roi*, (1625) was, in fact, substantially rewritten from de Pluvinel's notes, after his death, by a friend, René de Menou, who had been outraged when an earlier version, *Manèige Royal* (or *Maneige Royal)*, had been published two years earlier by the engraver, Crispin de Pas, whose own version of the text failed to match the quality of his engravings.

Antoine de Pluvinel instructing Louis XIII. Engraving from *Le Maneige Royal.*

It is generally reckoned that de Pluvinel introduced the idea of working a horse between pillars, and he is widely credited with advancing equitation by the application of gentler, more humane methods than were used by his mentor and most of his contemporaries; he undoubtedly had a much greater understanding of equine psychology than had been the norm during preceding centuries. His stricture: '…you must be careful not to bore him [the horse] or snuff out his gentleness…because…once it is lost it is gone forever.' is an often-quoted example of this. Although less respected as a horseman by de la Guérinière than his contemporary de la Broue, de Pluvinel was responsible for building the riding hall in the Tuileries in which de la Guérinière later worked, and his positive influence on the French royal family was to be a factor in Louis XIV's enthusiasm for the School of Versailles.

**descente de jambes**   A French term: reduction or cessation of the rider's forward-driving leg aids, especially to reward or acknowledge the horse's efforts.

**descente de main**   A French term: yielding the pressure of the hand and, consequently, the rein. As described by writers such as de la Guérinière and Baucher, this is done to check the extent of the horse's self-carriage; therefore the horse should not change his speed, balance or outline – he is sometimes said to be 'on parole'. This is thus a different effect from the descente d'encolure, in which the horse stretches his head and neck forward and down. However, in his book *Academic Equitation*, General Decarpentry points out that, at Saumur in the nineteenth century, the term descente de main was commonly used to describe what would now be considered descente d'encolure. In his book *Dressage for the 21st Century*, the American authority Paul Belasik discusses this divergence of definitions and asks the question 'How is [the horse] supposed to differentiate between a release of the reins that means "seek my hands, go long and low, extend your neck", or a release of the reins which means "stay on the bit, keep your balance, don't follow my hand or fill up the loose rein"?' Belasik's own answer to this is '…by feeling the rider's balance. If the rider maintains position as a "lever" and guides the horse with the seat, then softening the reins…as in descente de main will be only a momentary test of how self-sustaining this balance is. If, on the other hand, the rider leans forward with the back and seat, the horse recognizes and follows the shift of balance out further to the front.'

**descente de main et de jambes**  A French term: a simultaneous reduction in the demands of the rider's hand and leg aids. See individual descriptions of these two effects.

**descente d'encolure**  A French term meaning, literally, descent of the neck and shoulders; a degree of forward extension and lowering of the horse's neck and head. Commonly used to allow and encourage relative relaxation of these parts and give the dorsal (topline) muscles their free play, the effect being promoted by the rider yielding with the hands, thus recompensing the horse for previous efforts in working completely 'on the aids'. In this context, its effect is to produce a long and low outline. However, some French works on equitation also mention the term in respect of lengthening the stride and increasing the speed; as the rider's legs promote forward movement, the rider's fingers open a little to allow the forward impulse to develop and the horse's neck to assume a (somewhat lowered) carriage commensurate with the movement required.

**D'Esme, Dominique**  Born in France in 1945. A long-serving member of the French international team, representing her country at five Olympic Games (1976, 1984, 1988, 1992 and 1996), three World Championships, five European Championships and five World Cups.

**diagonal**  A diagonally opposite pair of legs. i.e. the left fore and right hind, or the right fore and left hind; usually named for the relevant foreleg. Also, an imaginary line running from one long side of a dressage arena to the other, at an angle of other than 90 degrees; the lines KM and HF (joining the extreme markers on opposite long sides) are commonly termed long diagonals; lines joining imtermediate markers (such as KB) are commonly termed short diagonals.

**diagonal aids**  Aids applied in combination to the opposite sides of the horse, for example, left rein and right leg, as distinct from lateral aids.

**Dierks, Clemens**  Born in Wismar, Germany, Dierks trained at Schwabisch and Warendorf, attaining the FNHDP qualification and becoming a member of the International Trainers Club. Having moved to Australia in 1973 he became an NCAS Level III Dressage Specialist

Instructor in 1987 and also an A Level Equestrian Federation of Australia judge and a member of the New South Wales Dressage Council. Almost from his moment of arrival in Australia he began to exert a major influence on the development of dressage in that country and New Zealand, training many riders and horses to Grand Prix level. In 1989 he became the Australian National Coach and in the following year as team coach he took Australia's first-ever international dressage team to compete in the World Equestrian Games at Stockholm. Throughout the 1990s he was coach to Australian teams that reached the finals of several World Cups, and also the team that attained 6th place in the 2000 Olympics in Sydney. In 2003 he announced his retirement from the post of National Coach in order to concentrate on private tuition.

**direct elevation**   Also referred to as active elevation. An actual or attempted raising of the forehand by the action of the rider's hands and the bit, the idea being that this will produce a consequent lowering of the haunches as required for collection. Direct elevation (as distinct from occasional corrections by the hands) is proscribed by most of the equestrian authorities, on the grounds that it creates physical strain and resistance, and in his book, *Academic Equitation*, General Decarpentry asserts that the whole concept of direct elevation is mechanically flawed because, lacking collar bones, the horse does not have a fixed point in his body that would provide the necessary fulcrum effect. Compare with **relative elevation**.

Direct elevation. Drawing by Klaus Philipp from Alfred Knopfhart's *Fundamentals of Dressage.*

**direct flexion**   Longitudinal flexion of the horse; the term is often used with specific reference to flexion of the poll and jaw and is associated with achieving the ramener. Much of the work on producing direct flexion was, historically, done in-hand, dismounted.

**directive ideas**   Comments added by the compilers of certain high-level dressage tests (such as the AHSA and the FEI) to direct the judge's attention to criteria deemed to be of particular importance in the execution of individual movements.

**direct rein**   Also known as open(ing) rein. A rein effect which acts on the side to which it is applied; an action of the inside rein used in motion on turns: the inside hand moves a little away from the horse and slightly forward; to assist correct response to this action without loss of impulsion, the outside rein contact is eased. On a well-schooled horse, all these actions are minimal.

**direct rein of opposition**   A rein effect which acts from front to rear, blocking forward movement on the side to which it is applied, increasing the loading on the same shoulder and causing displacement of the haunches in the opposite direction. A version of this effect is sometimes applied incorrectly by novice riders who effectively pull back on the inside rein when turning/circling, which blocks the inside shoulder and results in the loss of the quarters to the outside. Since its rearward influence tends to reduce impulsion, most authorities recommend discreet use of this effect in displacing the haunches, even when applied in conjunction with other aids on a trained horse. In rein-back, both reins act 'in opposition' in so far as they act softly against forward movement, but they must not be used to 'pull' the horse into the movement.

**direct transition**   A transition from one gait to another that misses out an intervening gait or gaits, e.g. a transition directly from walk to canter, with no intervening steps of trot. Direct transitions (especially downward) are more demanding of horse and rider than progressive transitions and are generally more prevalent in the higher-level tests.

**disabled riders**   Riders whose disabilities prevent them from riding in accordance with the normal rules and requirements of national organizing bodies are not necessarily debarred from taking part in competitions affiliated to these bodies: some form of dispensation may be made to accommodate their disability but specific inquiry to the organizing body prior to the event is advisable. British Dressage operates a scheme whereby disabled riders can apply to the Dispensation Committee for a Dispensation Certificate (renewable annually) which, upon entering a competition, is passed to the organizer to be lodged with the judge. British Dressage also holds dedicated Disabled Competitions, which are run under its own rules except where rules of the International Paraplegic Equestrian Committee (IPEC) take precedence. Other national bodies operate broadly similar systems.

**dishing**   Faulty action in which the lower parts of the limbs are thrown forward and outward during movement; usually rooted in conformation, but can become more marked in a horse who is both excited and under restraint. Dishing causes the movement to be biomechanically inefficient and horses who dish will not be favoured in dressage competitions.

**dismounting during the test**   If, during a test, a rider dismounts without a reason acceptable to the judges, no marks will be given for the movement during which the dismounting took place. See also **fall**.

**disobedience**   The behaviour of a horse who understands what the rider requires of him, is capable of complying, but does not conform to the requirement. A horse cannot properly be said to exhibit disobedience if he does not understand the rider's requirements (for example, a novice horse being asked suddenly to perform a movement for which he has had no prior training), or if pain or inappropriate restraint limit his ability to comply.

**dispensation**   A variation on the normal rules of a competition intended to accommodate special circumstances relating to horse or rider. Normally valid only if the pertinent rules recognize the possibility of it being necessary – for example, it is enshrined in the rules of British Dressage that riders with physical disabilities may apply for a Dispensation Certificate.

**disqualification**   The banning of an entrant from a competition, prior to the event, or their effective removal from it during or after the event, because they are found not to fulfil some criterion of qualification.

**distractions**   External influences which, whether schooling or competing, may attract the horse's attention and reduce his concentration upon the rider's commands. Since inattention is likely to compromise the performance of a test, astute riders see it as part of the training process to familiarize the horse with as many different sights and sounds as possible, in order to 'desensitize' the horse to such distractions and enhance concentration upon the rider's demands.

**disunited**   Said of the canter (and gallop) when the correct sequence of footfall is disrupted; for example, an unbalanced horse may canter with one 'leading leg' in front and the opposite' lead' behind (sometimes called cross canter).

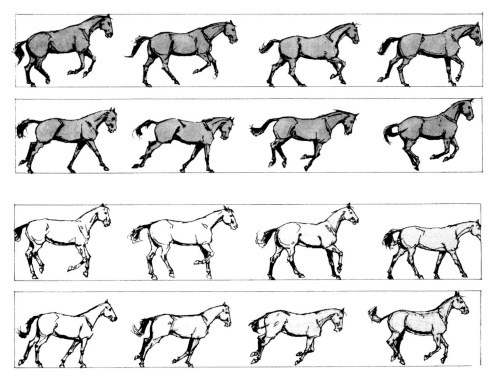

Disconnected canter: (top) hurried behind; the right hind has impacted before the left fore; (bottom) hurried in front; the left fore has impacted before the right hind.
Drawings from Ulrik Schramm's *The Undisciplined Horse.*

**diving**   A term sometimes used to describe the sudden, even violent, response of a horse who, having being subject to over-restraint by the reins, finds the rein contact released and thrusts his head downward as a relief. May also be a wilful act by a horse who simply wishes to escape the control of the reins. These actions are distinctly different from that of a horse ridden correctly and sympathetically who, when offered the chance to do so, takes

73

the contact forward and down in a measured fashion, thankful for the chance to stretch his topline, but happy enough to retain a light contact with the bit.

**doping**   The administration of a non-normal nutriment with the intention of artificially stimulating or sedating a horse. Forbidden under all rules of dressage and penalized by elimination/disqualification. See also **forbidden substances**.

An ornate double bridle being used by Portuguese rider, Carlos Couneiro. Photograph by Elizabeth Furth.

**double bridle**   A bridle that employs both a bradoon and a curb bit; in skilled hands, on a highly trained horse, it allows nuances of communication not achievable with a snaffle; compulsory for British Dressage Advanced Level and for all International (FEI) Level tests; not usually permitted at the lower levels (for example: in AHSA tests, not below Fourth Level; in British Dressage tests, not below Elementary.) See also **reins, holding of**.

**doux passage**   See **passage**.

**Dover, Robert**   Born in 1956 in Chicago, Illinois, into a theatrical family, Dover spent much of his childhood in Canada and the Bahamas until the family moved to Florida. He attended the University of Georgia with the intention of becoming a vet, but later changed direction and majored in philosophy.

At the age of thirteen, whilst living in Canada, he accepted an invitation to go riding and met Gerda Fredericks, who set about teaching him to ride in the classical manner, with great emphasis on developing his seat on the lunge. During this period he also learnt to vault. Whilst living in the Bahamas, he attended the local branch of the British Pony Club, where he did a great deal of bareback riding. During this time, he also played polo. On returning to America, he took part in endurance riding, but dressage always remained his real love. After taking his Pony Club A Test and then becoming a National Examiner, he trained with Elizabeth Lewis who was herself trained by Bengt Ljungquist. By the age of seventeen, Dover had trained his first Grand Prix horse. He went on to train under Ljungquist until the latter's death in 1979, subsequently training with Willi Schultheis and Georg Theodorescu.

In the 1980s, although competing at the highest level, Dover was dissatisfied with his results and so, in 1987, he took two horses to Europe to work with Gabrielle Grillo, who gave him a great deal of support. Later that year he won the Grand Prix Freestyle at Aachen on *Federleicht*, and finished

American Olympic rider Robert Dover on *Metallic*. Photograph by Elizabeth Furth.

3rd at the FEI World Cup Final, the highest placing by an American. He went on to represent the USA at the 1988 Olympic Games and has been a team member at all subsequent Olympics up to and including 2004, winning team bronze in 1992, 1996, 2000 and 2004. An adviser and trainer to a number of American riders, he draws on his own experiences to encourage participation in European training and competition.

**downgrading** An arrangement pertinent to competition dressage, operated by some national organizing bodies, such as British Dressage. Under such a scheme horses may, in certain circumstances and subject to specific criteria, have their grading points reduced. The main rationale is to accommodate relatively inexperienced riders who have taken over the permanent ride (e.g. through purchase) on a relatively highly graded horse but who need, for their own purposes, to compete for a while at lower levels. If the ride on a downgraded horse is subsequently taken over by a higher-graded rider (see **grading of riders**), the horse's grading will revert to its previous level.

**'downhill'** A term used to describe the undesirable characteristic of a horse whose back appears to slope downward a little from quarters to forehand, either because this is a fact of conformation (he is croup-high) or, in more common usage, because he is significantly unbalanced onto his forehand. Compare with **'uphill'**.

**dragging**    Action of the lower limbs and feet that signifies a serious lack of animation in the horse.

**draw reins**    See **auxiliary reins**.

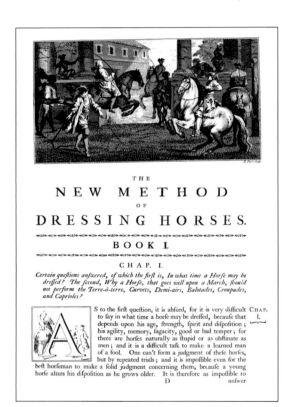

Chapter heading from the Duke of Newcastle's *A General System of Horsemanship.*

**dress**    An archaic term in English, derived from the French verb dresser, which had connotations both of straightness (e.g. 'right dress' was a command to either infantry or cavalry to straighten their line with reference to the next person on their right) and of overall training. Writers such as William Cavendish, Duke of Newcastle, referred to the act of training a horse as 'dressing' and to a fully trained horse as 'dressed'.

**dress, rider's**    Most organizing bodies require certain standards of dress for riders who wish to compete under their rules, and the FEI rules pertain to competitions run under their auspices. The rules of national bodies are subject to minor alteration from time to time, and there may be minor differences between the rules of one national or state body as compared to another. The rules of British Dressage, which are not universally applicable in other areas, but which may be taken as a general guide, are as follows:

*Advanced tests* – [appropriate equestrian] military uniform, or a tail coat with a top hat, or a black or navy-blue coat with a hunting cap, bowler or crash hat; and, other than with military uniform, a correctly tied white or cream stock.

*All tests below Advanced level* – [appropriate equestrian] military uniform, or a black, navy blue or tweed coat with correctly tied stock, or white American collar, or shirt and tie (not bright or multi-coloured), with hunting cap, bowler hat, crash cap (with black, brown or navy-blue cover) or dressage topper.

For all levels, breeches or jodhpurs must be white, cream or beige, except when they are part of an official military uniform. Boots must be black or brown. Under British Dressage rules gloves must be worn; there is currently no stipulation regarding colour; in America, gloves are not compulsory at the lower levels; in FEI tests everywhere, gloves (traditionally white) are required.

In excessively hot weather, most national bodies sanction the removal of jackets, subject to the discretion of the competition organizer.

Under British Dressage rules, it is compulsory for anyone mounted on a horse (i.e. grooms as well as riders) at an affiliated competition to wear a hat, and there is a fine for non-compliance. Should a competitor's hat come off during a test, it must be replaced immediately; the rider can either dismount to collect it, or it can be handed to them. The test will be restarted at the beginning of the movement in which it came off, and there will be no penalty. See also **spurs**; **whip**.

**dressage**    Derived from the French verb dresser, dressage means, essentially, training. Competitive dressage, in its present form, is a relatively modern development, arising to a large extent from the initial inclusion of dressage in the Olympic Games of 1912, at which point it was termed 'Individual Prize Riding'.

**dressage arena**    See **arena**.

**Dressage equitation class**    A form of competition, devised in the USA, to encourage relatively inexperienced riders to develop correct basics. It combines elements of a dressage test with elements of a showing class, in that most of the movements (walk, trot and canter, with the relevant transitions) are performed by all competitors simultaneously. Riders are judged on posture and the correct and effective use of the aids, as demonstrated by their horses' responses; judges may also introduce elements such as the individual execution of certain movements, and brief periods of riding without stirrups.

**dressage markers**   The letter markers at predetermined geometrical points around the arena as guide points for the designation and riding of test movements. In a 40 m x 20 m arena, the markers, clockwise from the entry point at A are: A, K, E, H, C, M, B, F; these appear as actual markers. Up the centre line are three imaginary markers: D (midway between K and F); X (the geometrical centre point of the arena) and G (midway between H and M). In the 60 m x 20 m arena, the perimeter markers, clockwise from A are: A, K, V, E, S, H, C, M, R, B, P, F. Up the centre line, in addition to the imaginary D, X and G are L (midway between V and P) and I (midway between S and R). These markers, and their relative placement, have been subject to some development and change since the beginnings of competition dressage. See also **arena**.

**dressage test**   Performed for the purpose of competition; a series of movements executed within a dressage arena that are marked by a judge or judges, the marks for the movements being supplemented by the collective marks, which relate to assessment of certain factors throughout the duration of the test. In most types of test, the form and order of the movements are prescribed; in freestyle tests, the rider has some choice of form and content, but is usually required to include certain compulsory movements.

**dressage whip**   Essentially, a whip long enough to allow the rider to supplement his own leg aids with it without letting go of the rein or disturbing the rein contact. Whips, and their correct use, are allowed in most, but by no means all, forms of dressage competition (for example, they are not allowed in FEI international competitions) and riders who wish to carry a whip should check the specific rules of the organizing body concerned for the class being competed in. See also **aids, artificial**; **whip**.

**Dressage with Jumping**   A form of competition in which horse and rider complete a dressage test and a round of showjumping, any penalties incurred in the latter being deducted from the marks awarded in the former. Competitions of this basic format have been held for many years, often under different names, including combined training (a term that has a different meaning in the USA); the term given here is currently in use by British Dressage. Generally, the dressage phase of such competitions is judged under the rules of the organizing dressage body (in this case, British Dressage) and the jumping phase under the rules of the relevant showjumping body (in this case, the British Show Jumping Association), although there are some modifications to BSJA rules.

**dresser**   A French verb, with various shades of meaning, including to raise, to draw or set up, to straighten and to train.

**dresseur**   A French noun, derived from dresser, meaning trainer.

**drifting**   A term sometimes used to describe a moderate but sustained loss of direction; for example, a horse may drift off the centre line or long diagonal. Most commonly seen in horses who are crooked and/or are not moving actively forward.

**driving aids**   Aids of the seat and legs intended to produce forward impulse in the horse.

**drugs**   See **forbidden substances**.

**dry mouth**   An undesirable state in the horse, since a modicum of saliva helps to lubricate the action of the bit. As in humans, it may also indicate nervousness. However, some horses seem naturally to produce less saliva than others, the physiology of the parotid (salivary) glands, the relative conformation of jawbones and neck, together with the general degree of flexion at the poll, possibly being contributory factors.

While a dry mouth is undesirable, this photograph by Elizabeth Furth shows the moderate salivation of a confident horse.

**Duarte, King of Portugal** (d. 1438) King of Portugal at a time of struggle for dominance of the Iberian Peninsula between the Moors and the native population, Duarte realized that it was a battlefield necessity for the Iberians to adapt from riding heavy horses in the deep-seated European medieval manner to riding lighter horses with shorter stirrup leathers, in the Moorish manner, or a la gineta, and wrote a treatise addressing this matter. However, his interest in equitation transcended the use of the horse in war; he founded the equestrian academy in Lisbon and wrote a second book on training. Duarte's writings stress aspects such as lightness and manoeuvrability and suggest that he was genuinely concerned with training the horse, as opposed to pursuing the rather brutal domination that was common practice in Europe at that time. In this respect, he seems to have preceded even the more enlightened elements of the Neapolitan school by more than a century and, consequentially, some commentators consider him a philosophical link between Xenophon and de Pluvinel.

**Duke of Newcastle** (1592–1676) Best known in equestrian circles by his ducal title, William Cavendish, Duke of Newcastle, was an English nobleman of great wealth, a cultivated man who wrote plays and poems and became friend and patron to many leading figures in the arts. In 1639 he became a Privy Counsellor to Charles I and, with the onset of the Civil War, Commander in Chief of the Royalist Northern Army. Initially, he was successful in this role but when the tide of war turned he was obliged to flee to Europe, where he tried in vain to muster support for his king. With Charles I executed and his own estates confiscated, Cavendish settled in exile in Belgium. Here, he devoted his time to training horses and writing *A General System of Horsemanship* – a book which was to have an influence on the thinking of pre-eminent figures such as de la Guérinière, the Comte d'Aure and Gustav Steinbrecht.

With the restoration of the monarchy and the accession of Charles II to the throne in 1660, Cavendish was able to return to England, where the remnants of his estates were returned to him. Although he became a Privy Counsellor to the new king, he was past the prime of life and had little influence at court. He therefore continued to devote his time to equitation, until failing health obliged him to give up even his own horses. He died in 1676 and was buried at Westminster Abbey.

**durchlässigkeit**  A German term, based on *durchlässig*, which literally means porous. The essence of being porous is to 'let through', thus durchlässigkeit is 'letting-throughness'; a state in which the energy produced by the hind limbs and quarters is allowed to travel freely through the horse's back. In English terminology, the horse who possesses this quality is said to be 'through'.

# E

**early**  A judge's remark signifying that a movement was begun or ended, or a transition performed, before the point or marker specified by the test sheet.

**earthbound**  Describes movement lacking suspension or elevation.

**Ecole de Cavalerie**  The original French name for the cavalry school at Saumur, and also the title of the famous book by de la Guérinière.

**écouté**  A French term meaning, literally, 'listen in'. Said of a school trot or walk, which one can 'hear' – that is, a precise, shortened, highly cadenced gait, the quality of which is identifiable aurally.

**écuyer**  A French term used throughout Europe from around the sixteenth century onward; a recognized riding master, originally often of noble birth and/or military rank, but more latterly conferred as a courtesy title upon recipients deemed worthy of it.

Ecole de Cavalerie, Saumur.

**educating**   The process of teaching a horse to really understand what is being asked of him; typified by the trainer breaking down exercises into component parts and building progressively towards the whole.

**Eilberg, Ferdi**   Born in Germany in 1953, Eilberg began riding at the age of ten and by sixteen he had decided to become a professional trainer. He completed his Bereiter apprenticeship with Reiner Klimke and also worked with other trainers including Harry Boldt, Willi Schultheis and Johann Hinnemann. During the 1970s he spent four years in the yard of Eva Pracht before becoming a freelance trainer. He achieved his Berufsreitlehrer, the highest German qualification, in 1978 and also holds the Reiter Abzeichnung, a gold medal awarded for success in both dressage and showjumping at advanced level. In 1980, he moved to England, where he quickly established himself as a prominent trainer, being dressage trainer to the British eventing team from 1982 to 1992.

Ferdi Eilberg on *Arun Tor*. Photograph by Elizabeth Furth.

In due course, he took out British nationality and rode for Britain on many occasions throughout the 1990s. In 1993 he was a member of the silver-medal-winning team at the European Championships and, riding *Arun Tor*, he became the first British rider in five years to win an International Grand Prix Special when he won at Rennes CDI in France. In 1995, riding the same horse, he won a Grand Prix Kür at the European Championships and the Horse of The Year Show Grand Prix World Cup. The following year, he was short-listed for the Olympic Games with *Arun Tor* and long-listed with another of his rides, the highly successful stallion *Demonstrator*. In both 1994 and 1998 he represented Britain at the World Championships.

In recent years, Eilberg has become increasingly involved in coaching and team management roles. In 2002 he became Director of Coaching for Britain's World Class organization and he was trainer to the British team that won the bronze medal at the 2003 European Championships.

**elasticity**   A quality that allows muscles to stretch and return to their original length; applied to the whole horse, it implies that the musculature associated with movement has high levels of strength and suppleness.

**Elementary**   Under British Dressage rules, the third level of tests, above Novice.

**elevation**   Most commonly refers to the degree to which the horse's feet are raised in movement. This depends partly on skeletal conformation and muscular development, partly on the degree of animation with which the horse is moving, and also on the gait variant being performed; for example, in the collected gaits, the steps are relatively short, but high. The term is also used in respect of the height achieved in the airs above the ground. See also **active elevation**; **relative elevation**.

Piaffe, showing both elevation and engagement. Drawing by Gisela Holstein.

**eligible**   Signifies that a horse, rider, or combination thereof, is qualified to enter a competition or participate as a team member.

**elimination**   A penalty that debars a competitor from further involvement in a competition; in dressage tests, may include factors such as prolonged resistance, using prohibited equipment, etc.

**embouchure**   An old French term; the mouthpiece of a bit.

**energy**   The capacity to do work. Since it is a principle of physics that energy cannot be created or destroyed, the common idea that the rider 'creates' energy in the horse is incorrect; the rider's actions induce the horse to expend energy that he already possesses.

**engaged**   Describes the hind limbs when, during the forward (stance) phase of movement, they are placed sufficiently forward beneath the horse's mass to enhance his balance and provide active forward propulsion. Some degree of engagement is necessary for the working gaits to be correct; true collection and extension require engagement at an advanced level. See **engagement**.

**engagement**   The quality of being engaged.

**enter**   To enter a competition, or a dressage arena at the start of a test. See **entrance**.

**entrance**   The start of a dressage test, which always entails entering the arena at the A marker. Depending upon the test being ridden, the entry will be performed in some variant of either trot or canter; since the requirement will always be to proceed straight along the centre line, astute competitors ensure that they ride the entrance from the most advantageous line of approach, with the appropriate gait properly established.

Under all rules, there is a requirement to enter the arena within a specified time after the signal to start has been sounded. Under FEI and British Dressage rules, the time limit is 45 seconds; exceeding this time entails elimination.

**equestrian**   As an adjective, relating to horse riding; as a (masculine) noun, a rider – the feminine form being: equestrienne.

**equilibrium**   A term, borrowed by equitation from the physical science of statics, in which it means the state of a body acted upon by two or more forces, which balance one another. It is certainly true that a horse in motion is acted upon by several forces and, provided that he remains balanced under the influence of these forces, including the weight of the rider, then the use of this term, to imply a refined state of balance, is justified.

**equine influenza**   An infectious viral illness, the spread of which most equestrian organizations are anxious to guard against. Whilst vaccination may not be a compulsory prerequisite simply for registration with some national dressage bodies, all recommend this practice, not only in the interests of equine health, but also because up-to-date cover is a requisite for

FEI competitions and simply for entry into some venues. The procedure for initiating cover is somewhat protracted and it is recommended that veterinary advice be sought some time before certification is required for competitive purposes.

**equitation**   Derived from the Latin, *equito*, means, essentially, horse riding, but nowadays has assumed connotations of skilled riding and training.

**error of course**   A mistake in the execution of a test, such as a wrong turn, wrong gait, or omission of a movement, that materially affects the execution of the test. Where such an error occurs, the judge (or President of the Jury), notifies the competitor by sounding a bell. The competitor is then shown, if necessary, the point at which the test must be restarted, and told the next movement to be executed.

In some cases, if sounding the bell to correct a minor error of course (e.g. a transition mistakenly performed one marker early or late) would unnecessarily interrupt the flow of the test, the judge/President of the Jury may use discretion in whether to sound the bell or not, but the error will be noted and the mark adjusted accordingly. Generally, if it is felt that the rider might repeat the error when the movement is performed on the other rein, a fair-minded judge will ring the bell to notify the competitor of the first error, thus providing a tacit reminder not to replicate it. There is, however, no obligation upon the judge to do this.

Errors of course (whether signalled by the bell or not) are penalized cumulatively as follows: 1st error, 2 points; 2nd error, 4 points; 3rd error, 8 points; thereafter, elimination.

**error of test**   A mistake in the execution of a test involving something other than an error of course, e.g. the competitor trots rising instead of sitting, or executes the salute incorrectly. Although the penalties are the same as for errors of course, it is rarely appropriate for the judge(s) to halt the test to correct such an error.

**evasions**   Overt actions by the horse with the intention of avoiding doing something that is required by the rider. Compare with **resistance**.

**eventing**   See **horse trials**.

**exercise**   Work, either on long reins, the lunge, or under saddle, carried out primarily to improve or maintain physical condition. As such, differs in certain aspects from exercises and training or schooling.

**exercise bandages**   Bandages applied to the lower limbs to provide soft tissue support during work or riding in. These, and other forms of leg protection, may sometimes be appropriate at such times, but they are not permitted during standard tests and their use will entail elimination. They may, however, be allowed during specialized classes such as pas de deux and quadrilles.

**exercises**   Movements performed either under saddle, or in-hand, with the aim of producing some specific development of the horse's understanding and/or way of going. The potential difference between exercise and exercises might be seen in the following example: a horse might be exercised at canter with the primary intention of developing physical fitness; he might do exercises in canter, such as serpentines involving counter-canter, with the primary intention of increasing obedience, suppleness and the overall quality of the gait.

**extension**   In each gait, the lengthening of the strides to the practical maximum that the individual horse can achieve without compromising

Isabell Werth and *Gigolo* in extended canter. Photograph by Elizabeth Furth.

balance and the regularity of footfall. The amount of extension achievable will be ultimately limited by a horse's skeletal conformation, but progression towards the practical maximum will be assisted by the development of joint flexibility and muscular strength, and the enhancement of balance and impulsion.

**extravagant**  An adjective sometimes used to describe particularly eye-catching movement; for example, a horse might be said to have an 'extravagant trot'. Provided that such movement is fundamentally correct, it may find favour with the judge(s). However, connections of such horses should be mindful that meanings of this word, closer to its root, include 'going beyond what is reasonable', 'not closely controlled' and that movement fitting these descriptions, however striking, will not impress a discerning judge.

# F

**fall**  If a horse and/or rider fall(s) during the execution of a dressage test, they will not be eliminated, but will be penalized by the effect of the fall upon the movement in which it occurs and, as appropriate, in the collective marks.

**fall apart**  A term sometimes used to describe a serious loss of balance and impulsion by the horse, with the probable consequence that the gait and or movement being performed will break down.

**fall in**  Said of a horse who, when going through a corner or otherwise on the arc of a circle, leans to the inside of the figure with his inside shoulder and loses the correct inside bend. May be related to loss/lack of balance and/or marked crookedness, but is commonly caused or provoked by the rider's faulty posture and inappropriate use of aids, especially those of the inside leg and outside rein.

**fall into**  To perform a downward transition in an unbalanced manner, with the horse tipping onto the forehand and rhythm being lost.

**fall out**  Sometimes elaborated as 'falling over the outside shoulder'; the horse, incorrectly bent to the inside, veers to the outside of the required figure, with his outside shoulder effectively leading the movement. Sometimes seen in faulty attempts to execute shoulder-in, as well as turns and circles; while crookedness and lack of balance may be contributory factors, the main cause is often overuse of the inside rein in a backward-pulling fashion, which more or less obliges the horse to move in this way.

**false bend**  A term that describes lateral bend in the horse that appears superficially correct (i.e. the overall tendency is for the horse to be curved to the left or right, as intended) but involves some biomechanical flaw. For example, a horse falling out through the outside shoulder will still show a crude approximation of bend to the inside, but the curvature will be accentuated and 'broken' from the wither forward and his movement will be crabbed and lacking impulsion. A more subtle example may be produced by a rider who takes too much contact on the outside rein, thus, while the overall bend may seem correct, the horse's neck will be somewhat warped and contracted.

Drawings of false bend by Brian Tutlo, from Paul Belasik's *Dressage for the 21st Century.*

**false canter**   A term, rare in current usage, that has sometimes been used to mean counter-canter. The latter is a more precise description of a gait which, when ridden intentionally and correctly, has nothing 'false' about it.

**false extension**   Sometimes referred to by figurative phrases such as 'goose-stepping' or 'shooting the cuffs'; a faulty form of extended trot, suggestive of tension, in which the forelegs and toes are hyper-extended whilst in the air, the feet then being snatched back and grounded short of the vertical line to which they reached whilst above the ground. This form of movement has long been criticized as incorrect by various equestrian authorities and is contrary to the widely accepted precept that the forefeet should touch down on the spot towards which they were pointing while still suspended.

**fatigue**   The effects of physical fatigue upon the horse are sometimes overlooked by riders and trainers overanxious to achieve rapid results, or to overcome a particular schooling problem in a single session. Young horses often tire (and lose concentration) surprisingly quickly; collected work, especially in the early stages, when horses may not have acquired their full strength, places great demands upon the muscles and joints of the hindquarters and limbs, and active lateral work places considerable stresses on tendons and ligaments. Working a horse who is significantly fatigued not only risks physical injury, it is also likely to prove counter-productive in terms of quality; and there is the added factor of provoking resistances if the physical demands are such that the work becomes uncomfortable.

**faults**   When assessing movements in a dressage test, judges may have in mind overall categories of faults which will have a greater or lesser impact on marks given. The categories usually applied are: basic faults (fundamental flaws which are heavily penalized – for example, impure gaits, not accepting the bit); main faults (which are significantly penalized, examples being poor transitions, poorly formed figures); and minor faults (transient errors arising from momentary inattention etc., which will be quite lightly penalized). Some organizing bodies, such as the USDF list these categories and related faults in detail in their literature.

Emile Faurie. Photograph by Elizabeth Furth.

**Faurie, Emile** Born in 1963, Faurie spent his early years in South Africa, where he started riding at the age of fifteen at a local riding school. In 1980, he moved to England where he spent three years at the Talland School of Equitation, starting as a working pupil but later riding the proprietor's, Molly Sivewright's, advanced horses. After that he went to Germany where he worked for Performance Sales International, backing and preparing young horses for auction. On returning to England he was offered the ride on *Virtu*, on whom he represented Great Britain at the 1992 Olympic Games and the 1993 European Championships, winning team silver and individual bronze medals in the latter event. The partnership also won the British National Champion title in 1993 and 1994. Following *Virtu*'s retirement in 1995, Faurie has continued to compete successfully on a number of horses, being a member of the British Olympic team in 2000 and travelling reserve in 2004. He has also ridden in three World Equestrian Games and three European Championships, winning team bronze in the latter event in 2003.

**Federation Equestre Internationale** (**FEI**) Created in 1921 and based in Lausanne, Switzerland; the governing body of most major equestrian sports (except racing) worldwide. National organizing bodies of the sport of dressage are affiliated to the FEI and base the rules for their own internal competitions closely on those of that body. Tests for the higher levels (Prix St Georges upward) are produced by the FEI and are normally run under their rules, as are all official international competitions.

**feeling the hair** A term originating in Germany which describes a light, steady contact of the rider's legs resting against the horse's sides; the basis from which specific leg aids can be given with immediacy and without undue movement.

**FEI** See **Federation Equestre Internationale**.

**Felton, W. Sidney**  The author of an informative book *Masters of Equitation*, which plots the development of dressage in Europe and America from its roots in the Renaissance era. Felton was born in Massachusetts in 1895: a graduate of Harvard Law School, he served as a US Aviation Officer in the First World War, and subsequently practised law in Boston. A lifelong rider and highly analytical equestrian scholar, he was a keen follower of hounds, an amateur instructor and judge and a leading figure in the organization of the US Pony Club. Felton was well respected by many leading riders of his era, and the foreword for *Masters of Equitation* was provided by Henry Wynmalen.

**Ferrer-Salat, Beatriz**  Born in Barcelona, Spain, in 1966, the daughter of a National Champion tennis player, who represented Spain in the Davis Cup. Highly educated and multi-lingual, she did not start competitive riding until the age of sixteen. Trained by the German, Jan Bemmelmans, she has represented Spain with distinction at three Olympic Games (1996, 2000 and 2004), winning team silver and individual bronze in 2004, three World Championships (1994, 1998 and 2002), four European Championships and one World Cup.

Beatriz Ferrer-Salat on *Brilliant*. Photograph by Elizabeth Furth.

**Fiaschi, Cesar** (or **Césare**)  (d. 1575) An Italian trainer of the sixteenth century, with a school at Ferrera. Fiaschi was a contemporary of Federico Grisone, some of whose ideas he apparently adopted and developed. He may, in effect, have been the instigator of dressage to music, in that he introduced music during riding to promote rhythm. His most famous pupil was Giovanni Pignatelli, who himself went on to found perhaps the most famous and influential school of the Neapolitan era.

**figure of eight**  A figure consisting of two same-sized circles, ridden in opposite directions; on completion of the first circle, the horse is

91

momentarily straightened then the second circle is started on the opposite rein; promotes bilateral suppleness in the horse and is an exercise in control and application of the rider's aids.

**figures**   Geometrical patterns ridden in the school to educate, balance and supple the horse and to promote accurate riding.

**Filatov, Sergey**   Rider from the Soviet Union who won the individual gold medal at the 1960 Olympic Games in Rome, riding *Absent*, and the individual bronze medal in Tokyo four years later on the same horse. Subsequently viewed as his country's most celebrated exponent of dressage, he was invited to work as senior instructor and was instrumental in launching the career of Yelana Petushkova. However, allegations began to surface about some of his training methods and, in the light of these, he seems to have removed himself from the dressage scene.

Photograph of James Fillis from *Breaking and Riding*.

**Fillis, James**   (1834–1913) Born in London, Fillis went to France at an early age. There he met François Baucher and, greatly impressed by his methods, studied them under Baucher's pupil, François Caron. (Later in life, Fillis found himself at odds with some of Baucher's ideas – as his 'Commentaries on Baucher' in his book *Breaking and Riding* show – but he always retained an overall admiration for him.)

After running his own school in Le Havre, Fillis moved to Paris, where he supervised the stables of various members of the nobility. Then, wishing to promote his method more widely, he followed the same course as Baucher, and began to perform in the circus, to great acclaim. Pressed to produce a book, Fillis was offered editorial assistance by a long-time pupil, the French politician, Clemenceau. Published in 1890, the book was subsequently translated into English by the eminent veterinary author, Horace Hayes.

From 1891 to 1897, Fillis was based in Germany. He then went to Russia with Circus Ciniselli and created such an impression that he was offered, and accepted, the post of Colonel and Ecuyer-en-chef of the Russian Cavalry School – a position he held until retiring in 1910. During his period of office, a visiting American Army Commission decided to adopt his method, and *Breaking and Riding* became the official textbook of the US Cavalry School.

After his retirement, Fillis moved back to Germany to coach his daughter Anna (who became a famous circus écuyère) and two sons and, when they moved to America, he returned to Paris, where he died. Although some of his ideas were seen, in some quarters, as controversial, Fillis's work had a considerable impact on the equestrian world and many eminent riders and trainers of following generations made reference to it.

**first position**   See **position** and **shoulder-fore**.

**fitness**   Correct and progressive dressage will produce an advanced degree of fitness in the horse; there are various accounts, from eminent figures such as Podhajsky, of horses trained almost entirely in the arena coping admirably with a hard day's hunting. However, a horse's current level of fitness (also suppleness and strength) must always be taken into account during training, especially where the more physically demanding movements are concerned.

**flapping**   Said of the rider's legs if they are used continually in an unrefined or unconstrained fashion, being alternately taken off and re-applied to the horse's sides, often with no correlation to the action of the horse's limbs.

**flat**   Said of steps or strides that lack sufficient elevation for the gait or gait variant being performed.

**flexibility**   Of a horse, the capacity to bend readily in the lateral and longitudinal planes and to articulate the joints readily and fully; thus closely related to suppleness.

Lateral exercises such as shoulder-in help to develop flexibility. Photograph by Karl Leck from *Dressage for the 21st Century.*

**flexion**  Bending; in equitation, most commonly used with reference to the joints of the limbs, poll and lower jaw and to describe moderate degrees of lateral bend.

**flexions in-hand**  Exercises carried out from the ground with the bridled horse, aimed at educating him as to the required responses to contact with the rider's hands and at promoting direct flexion (yielding) of the jaw and lateral flexion of the head and neck. Work of this sort was popularized during the nineteenth century and beyond by François Baucher and his disciples. Michel Henriquet who, in *Henriquet on Dressage*, refers extensively to the legacy of Baucher, comments: 'The aim of all these flexions is to obtain a light, two-way rapport between the hand of the rider and the mouth of the horse', and adds that they 'demand the competence, experience and tact of a master'. In *Breaking and Riding* James Fillis, a former pupil of Baucher, explores these flexions in detail and also highlights some faulty practices (including those he considers to be some of his former master's) and warns: 'flexion is such a delicate thing that an incapable horseman who practises it, will often spoil a horse instead of improving him'.

Drawing of lateral flexion in-hand, from James Fillis's *Breaking and Riding*.

**flies, protection from**  In certain seasons and climates, flies may prove a major distraction to horses, and riders schooling at home have various options with regard to minimizing such nuisance. Some of the means of protection are also permitted in some circumstances under competition rules. For example, British Dressage rules permit the use of fly fringes, ear covers and gauzes whilst riding in, but not during the test. (Under certain circumstances, there may be a written dispensation for a confirmed 'headshaker' to wear a nose gauze, but this would normally be for reasons other than fly nuisance.) They do, however, permit the use of impregnated browbands and fly repellent discs both for warming up and during the test. FEI rules permit the use of fly hoods under extreme circumstances and subject to the discretion of the President of the Ground Jury. Given global differences, rules relating to this issue may vary, encompass exceptions and dispensations and be subject to revision, so competitors would be advised to check current rules relating to any specific competition.

**floating**   A term sometimes used to express the quality of light, active movement of a horse; there will be free movement of the back and limbs, and a significant degree of suspension; a contrast to hovering movement, which is typified by tension and a relative lack of forward progression.

**flying change**   A change of canter lead, executed in close connection with the moment of suspension that takes place at the end of each stride of that gait.

**forbidden substances**   All dressage competition organizing bodies produce lists of substances, the presence of which is forbidden in competing horses and riders. The lists are generally based on those compiled by the FEI and, where appropriate, the International Olympic Committee, and are subject to updating. In addition to substances that could have an obvious stimulating or sedating effect, the lists include such substances as anti-inflammatories and various analgesics, steroids, hormones, etc., and they are subject to continual updating. So far as horses are concerned, some of the substances are not absolutely forbidden, but are subject to maximum thresholds, the level of which must not be exceeded.

Random testing for forbidden substances, in both horses and riders, may be carried out by the organizing body concerned. Therefore, if it is necessary for a rider to take medication shortly prior to or during a competition, perusal of the relevant list of forbidden substances for riders should be made in consultation with an appropriate health professional. If it is necessary to administer medication to a horse in the period leading up to a competition (let alone during the competition period), expert veterinary advice should be sought – and it should be noted that some substances have been known to remain in a horse's system for longer than veterinary opinion predicted.

**forehand**   A general term for the front part of a horse, including the head, neck, chest, shoulders and forelegs. In his natural state, a horse will generally make significant use of the forehand to support his weight and assist in movement; it is axiomatic of correct training that he will learn to make greater use of his hindquarters to carry and propel his own weight and that of his rider, the role of the forehand in these respects thus reducing. (See also **collection; rassembler; self-carriage**.) A horse in whom these adjustments have not been made is said to be on the forehand.

**forging**   The striking of a front shoe by the hind shoe on the same side when the horse is trotting. This can only occur if the timing of the footfalls is incorrect, often as a consequence of fatigue, lack of balance, inactivity or some combination thereof. Forging during a test will be penalized severely.

**Fort Riley**   At the start of the twentieth century, a simple cavalry and artillery post in Kansas, at which there was little training in horsemanship or horsemastership. When Guy Henry was sent there in 1902 he, along with Capt. W.C. Short, began to place more emphasis on these aspects. Following his attendance at Saumur, Henry returned to Fort Riley in 1907 and went on to reorganize the entire American military system of instruction along the lines of the French training system. As a result of Henry's work, Fort Riley became increasingly influential as a training centre. A number of top American military riders, including Isaac Kitts, Hiram Tuttle and Robert Borg had official roles there.

**forward**   Towards the front. The horse's willingness to move forward with minimal encouragement (see **free forward movement**) is an essential building block of correct training; a horse who displays this quality is sometimes described as being 'forward'.

Horse in-hand showing free forward movement in trot. Photograph from Alfred Knopfhart's *Fundamentals of Dressage.*

**four-time**   Describes a gait in which the horse's four feet strike the ground independently; the walk and gallop are four-time gaits. The canter, which is a three-time gait, can become four-time if the normally single beat of the diagonal pair of legs becomes split: the canter is then considered incorrect. However, some authorities maintain that, when pirouetting in canter, it is almost or actually inevitable that the canter will become four-time to some degree.

**Franke, Käthe** (1897–1976) Born Käthe Cobau in Berlin, to parents who owned a Thoroughbred stud farm, she displayed an enormous enthusiasm for riding from a young age and, at fourteen, was allowed to work with the highly regarded trainer August Staeck. Unusually for a female in the Germany of that period, she was initially taught to ride astride rather than side-saddle; she was also introduced to showjumping. A period at boarding school and then the war years called a temporary halt to her riding but, in 1918, she once again attended Staeck's yard, taking with her two of her father's horses. It was at this point that she learnt to ride side-saddle in order that she would be able to compete at shows. In 1919, the first post-war show was held in Germany and Franke was placed second in a riding-horse class, behind Oskar Stensbeck. The following year she had her first victory in a dressage competition riding astride, and in 1922 she won her first dressage competition riding side-saddle. This was the start of an amazing period of competitive success in Germany that extended to the start of the Second World War: in 1927 she won sixteen hunter classes, eleven dressage competitions, one horse trial and eighteen combined classes; in 1927, 1931, 1932 and 1933 she won the ladies' showjumping championship and every year from 1925 to 1939 she was the lady riders' dressage champion.

Throughout this period of success, she continued to be supported by Staeck, riding many horses he found and produced and, in due course, becoming first his assistant and then partner in his enterprise. It was a great blow to her when, in 1942, Staeck died. After the end of the war, however, she went to work on the famous Thoroughbred stud farm owned by Werner Schauerte, where she quickly built up an influential dressage (and driving) yard. She produced the highly successful dressage horses, *St. Georg*, *Matador* and *Brilliant* and developed a passion for training young riders, being a major influence on both Harry Boldt and Reiner Klimke.)

Drawing of Käthe Franke, from General Decarpentry's *Academic Equitation.*

**Frank, Oscar**   Born in 1894, Frank served as a member of the Swiss Armed Forces for some forty years, first in the artillery at Thun and later as a riding officer and head trainer for the cavalry in Bern. Always a highly gifted rider and trainer, he was especially influenced by the period he spent at the Spanish Riding School in 1929. On his return to Switzerland, he started work on a report: 'The Spanish Riding School of Vienna'. Up to that time, the teachings of the School had been largely handed down by oral tradition, the only real exception being the short Directives, written by the former Director, von Holbien, at the end of the nineteenth century. Frank's work thus attracted a good deal of attention and subsequently his superiors instructed him to produce a book of Swiss Riding Directives. In 1940, Frank published another book, *Reiten*, which included further explanations of the various directives along with various hints for riders and trainers. This book became very popular with a wide audience, and was referred to informally as 'Der Frank'. Frank retired from the military in 1956 and, following serious illness, died in 1963.

**free**   Unconstrained, as in free walk.

**free forward movement**   A term used to describe the physical consequences of a horse's willingness to go forward; implies that he will continue to do so in a designated gait, with a minimum of reinforcing (driving) aids from the rider, until instructed to do otherwise.

**freestyle tests (and freestyle to music)**   The essence of a freestyle test is that it is one in which, rather than the sequence of movements being prescribed, competitors effectively 'design' their test. There are, however, certain constraints to this, which may vary in points of detail depending upon the rules of the organizing body and the level of the test. Generally, there will be some compulsory movements (which must be performed at some point in the test); there may also be prescribed *forms* of movements (for example flying changes every two strides, a minimum of five times consecutively) and, in some cases, certain movements may be forbidden (these may include movements deemed to exceed the degree of difficulty of the level of test being performed.) In marking freestyle tests, judges take account of the 'technical execution' – the manner in which the compulsory movements are performed – and other factors, similar to normal tests, such as harmony between horse and rider, rider's position and seat, etc., but a mark is also given for the composition of the programme.

Freestyle tests achieved a level of popularity in the latter part of the twentieth century – In Britain they were used for a while for Young Horse Tests – but it was not long before the basic form was pretty much superseded by the addition of music to the freestyle. This is music chosen in advance by the rider, around which the freestyle programme is based, played from a pre-recorded medium for the duration of the test. Essentially, the interpretation of this music adds the dimension of 'artistic presentation' to the riding and judging of the test. Initially, in tests ridden under FEI rules, this dimension was assessed in a collective mark which covered how the programme was composed and choreographed to the music, and the degree of difficulty of the movements. However, in freestyle tests at Grand Prix level this basic concept has been developed to include specific elements such as use of arena, inventiveness, well-calculated risks and choice and interpretation of the music. Since 1996, the Grand Prix Freestyle has become an integral component of the Olympic dressage competition, following on from the Grand Prix and Grand Prix Special tests and determining the final placings of the leading individuals.

Freestyle competitions at various levels are nowadays run under the rules of most national organizing bodies; these rules include various points of detail about the timing of the music, failure of the sound system, etc. Riders wishing to participate in such competitions will need to be familiar with the precise rules that pertain to their competition of choice.

**free walk on a long rein**   A form of walk in which, while the horse is allowed complete freedom to lower and stretch his head and neck, the rider nevertheless retains a light rein contact. The walk should be free, regular, swinging and long-striding (with marked over-tracking) but without haste.

Free walk on a long rein. Drawing by Maggie Raynor.

99

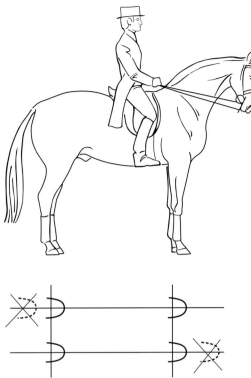

Drawings by Gisela Holstein indicating the elements of a correct full halt.

**fresh**  A term used to describe a horse who, through relative lack of exercise or sheer high spirits, is over-exuberant in the early stages of work.

**full bridle**  Another term for double bridle.

**full halt**  A complete, established halt; with connotations of correctness, balance and attention.

**full pass**  An old dressage movement, not required in modern-day tests, in which the horse is deemed to move laterally, without any forward movement. In practice, since the horse's outside lateral legs have to step in front of the inside lateral pair, this cannot be achieved unless the horse is, to some extent, bent laterally toward the required direction of movement, as is shown in old diagrams of the movement.

**gait**  A distinctive, repeated sequence of footfall that characterizes a specific mode of equine locomotion. The gaits currently employed in competition dressage are walk, trot and canter, each of which may be sub-divided into its gait variants. A number of other gaits may be observed in horses, some of which are more or less natural in particular breeds, others of which are engendered or developed by training.

**gait variant**  The different shades of movement that are available to a horse within each gait. As currently defined for training and competition purposes, these are collected, working, medium and extended in trot and canter – collected, medium, extended and free in walk. However, with the possible exception of the extended form, which is generally defined as the maximum length of stride that an individual horse can perform (without loss of balance and rhythm), the others mentioned are, despite their practical value, essentially arbitrary definitions that each cover a span of the overall movement available to the horse within each gait. By way of illustration, it is common practice, once a novice horse has established a more or less consistent working trot, to ask for some relative lengthening and shortening of this form of the gait. However, the changes of stride length achieved do not, at this stage, constitute 'collected' or 'medium' trot – they are minor changes within the working gait. To illustrate the point further, in his book *Reflections on Equestrian Art,* the late Nuno Oliveira made the observation 'In the gait known as trot, there are at least ten variations...'

**gallop**   A rapid, four-time gait, usually transverse in form, the sequence of footfall being one hind leg, the opposite hind leg, the foreleg on the same side as the first hind leg, the foreleg on the same side as the second hind leg, followed by a period of suspension. The gait is not required in dressage tests being (apart from other considerations) too rapid and ground-covering for much practical display within the confines of a dressage arena. However, some riders (especially those who have experience of three-day eventing), make occasional, judicious use of controlled gallops as part of their overall training programme, believing that it can help to exercise the topline muscles and ligaments, and encourage the generation of impulsion.

**galop**   The French word that serves for both the three-time gait of canter and the faster four-time gait of gallop (although occasionally the term petit galop is used to distinguish the former). In some books translated from French, galop is rendered in all cases as gallop, despite it being clear from the context that the author's intended meaning is canter.

**giravolta**   A form of turn on the forehand or reversed pirouette performed in-hand by some trainers to teach young horses to accept the action of the bit

The giravolta. Photograph by Karl Leck from Paul Belasik's *Dressage from the 21st Century*.

and to step sideways away from lateral pressure (in this case light pressure from the whip) as preparation to responding to the leg aids.

**give and re-take the reins**  A test command (the form used in the British Dressage rules) that requires the rider to push both hands forward to release the rein contact and then re-take it, in a smooth, continuous movement. The object is to demonstrate that the horse is in self-carriage or, at least, in balance. If this is the case, he should retain balance, outline, rhythm and tempo. If, however, he was previously being restrained or propped up by the rider's hands, he will run or fall onto the forehand. See also **uberstreichen**.

**gloves**  See **dress, rider's**.

**GMO**  See **Group Member Organization**.

**going**  Also known as footing; the state of the arena surface, or ground condition.

The surface of a modern all-weather dressage arena. Photograph from *All-weather Surfaces for Horses* by Ray Lodge and Susan Shanks.

102

**going short**   One (or sometimes more) of the horse's limbs not advancing to the same extent as the other limbs, as would accord with regular movement in the current gait. It is generally a sign that some injury, discomfort or imbalance is affecting movement of the limb(s) concerned.

**go large**   A command or action within the manège or arena; to go around the perimeter or outside track.

**good hands**   An old term that signifies astute and sympathetic use of the rein aids, in harmonious conjunction with the other aids and with appropriate reference to the horse's actions and responses.

**good mouth**   Traditionally said of a horse with a sensitive mouth, who willingly accepts the bit and light rein aids; signifies submission of the jaw and at the poll.

**grading of horses**   A scheme operated by national organizing bodies such as British Dressage whereby horses are graded on the basis of percentage scores achieved in competition, rather than placing or prize money. For example, under the British Dressage scheme, a horse who achieves a percentage mark of 67 per cent in a test will be awarded seven points, regardless of whether he wins the class or comes, perhaps, twelfth. On the other hand, a horse who wins a class with a percentage score of less than 60 per cent, will receive no points. (Some types of competition are exempt from this scheme.) The rationale behind this system is that a horse should progress through the competition levels on the basis of his own adjudged merits, rather than by comparison with others. As a corollary to this, the various competition levels each have a points limit and horses may not compete at a particular level once they have gained more points than this (e.g. the points limit for Novice is 74, so a horse who has gained 80 points cannot compete in official competitions at Novice level). However, in certain circumstances, a horse may be downgraded. See **downgrading** and also **ungraded**.

**grading of riders**   National organizing bodies generally operate schemes that grade riders for competition purposes, the grades relating to points won in competitions at various levels. These grades, together with those of the horses ridden, determine the eligibility of horse/rider partnerships for individual classes and competitions.

**grand passage**   See **passage**.

**Grand Prix**   The top level of competition under FEI rules.

**Grant, Charles Dudley** ('Chuck')   (1914–1990) A major driving force behind the development of dressage in America, Grant's fascination with horses began in early childhood when he rode the plough horses bareback at his family's farm in Michigan. Later, when the family moved to the Chicago area, Grant enrolled at college, planning to become a marine engineer. In Chicago, however, his riding opportunities were strictly limited and, missing horses, he joined the 122nd Field Artillery so that he could indulge his passion. Soon, he was riding almost continually – a circumstance enhanced by the fact that he had also become involved with schooling polo ponies. At this time, an acquaintance gave him a copy of Fillis's *Breaking and Schooling* and he began to apply the principles he learned to the polo and military horses in his charge.

In 1938, military reorganization meant that the horses in Grant's care were sent elsewhere, so he went to work at the Christensen Riding Academy, a large outfit in Chicago. At the outbreak of the Second World War, he enlisted in the army and saw service in North Africa and Italy, where, at one time, he was put in charge of a large number of horses captured from the enemy.

After the war, Grant returned to the Christensen Academy, where he taught and rode dressage, and also took part in jumping events, polo and racing. In 1947, he and a partner opened their own training centre and, in 1948, he judged the first civilian dressage competition in America. However, with interest in dressage still in its infancy, he moved to Michigan to work with the Bloomfield Open Hunt Club. Here, he promoted equal attention to dressage and jumping, with great success. In 1952, he was invited to give a dressage exhibition at the Michigan International Show and, with his horse *Shining Gold*, he went on to achieve great success in America and Canada. In due course, he established a new centre at Shine-A-Bit Farm where, under his guidance, an increasing number of pupils trained their horses to ever-higher levels. During the 1980s, failing health saw a (relative) reduction in the amount of riding and teaching he could manage, but he continued to instruct through books (including *American Dressage* and *Training the Haute Ecole or High School Horse*) and articles up to the time of his death.

Grant trained seventeen horses to Grand Prix level, and many of his human pupils achieved great success. However, it is notable that he was always happy to work with enthusiastic pupils of any standard, and he remained interested in all breeds and all disciplines, training high-school dressage and Western reining with equal facility. In 1997, he was inducted posthumously into the USDF Hall of Fame.

**grinding the teeth**    See **teeth, grinding**.

**gripping**    In dressage terminology, usually refers to the rider's legs when clamped constantly against the horse's sides; may be a misconceived attempt to maintain/increase activity, or a consequence of poor seat/posture.

Drawing of gripping legs, from Ulrik Schramm's *The Undisciplined Horse.*

**Grisone, Federico** (also rendered as Federigo or Frederic, and Grisoni) A pre-eminent Italian Renaissance trainer of the sixteenth century, generally considered to be the founder of the Neapolitan School. He based his ideas on the mechanics of riding on the written work of Xenophon and particularly emphasized the importance of the rider's legs in schooling; wrote *L'Ecurie de Sieur Grison* (c.1550) and *Gli Ordini di Cavalcare* in 1555. The latter, the first book on riding ever published in Italy, found a wide audience and was subsequently translated into French and German. Grisone's teacher, Colas Pagano, was a grandson (outside wedlock) of the King of Aragon and it may be that there were some Spanish influences in Grisone's own teaching. Grisone's ideas were further developed by Cesar Fiashi and his illustrious pupil, Giambattista Pignatelli.

**Grisoni**    See **Grisone, Federico**.

**ground jury**    In competition dressage, the ground jury consists of the presiding judge, or judges – thus judge and jury are effectively the same thing.

**Group Member Organization**   In America, a body that is affiliated to the United States Dressage Federation (USDF); local and regional 'clubs' that organize and promote competitions and educational events within their locality.

**Gunther, Maria**   Born Maria Buhling in 1925, the daughter of a German hussar and a mother who was a keen rider, she was given professional riding lessons from a very young age. Her early, distinguished, trainers included Käthe Franke and Felix Bürkner. During the Second World War she trained riding horses and carriage horses, only to see them sent to the front to their possible deaths. She subsequently moved to the stables of the Royal Horse Guards in Westphalia, where she met Walter ('Bubi') Gunther, whom she married in 1949. In 1963, she won the German National Dressage Championships on *Sambesi* on the same day that her husband became the (similar sounding) National Dressage Champion. Following her husband's death in 1974, she continued to compete for a while, her successes including the Swedish Dressage Derby. When she retired from competitive riding, she began training at home, and also visited Great Britain and the USA. In 1985, she became Germany's first woman international judge.

**Gunther, Walter ('Bubi')**   Born in 1921, the son of the owner of a showjumping yard in Germany, Gunther became successful in that discipline, but dressage was his principle love and he became a trainer in the classical mould. In 1949, he married Maria Buhling and, in 1963, at the Olympic Riding Stadium in Berlin, Gunther became National Dressage Champion riding *Adjutant* and, an hour later, Maria on *Sambesi* took the (similar sounding) National Dressage Championship – this husband and wife triumph being a first such in German sporting history. In the years that followed, Gunther achieved international success, with wins at Dortmund in 1970, 1971 and 1972. His classical school won acclaim and he was very much in demand as a trainer. He was official trainer to the German national dressage team up until his death in 1974.

**gymnastic training**   One of the key roles of dressage is to increase the horse's suppleness and strength; in modern parlance to 'gymnasticize' the horse. This process makes it easier for the horse to respond to the rider's commands and provides the physical wherewithal to perform the more demanding movements and exercises. The importance of the gymnastic side of training has been emphasized by all the great Masters, and Gustav Steinbrecht actually entitled his famous work *The Gymnasium of the Horse.*

# H

**habit**   The traditional dress of a female side-saddle rider. Also, a (usually undesirable) action that becomes ingrained through repetition and may continue long after the cause that initiated it has disappeared.

**hackamore**   A type of bitless bridle, not permitted in dressage competitions.

**hacking**   Exercising a horse by riding in the open, mainly in the slower gaits. It provides variety for both horse and rider, and relative mental and physical relaxation as compared to the rigours of the more demanding exercises.

Hacking and schooling can quite well be combined, so as to add to the rider's interest and to the horse's education. The picture shows a half-pass across a road.
The value of hacking, as shown in Henry Wynmalen's *Equitation.*

**half-halt**   This is, essentially, an application of the aids with the purpose of improving the horse's longitudinal balance. While this is the primary aim, in some circumstances (for example, if the horse is leaning a little on one shoulder) the lateral balance may also be improved. Since any improvement in longitudinal balance will be consequent upon a relative increase in the weight taken on the haunches, a correctly applied half-halt can be said to have a collecting effect. Related to the improvement in balance is a preparatory effect; the half-halt is sometimes used both to physically facilitate some form of transition and to forewarn the horse that a change is about to be required of him.

Individual horses vary greatly in their conformation, level of training and degree of balance at any particular moment, and these variations affect the precise aims and requirements of any particular half-halt. Therefore, while many attempts have been made to produce firm definitions of the effect, it is difficult for writers to progress beyond describing it in general terms as an almost simultaneous co-ordination of the seat, legs and hands. In addressing this issue, Paul Belasik (*Dressage for the 21st Century*) has made the point that 'the real definition of each half-halt is peculiar to its use'. However, in line with the principle of the collecting, rebalancing effect being consequent upon the action of the haunches, it can be assumed that any influences from the forward-driving aids should fractionally precede those of the hands. It can also be said that any effective half-halt will be momentary in duration, and followed by a fractional lightening of the rein contact.

The needs for, and precise application of, half-halts are determined by astute riders who have their horses on the aids and are constantly monitoring all aspects of movement, including balance. Such riders tend to apply quite numerous, but small, light, half-halts to correct any incipient loss of balance, this being more effective than attempting major corrections after balance has been lost.

Picture sequence by Maggie Raynor showing the application and effects of the half-halt.

108

**half-pass**  A lateral movement performed along diagonals of the arena, rather than along the outside track. The horse is bent slightly round the rider's inside leg, and looks in the direction of the movement; his outside legs pass and cross in front of the inside legs. There is a general requirement that the mean inclination of the horse's body should remain as nearly as possible parallel to the long sides of the arena, this 'approximate' requirement relating to the facts that there is a little bend in the body and that the forehand should be slightly in advance of (leading) the hindquarters, these characteristics assisting with the maintenance of impulsion, balance, freedom and lightness of the movement. The half-pass can be performed at varying angles but the greater the angle (the greater the degree of sideways movement required), the harder it becomes for the horse to maintain the desirable characteristics of the movement. The half-pass forms the basis for the counter-change of hand and zigzags.

Half-pass in trot. Photograph from John Winnett's *Dressage as Art in Competition.*

**half-pirouette**  Also known as demi-pirouette; a pirouette figure involving a turn through just 180 degrees.

**half-volte**  A volte figure performed through 180 degrees.

**halt**  Essentially, cessation of motion. However, it is universally desired that the horse should learn to halt straight and square, with relative engagement of his hindquarters, so that he remains in balance under the rider and alert and ready to move forward with optimum efficiency as soon as he is asked to do so. Other desirable characteristics of the halt are that the poll should be the highest point, with the horse correctly on the bit, all of these attributes being essentially complementary.

Hans Handler. Photograph from Waldemar Seunig's *Horsemanship.*

**Handler, Hans, Col.** (1912–1975) Born in Austria, Handler became an officer in the cavalry and was, for a time, assigned to the Spanish Riding School as a pupil. During the Second World War he was wounded in action and imprisoned in Russia but, in 1947, he returned to the Spanish Riding School. Here, he proved to be an outstanding rider and later, following the retirement of Alois Podhajsky, he became its Director. Like Podhajsky, Handler had a great enthusiasm for travelling to promote the School and its teaching, and he made many trips abroad, including a number to America, where he conducted numerous clinics. Handler died of a heart attack whilst heading a ride at the Spanish Riding School.

**hands**   The natural aids by which, via the reins, the rider is in direct communication with the horse's mouth. The hands mete out the forward movement initiated by the forward driving aids and guide the horse's forehand in the required direction in unison with the directional aids of legs and seat.

**Hanna, Mary**   Born in Australia in 1954, Mary was married to Danish FEI rider and trainer, Gert Donvig until his untimely death in an automobile accident in 1989. Subsequently, she married showjumper Rob Hanna. A highly influential figure in her roles as rider, trainer and breeder, she has worked with such notable figures as Tineke Bartels, Anky van Grunsven and Kyra Kyrklund, from whom, in 1998, she acquired her horse, *Limbo*. Prior to this acquisition, she was particularly well-known for her partnership with the New Zealand-bred *Mosaic II*, on whom she won the Australian National Championship in 1993 and the Pacific League Finals in 1995, 1996, 1997 and 1998. This partnership also competed at the World Equestrian Games in 1994 and 1998, the World Cup in 1996 and the Atlanta Olympics in 1996, in which a top-twelve finish qualified them for the Kür. On *Limbo*, she has competed at Aachen and Hickstead (1999) and the World Equestrian Games (2002); she was a member of the Australian team for the Sydney Olympics (2000) and rode as an individual at the 2004 Olympics. A World Cup finalist in 1996, 1997 and 1998, she has achieved many other successes, both as an Australian team member and an individual, including winning the Australian Young Dressage Horse championship on the imported colt, *Rituel* – a victory that underscores her efforts to improve the standard of Australian-bred dressage horses by standing at stud imported stallions who have competed at Grand Prix level.

**hard-mouthed**   A term sometimes used to describe a horse who takes a strong, rather 'dead' contact with the bit and does not submit easily to light indications from the rider's hands. This condition can arise from basic insubordination (which is not dealt with adequately by an interplay of the rider's seat, legs and hands), or as a result of heavy-handiness on the rider's part. Bad cases, of whatever origin, can be worsened by actual injury to, and deadening of, the horse's mouth.

**harmony**   The co-existence of individually distinct entities, forces or parts as a pleasant, consistent whole. Harmonious use of the rider's aids occurs when the aids are complementary to each other and send consistent, acceptable and intelligible signals to the horse. Horse and rider are said to be in harmony with each other when there is positive two-way communication between them, evidenced by rapport and a happy partnership.

**Harris, Charles**   (1915–2001) An engineer by profession, Harris qualified as a riding instructor in 1932 and went on to become a Fellow of the Institute of the Horse, a Fellow of the British Horse Society and a Fellow of the Association of British Riding Schools.

From 1948 to 1951, through the support of Col. V.D.S. Williams, a leading figure in British equitation at that time, he became the first and only English rider to complete the full three-year course at the Spanish Riding School. There, he trained under Commandants Alois Podhajsky and Hans Handler, and with such luminaries as Franz Rochowansky, Georg Wahl and Franz Mairinger.

A fervent devotee of classical principles, Charles Harris was an advocate of using precise equestrian terminology to ensure that these

Charles Harris long-reining a horse at the Spanish Riding School. Photograph from *Workbooks from the Spanish School.*

principles are conveyed exactly and concisely to pupils and students of equitation, and his many writings reflect this fact. Always accessible to club-level riders, for whom he gave numerous clinics, he also had a great influence on the careers of some major figures, usually behind the scenes. *Workbooks from the Spanish School*, which includes a facsimile edition of notes and sketches made during his stay there, was published posthumously in 2004.

**haunches**   The part of the horse consisting of buttocks, hips and upper thighs and thus a significant component part of the hindquarters; however the term is often used rather more loosely than this and for practical purposes it can, in many cases, be considered more or less synonymous with hindquarters.

**haunches in**   See **travers**.

**haunches out**   See **renvers**.

**haute école**   The French term for high school.

**head carriage**   The position and manner in which a horse carries his head and neck. The neck being a continuation of the spine, and part of the horse's natural balancing mechanism, the head carriage will both influence, and be influenced by, the movement, carriage and balance of the rest of the horse's body.

**headshaker**   A horse who shakes his head violently from side to side or up and down, often snorting and sneezing and attempting to rub his nose on himself or other objects, as a result of affliction by a (usually) seasonal

112

disorder, causing an apparently allergic response of the central nervous system. Headshaking of this sort is a recognized condition, unrelated to general fidgeting, or attempts to evade the bit. During periods when a horse prone to the condition is afflicted, it is practically impossible to school or compete. However, in some cases under some rules (e.g. those of British Dressage) it may be possible to obtain a dispensation to allow a headshaker to compete wearing a nose gauze – a device sometimes used to minimize the effects of the affliction.

**head to the wall**   See **travers**.

**Henriquet, Michel**   Born in 1924 in Gérardmer, France, Henriquet first studied under René Bacharach, whose own equestrian education was rooted in the school of François Baucher. While he was a confirmed Baucherist, Bacharach had a wide knowledge of the classical works of equitation and introduced Henriquet to such writers as de la Broue, de Pluvinel and de la Guérinière. It was the work of the last-named and the tenets of the riders comprising the School of Versailles that particularly captured Henriquet's attention and, preferring their philosophy to that of the purely Baucherist school (although his own work continues to meld the best of both), he decided to go in search of suitable horses of the old, baroque stamp on which to practise this form of classical equitation.

Looking for such horses in the Iberian Peninsula, Henriquet met Nuno Oliveira who, at that time, was little known beyond the environs of Lisbon. Captivated by Oliveira's genius in the saddle and his open-minded philosophy, Henriquet became his first regular foreign pupil, starting a relationship and friendship that was to last up to the time of Oliveira's death. Upon returning to France, Henriquet wrote articles about Oliveira in the equestrian press and subsequently invited Oliveira to a reception at his establishment, to which the Staff Officer of Saumur and a number of

Michel Henriquet. Photograph courtesy of M. Henriquet.

eminent riders and judges were invited. He thus became one of the first people instrumental in bringing Oliveira to international attention.

No fan of competition dressage (although his student, Catherine Durand, won the French Freestyle Championship in 1993 and represented France in the 1992 Olympics), Henriquet pursues equitation as an art form. While he trains horses of various breeds, he continues to champion Iberian stock. He attracts many visitors to his establishment near Paris and his major work *Gymnase et Dressage* has recently been translated into English (as *Henriquet on Dressage*) by Hilda Nelson.

**Henry, Major-General Guy, V., Jr.** (1875–1967) Born in a log cabin during a freezing Nebraska winter, the son of an army officer, some of Henry's first companions were friendly Sioux. His formative years were spent among these people, along with soldiers and frontiersmen, and it was here that he first developed his riding skills on his pony, Prince. From the age of seven, he set his sights on going to West Point military academy; once there, he found the academic work strenuous, but was far ahead of his classmates in equitation and practical soldiering.

In 1905, he became the first American officer to attend the full course at the French Cavalry School of Saumur and by 1911 he was head of the Department of Equitation at the American Cavalry School at Fort Riley. At this time, the American army agreed to take on the task of preparing teams for the first equestrian Olympics, to be held in Stockholm the following year, and Henry was put in charge. Despite the fact that, at that time, there was really no programme of competitions in the major equestrian disciplines in America, the team won bronze in the militaire (precursor of the three-day event) and came 4th in the showjumping. Henry himself rode in all three disciplines: the militaire, showjumping and dressage.

Henry's long and distinguished military career spanned fifty years; he served in both the Spanish American War and Second World War. In terms of rank, he became Director of Equitation at the US Military Academy in 1916, was Chief of Cavalry from 1930 to 1934 and Commandant of Cavalry at Fort Riley from 1935 until his retirement in 1939. In a broader equestrian context, he was the only American so far to be President of the FEI (1931–1935), he coached two American Olympic teams, was chef d'équipe to the 1936 and 1948 teams and judged at two Olympic Games; he was Director of the first civilian American equestrian team and also of the AHSA and New

York's NHSA and Chairman of the US Olympic Equestrian Committee. He can truly be described as a pioneer and founding figure of American equitation.

**Herbermann, Erik** Born in Amsterdam in 1945, Herbermann moved at an early age with his family to Johannesburg and ten years later, moved to Canada. His initial equestrian training was with Patricia Salt FBHS, herself a pupil of Richard Wätjen and Oberbereiter Lindenbauer at the Spanish Riding School. Herbermann subsequently studied under the celebrated classical riding teacher, Egon von Neindorff.

Erik Herbermann. Photograph from *Dressage Formula.*

Now residing in the USA, Herbermann devotes much of his time to lecturing, teaching and conducting clinics internationally. In addition to producing three editions of his book *Dressage Formula,* he has also written numerous articles for equestrian publications.

Herbermann is a staunch advocate of classical ideals, and his ideology is based on an objective study of the horse's nature, which seeks the depth of understanding and quality of work perceived in the greatest of Renaissance Masters. In common with these luminaries, he views equitation as a self-improving art, rooted in the utmost affection and respect for the horse.

**Hess, Christopher** Born in 1950 in Delmenhorst, Germany, Hess displayed an enormous enthusiasm for riding from a very early age. He began studying equitation at various competition yards and his more advanced training included a spell at Warendorf. In addition to studying the jumping disciplines under eminent trainers, he also trained with Seigfried Peilike and went on to qualify as a riding instructor. On the academic front, he completed his studies with a degree in education (and found time to be the 1976 German Universities Showjumping Champion). He also competed successfully at advanced-level dressage competitions and novice-level eventing. Since 1978, he has worked for the German National Equestrian Federation and for the German Olympic Committee, his current role being Director of Training for the German Olympic Committee for Equestrian Sports (DOKR). He is also an International level FEI Judge and spends much of his time conducting seminars and clinics for judges, trainers and riders in Germany and abroad.

Carl Hester on *Giorgione*. Photograph by Elizabeth Furth.

**Hester, Carl** Born in 1967 on the Channel Island of Sark, where no cars were allowed, Hester's first riding experiences were on the backs of carriage horses. He initially wanted to be a jockey, but quickly grew too tall. Having decided instead to concentrate on dressage, he showed a prodigious natural talent in this discipline, becoming British Young Rider National Champion in 1985, only eighteen months or so after taking it up. In his early career, he had assistance from Harry Boldt, later going on to train with Conrad Schumacher. In 1988 he became a member of the British Young Riders team and in 1990 competed at his first World Equestrian Games. In 1989, he was offered the chance to ride horses owned by the German enthusiast Dr Wilfred Bechtolsheimer, and quickly established a successful relationship with them. In 1992, on *Giorgione*, he represented Great Britain at the Barcelona Olympic Games, where he was the youngest member of an Olympic equestrian team. In the same year, also on *Giorgione*, he became British National Champion and was awarded the title Dressage Rider of the Year.

Hester's ascendancy as a trainer was almost as rapid as his progress in the saddle. In 1994, his pupil, event rider Vaughn Jeffries became individual gold medallist at the World Equestrian Games in The Hague and Hester was subsequently asked to be the New Zealand eventing team's dressage trainer at the 1996 Olympics. His hard work and dedication as a trainer was recognized

116

in the same year when he won the Dressage Trainer of the Year award.

It is a measure of Hester's sustained dedication and professionalism that he competes a large number of horses at different stages of training, and his list of successes at Advanced Medium, Intermediaire and Prix St Georges levels is immense. His major triumphs include winning the Pas de Deux at the 1995 European Championships (in partnership with Vicky Thompson) and three consecutive Grand Prix National Championships (1997, 1998 and 1999) on *Legal Democrat*. Since his debut at Barcelona, he has also represented Britain in the 2000 and 2004 Olympic Games, in the latter event finishing highest-placed of the British team, riding *Escapado*. In the same year, he was National Champion at Grand Prix level.

**Heydebreck, Hans von** (1866–1935) German cavalry officer (retired with rank of Colonel), who studied under Steinbrecht's pupil, Paul Plinzer, and became a major force in promoting Steinbrecht's work. He was co-author in 1912 of the *German Cavalry Manual* and, following the First World War, his dream of an academy for civil riding instructors became a reality (in Belgrade). He spent his last years (during which he continued to ride himself) as an instructor at Felix Bürkner's riding school in Düppel. He was also a tireless judge, with excellent powers of observation and an incorruptible sense of what was right. As a literary figure, he made exemplary contributions to professional journals and wrote books on equitation including *Das Gebrauchspferd*, about which Waldemar Seunig said: 'This is a book you have to read again and again – in short, a masterwork.'

**high airs** An old term for the airs above the ground.

Some of the high airs as illustrated in de la Guérinière's *Ecole de Cavalerie*. (The pesade is included as a preparatory exercise; the courbette is shown with the hind legs in stance phase.)

**high school** The term used in classical equitation to describe training and performance of the highest level.

**hindquarters** The rear or hind part of a horse, essentially the area from the croup backward, including the hind legs.

**Hinnemann, Johann** Born in 1948 to parents who farmed in the Münster region of Germany, Hinemann devoted himself to riding from an early age. From 1968 until 1971, he studied at the St. Georg riding club in Münster, where his trainers included Reiner Klimke, Albert Stecken and Harry Boldt. In 1972, he set up his own business as a professional rider, taking over a stable in Voerde and in 1976 he passed his professional instructor's exams. In the same year, he achieved his first victory in an advanced-level dressage competition, heralding a ten-year period of success as a professional rider. During this time he twice finished 2nd in the German Championships for professional riders (1981 and 1984) and twice 3rd (1983 and 1985) and was also a member of successful national (professional) teams. His record led to him being awarded the German Golden Rider's Badge and, in 1986, he was 3rd in the world rankings published by *L'Année Hippique*.

Despite these successes, Hinnemann's professional status at the time debarred him from competing at a number of major events, so he decided to adopt amateur-rider status, renting out his farm and working as an employee. In the same year (1986) he was picked for the German national (amateur) team and participated at his first World Championships, winning team gold and individual bronze medals. His mount at the World Championships was the Dutch-bred *Idaal*, owned by his wife, Gisela, and a group of friends. The following year, the partnership won the German Championship and individual bronze and team gold at the European Championship and also competed successfully at a number of national competitions.

Unfortunately, *Idaal* was ruled out of the 1988 Olympics after concerns about a prohibited substance, but Hinnemann went on to further successes with *Malte* and *Ribot* before retiring from competition in 1993. Throughout his riding career, he had also continued as a trainer (in addition to working with a number of eminent individuals, he was trainer to the Canadian national team from 1981 to 1985) and from 1993 to 1998 he worked as an honorary trainer for the German Equestrian Olympic Committee. In December 1996, he was given the title of écuyer, the highest award of the German National Equestrian Federation and in the same month, together with Klaus Balkenhol, he was appointed coach to the German national dressage team, a position he held until 1999.

**holding back**   A term sometimes used to convey the idea that a horse is not committing himself fully to energetic forward movement.

**hollow-backed**   Also described as hollow outline; the horse exhibits a marked concavity of the back. While this can be a feature of undesirable conformation, it can also be produced by a horse tensing his back muscles and literally hollowing them away from the rider, perhaps because of discomfort from the saddle or because the rider is sitting too heavily and/or overusing crude driving actions of the seat. If incorrect riding is accompanied by high, restraining hands, causing the horse to raise his head and neck, this posture will also be reflected in a hollowing of the back. While the back is hollow, the forward impulse of the hind legs will be blocked and the horse will not be 'through'.

**hollow side**   The side to which a horse, who is not yet fully suppled and straightened, naturally shows a lateral concavity. See also **concave**.

**Holzel, Wolfgang**   (1943–1999) Born in Stuttgart-Bad Cannstatt, the son of a riding school proprietor, Holzel undertook an early apprenticeship as a toolmaker but then went into teaching riding at his father's school. His own success in various competitions soon brought him to the attention of the German riding establishment and, at the age of twenty, he was awarded the German Gold Riding Medal for his achievements in dressage, showjumping and cross-country riding. Following on from this, Holzel took his riding teacher examinations at the Westphalian Riding and Driving School, and embarked upon a university-level study of education at Ludwigsburg. Having gained a PhD, he took further exams in professional riding instruction at Warendorf and, in 1976, was appointed to head the German Riding School, a position he held until moving to Australia in 1985. From 1985 to 1989 he was the Australian National Coach, training many riders including Erica Taylor, Australia's first representative in the Dressage World Championships (1986) and sole dressage representative at the Seoul Olympics (1988). In addition to his teaching, he was a prolific author of articles and books, many of which were written in conjunction with his wife, Petra. His best-known work is *The Riding Badge*, which was written primarily to assist in the preparation for German FN equestrian exams.

**hoof print**   The indentation made in the ground surface by a horse's hoof. Examination of hoof prints in series can provide useful information about how the horse is moving in the various gaits and exercises.

**hors concours**   A French term, meaning 'outside the competition'; an arrangement whereby a rider performs a prescribed test and is marked according to the rules, but their performance is not counted in terms of placing, prize money, points, etc. There are various reasons why hors concours arrangements may occasionally suit riders, organizers and selectors. However, if a rider has a unilateral wish to ride hors concours, it is usually necessary to state the fact on the entry form, and to obtain permission from the competition organizer. In such cases, the standard entry fee will usually remain payable.

**horsemanship**   The art of riding horses with technical skill and with an understanding of equine physiology and psychology.

**horsemastership**   A generic term implying knowledge and good practice applied to the all-round care and training of horses.

**horse trials**   Commonly known as eventing and, in the USA, combined training; equestrian competitions that consists of dressage, cross-country jumping and showjumping elements (in major competitions, steeplechase and roads-and-tracks elements may precede the cross-country). Penalties from the various phases are combined to compute the final standings. It should be noted that, under horse-trials rules, the tack and equipment allowed in the dressage phase may vary from that usually permitted under pure dressage rules.

**hovering**  See **passagey trot.**

**hurrying**  Said of a horse moving in any gait, when the rhythm of the gait is faster than desirable in terms of maintaining good balance and appropriate length of stride (horses who hurry do so by increasing frequency of stride at the expense of stride length).

A horse hurrying in trot. Drawing by Maggie Raynor.

**impulsion**  A term used to describe the propulsive energy generated from the horse's hindquarters.

**inactive**  Moving with a degree of energy insufficient for the work being performed.

**inattentive**  A horse insufficiently focused on the rider's commands; may be the result of ineffective riding or distraction by an outside agency or, to some extent, a combination of the two.

**independent seat**  Said of a rider who maintains correct balance and posture in the saddle and makes no reliance on the reins or gripping legs; a basic prerequisite for any rider wishing to improve the horse's way of going.

**indirect rein**  A rein effect that places the horse's head to the side on which it is performed and advances/increases the load on the opposite shoulder. For example, on the right rein, the right hand moved to the left

121

and fractionally forward places the head to the right and acts on the left shoulder. Used when a light flexion is required to the outside and in a corrective capacity.

**indirect rein of opposition**  Depending on how it is applied, this produces two rein effects. Used in front of the withers (i.e. at a marked angle to the mean inclination of the horse's body), it brings the head and neck in the direction of the rein applied and produces a pivoting effect of the haunches in the opposite direction; used behind the withers (i.e. at a lesser angle to the inclination of the horse's body, towards the horse's opposite hip), it produces a  lateral effect to move the horse in the opposite direction from the side to which the rein is applied (for example, right rein used towards left hip produces lateral effect to the left).

**influenza**  See **equine influenza**.

**in front of the leg**  An idiomatic phrase implying that the quality of free forward movement is present in the horse, such that he moves freely forward with a minimum of encouragement from the rider's leg aids, and responds promptly and willingly to any specific aid from the leg; the opposite of behind the leg.

**in front of the vertical**  Describes the angle of the horse's face when it is in front of a line perpendicular to the ground. In most circumstances (other than in a fully and correctly collected horse, whose whole face may be just about perpendicular to the ground), the face should be somewhat in front of the vertical, but the degree to which it is so should relate to the combined factors of conformation, state of training and the movement being performed. The key indicators of whether or not the angle is appropriate are the flexion at the poll and the degree to which the horse is accepting the bit. A face substantially in front of the vertical, accompanied by setting of the jaw, stiffening of the poll and contraction of the muscles in the top line of the neck, signifies problems in training.

**in-hand**  The exercising or schooling of horses whilst dismounted, either using some form of line(s) to connect trainer to horse, as with

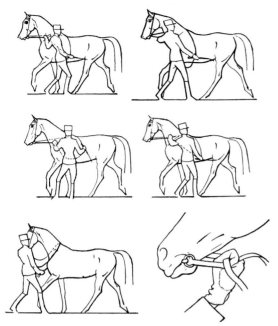

Drawings of work in-hand from General Decarpentry's *Academic Equitation.*

lungeing or long-reining or, working directly from the bridle, as with flexions in-hand.

**inside**   Generally, the inside leg/rein/hand etc. is that nearer to the centre of the arena. However, in some particular cases, the reference may be to the horse's bend, rather than to arena location. For example, in counter-canter, where the horse is likely to have some slight incurvation away from the direction of travel, the 'inside' rein may be that towards the outside of the arena. Similarly, in a half-pass that has travelled beyond the centre line, the 'inside' rein, with reference to the horse's bend, may in fact be further from the centre of the arena than the 'outside' rein.

**inside hand**   Generally, the rider's hand that is nearer to the centre of the arena. However, in some circumstances, the reference may be made with respect to the horse's bend. See **inside**.

**inside leg**   Generally, the rider's leg or horse's leg(s) that is/are nearer to the centre of the arena. However, in some circumstances, the reference may be made with respect to the horse's bend. See **inside**.

**insterburger**   A German term; a harsh action of one rein, up against that corner of the mouth, to punish a horse who locks his jaw as an act of flagrant disobedience. The French equivalent is remonte des dents: a lifting of the teeth. In *The Way to Perfect Horsemanship*, Üdo Burger points out that the action does not have to involve a vicious wrenching of the hand, but can be implemented primarily by 'an energetic bracing of the loin'.

123

**insubordinate**   A term favoured by some writers to describe horses who do not comply with their rider's wishes. This term should be applied and interpreted with great discretion; dictionaries generally define insubordination as 'disobedient, rebellious' and these are not necessarily the same thing. The second definition implies an overt and calculated act of defiance as when a horse, simply asked to go forward, responds by rearing. However, while this is certainly disobedient, 'disobedience' – when meaning a failure to obey – can have various other causes, including not understanding what is required and, in the case of the ridden horse, actually being prevented by the rider from doing what the rider requested. See also **disobedience**.

**interfering**   See **brushing**.

**Intermediare**   The second level of 'international' tests, produced by the FEI.

**International**   A competition between teams or individuals representing different nations.

**ipsilateral**   Belonging to or occurring on the same side of the body; not to be confused with unilateral.

**irregular**   Said of movement in any gait that lacks the consistent (correct) rhythm; causes may include lack/loss of balance or unsoundness.

**Ishoy, Cynthia**   Born Cynthia Neale in 1952, Canadian by nationality, her early years were spent in Germany where her father was stationed with the Canadian Air Force. Having taken an interest in horses in her early teens, she attended a local riding school where she was told that she was 'too small' for dressage and therefore channelled her equestrian enthusiasm into vaulting, which she later said gave her a lot of confidence. However, when her father was transferred back to Canada, she started to attend a local Pony Club and a year later began to pursue a career in dressage. Without financial resources, she went as a working student to the Canadian rider Christalot Boylen (née Hansen). There, she spent five years grooming, riding and training until, in 1971, she was selected as a reserve rider for the Canadian dressage team at the Pan-American Games in

124

Columbia. She travelled to the games with her employer, Hansen, and when another rider was taken ill, she took her place in the team that went on to win the gold medal (Hansen won the individual gold). The following year she was selected to represent Canada at the Munich Olympic Games where, at twenty, she was the youngest equestrian competitor. Here, she had the opportunity to meet the German trainer Willi Schultheis, who had been working with Canadian riders for several years and, in the aftermath of the Olympics, she travelled to Europe where she trained with Seigfried Peilicke for a year.

On her return to Canada, finding herself only reserve for the national team for the 1976 Olympics, she relinquished her dressage career and began training racehorses. However, this was a short-lived diversion as she soon returned to dressage with renewed determination. In 1978 she went to the World Championships at Goodwood where, as the only representative from Canada, she finished 8th. She then remained in Europe for three years, training with Schultheis and Peilicke and in 1979 she became the first Canadian to win a Grand Prix in Europe. In 1980 she purchased *Dynasty*, and subsequently took the horse back to Canada, where she married eventer and dressage rider Neil Ishoy. Having given *Dynasty* time to mature, she finished 7th on him at the 1986 World Dressage Championships, held in Canada, and the pairing went on to be placed 2nd in the 1988 World Cup and 4th in the individual placings at the 1988 Olympics, where they were members of the Canadian team that won bronze. Unfortunately, *Dynasty* died from colic in 1989, but Ishoy returned to the Olympics in 1992 on *Dakar* and was again a member of the Canadian team in 2004 riding *Proton*.

**Iwanowski, Lt. Col. George**   Born in Poland in 1907, Iwanowski grew up on his family's estate. He attended university in Warsaw and obtained an MSc in agriculture. Involved with horses from an early age, he participated in dressage, showjumping, steeplechasing, hunting and driving.

Fighting with the 1st Polish Lancers during the Second World War, he was wounded, captured and interned in a Russian field hospital, but escaped and made his way to France to join the Polish unit there. In 1944, as an officer of the 1st Polish Armoured Division, he was involved in the Normandy landings, and was subsequently awarded the Polish Military Cross of Valour.

After the war, on orders of the Rhine Army, Iwanowski spent two years collecting Polish Thoroughbred horses scattered in occupied Germany. During this time, he met Otto Lörke and had lessons with him.

In 1948, having been discharged from the army, Iwanowski emigrated to South Africa, where he started a riding school near Johannesburg. Although he rode in many disciplines, he had developed a passion for dressage and decided to devote most of his efforts to passing this on. He was greatly assisted in his aims when, at a horse show in Natal, he met Count Jankovich Besan, who had emigrated from his native Hungary, saving some of his best Lipizzaner stock from war-ridden Europe. The Count gave Iwanowski his first Lipizzaner, *Maestoso Erdem*, an exceptionally gifted horse, on whom he was able to compete and give public displays. This horse became the foundation of the Lipizzaner team which Iwanowski created, and was followed by another outstanding stallion in *Neapolitano Cypriana*. The team eventually built up to eight in number and remained, after Iwanowski's retirement, an institution in South Africa.

Another fruitful meeting occurred in Zambia, where Iwanowski met Hans Handler, then Director of the Spanish Riding School, who was judging at a show. Iwanowski's invitation to Handler to conduct a dressage course at his establishment was the beginning of a long friendship and collaboration with the Spanish Riding School, which was a great help in the development of the Lipizzaner team and the promotion of dressage in South Africa.

At that time, South African riders focused mainly on showjumping and showing, but Iwanowski's displays were a significant factor in promoting an interest in dressage. Initially, the attitude of many of the South African 'old guard' to dressage was such that the Chairman of the Horse Showing Association suggested holding a debate as to whether dressage was a useful discipline or not. This took place, with Iwanowski promoting the values of dressage, and the final vote was overwhelmingly pro-dressage. A dressage committee was established, elementary dressage was soon on the programme of many shows and the National Dressage Championship (which Iwanowski won six times in succession) was inaugurated. He was subsequently appointed Director of the National Equestrian Centre. In recognition of his achievements, Iwanowski has been awarded the South African Equestrian Federation medal, the German Silver Equestrian badge and the Polish Golden Badge. After retiring, he went to live with his daughter, in France.

**Janssen, Sjef**  Dutch rider and trainer, born 1950. With a number of other sporting interests, Janssen did not start riding until he was twenty-eight years old. Initially, he rode just for fun but, having acquired two horses (one of whom, *Oron*, became his first Grand Prix horse), he began to take the sport more seriously. When the riding school where he took his lessons went bankrupt, he ended up buying it. Shortly afterwards, a school that taught classical dressage opened in Belgium. Its proprietors had studied at the Spanish Riding School and with Nuno Oliveira in Portugal. Since this school had about thirty horses who could perform the high-school movements, Janssen decided to go there to get a firm grounding in dressage. For two years he rode for seven hours a day.

After this intensive period of study, Janssen started to compete. He represented Holland at the 1983 European Championships, riding *Oron* and won a bronze medal at the 1991 European Championships riding *Olympic Bo*, the horse he later sold to Sven and Gonnelien Rothenberger.

Sjef Janssen. Photograph by Elizabeth Furth.

These successes notwithstanding, Janssen, who had always had a fascination with the philosophies of sports training, felt increasingly drawn to the challenges of training horses and riders. Focusing on training, he was voted Trainer of the Year by the International Trainers' Club in 1995 and, during

2002–2003, he completed a course to become a Mastercoach in Sports. In 2005 he was appointed as the new Dutch team manager, succeeding Bert Rutten in that role. In addition to being the personal trainer of the vastly successful Anky van Grunsven (whom he married in 2005), Janssen has trained a number of international competitors, discovered many successful horses (including van Grunsven's Olympic gold-winning *Salinero*) and trained numerous horses from novice standard up to Grand Prix.

**Jensen, Anne-Grethe (née Törnblad)**   Highly successful Danish rider, married to Danish rider Tonny Jensen. National Champion of Denmark on ten occasions and Nordic Champion twice. Best-known for her remarkable partnership with *Marzog* on whom she was European Champion in 1983 and 3rd in the European Championships in 1985, silver medallist at the 1984 Olympics and both World Champion and World Cup winner in 1986. Following these successes and based on performances in major competitions, *Marzog* was voted the Top Dressage Horse since the Second World War by a panel of top riders, judges and trainers. Following *Marzog's* retirement, Jensen represented Denmark at the 1988 and 1992 Olympics on *Ravel*.

**jogging**   A shortened, impure and usually crooked travesty of trot characterized by tension; often displayed by inexperienced or over-excited horses when in strange surroundings and/or when restrained from rushing after their companions. While jogging signifies that the horse is to some extent ignoring or disobeying the rider's aids, it will be aggravated by fussy, nagging hands and insufficient use of the seat and legs. If it occurs in a dressage test, jogging will be penalized severely.

'The wrong way to sit on a jogging horse'. Drawing from Ulrik Schramm's *The Undisciplined Horse.*

**Jousseaume, André**   (d. 1960) A graduate of Saumur and a cavalry officer for most of his lifetime, Jousseaume won the individual silver medal for dressage at the 1932 Olympics when a member of the French gold-medal-winning team. Having been cited for valour during the early stages of the Second World War, he was then captured and held prisoner, during which time he wrote the first draft of his book *Progressive Dressage*. After the war, at the 1948 Olympics, he repeated his feat of winning individual silver and team gold medals. He also took the individual bronze medal in 1952. He subsequently retired from the French army with the rank of Colonel and taught at the Cercle Hippique until his death.

**judge**  An official who assesses competitors' performances in dressage tests. In competitions affiliated to national organizing bodies (and at international level), judges from an official panel are used; the organizing bodies have their own criteria and processes by which judges join the panel (become 'licensed' in the USA) and then proceed through various 'levels', but the general procedure is that, as judges increase in experience and pass various assessments, they become qualified to judge at increasingly high levels.

**judge's writer**  Also known as scribe; the person who records the judge's comments and marks during a test. In the interests of accuracy and the smooth running of the competition, it is desirable for a writer to have a good practical knowledge of the test and the movements required.

**jumping**  Historically, some degree of jumping was required in many early dressage tests, including early Olympics, and it is still required in some

Reiner Klimke's Olympic dressage horse *Dux* jumping as a gymnastic exercise. Photograph from Klimke's *Cavalletti*.

lower-level tests in certain countries. Correctly performed, jumping – especially gymnastic jumping, or gridwork – encourages activity, engagement and a rounding of the topline, and it is incorporated into the training programme by a number of successful dressage competitors. Many equestrian authorities in the past naturally included jumping in their books on training and some pre-eminent figures in the world of dressage began their careers concentrating on competitive jumping.

# K

**Kemmer, Heike**  (b. 1962) Born in Berlin, Germany, Kemmer initially became a dressage rider because her father considered jumping was not for girls. She began competing at the age of thirteen, and went on to win the European Championship for Young Riders. In her formative years, she competed on horses trained by others, but subsequently moved on to breeding as well as training; in 2003, she was a member of a gold-medal-winning team at Hickstead competing on a horse she bred and produced herself. Kemmer trained for ten years with Johann Hinnemann then, after he introduced the pair in 1998, she and Ulla Salzberger assisted each other. As a member of the German team, she also worked with Holger Schmezer, the German National Dressage Trainer, and both Kemmer and Salzberger were members of the team that won Olympic gold in 2004. Kemmer holds Germany's Silver Laurel Award for sporting achievement.

**kicking out to the aids**  Normally considered a disobedience, this will be almost certainly presumed the case for the purpose of marking a dressage test. However, while it may be simply an act of bad temper or defiance, where it is uncharacteristic of a particular individual, it is quite probable that it is indicative of pain, or of stiffness which renders a solicited movement difficult. Whatever the root cause, kicking out against the aids is likely to be exacerbated by inappropriate use of the spur. Clumsy use of the spur, whether intentional or not, is likely to provoke this response in a sensitive or temperamental horse. Applying the leg (with or without the spur) abnormally far back, with the intention of stimulating either forward or lateral movement may also provoke this response, since the sensitive abdominal wall in this area has no immediate connection with the musculature that produces the movement required.

**Kisimov, Ivan**   Rider from the Soviet Union who enjoyed an enduring and successful partnership with *Ikhor*. In 1964, at the Tokyo Olympics, they were members of the Soviet team that won the bronze medal; in 1968 they won the individual gold medal in Mexico City and were members of the Soviet team that won silver, and in 1972 in Munich they were members of the Soviet team that won the gold medal.

**Kitts, Col. Isaac L.**   (1896–1953) Born in Oswego, New York, Kitts was studying for the priesthood when the First World War broke out and he joined the army (he later continued his studies and became ordained in 1940.) Attending the Army Equitation Schools at Forts Riley and Sill, he took their advanced equitation courses and later returned to teach at both centres. Kitts' equestrian talents were first demonstrated in the showjumping arena and on the polo field but in 1931 he began to study dressage, working largely from the books of writers such as Baucher, Fillis and L'Hotte. Since there were hardly any dedicated dressage instructors in the USA at that time, he and his colleague, Hiram Tuttle, would get together and teach each other. In the early 1930s, the army assigned to Kitts an ex-steeplechasing mare, *American Lady*, who had been injured whilst racing and was proving a difficult ride. Within a year, Kitts had schooled her to Grand Prix level and they were members of the American team that won a bronze medal at the 1932 Olympic Games.

In 1936, Kitts, with the mare and his entire family, travelled to Berlin in order to gain more experience of European dressage competition in preparation for the Olympics of that year. Although they did not return with any medals, their venture helped to establish an early precedent for American dressage riders to venture to Europe. Following war years spent in the USA and China, Kitts retired from the army in 1946, only to rejoin as Director of Horsemanship at Culver Military Academy, a post he held until his death. His son, Col. Alfred Kitts, shared his father's interest in dressage and had a significant influence on its development in the USA.

**Klimke, Dr Reiner**   (1936–1999) Born in Munster, Germany, Klimke began his association with horses when, evacuated to a farm during the war years, he journeyed to school by horse and cart. After the war, he took lessons at Stecken's Westphalian Riding School and, in 1953, he came to the notice of Gustav Rau, who did much to revive Germany's equestrian fortunes in the post-war era. Rau invited Klimke to train at Warendorf, where for three years his room-mate was the great showjumper, Alwin Schockemöhle. At that time Schockemöhle was concentrating on eventing but, in 1956, he decided that his future lay in showjumping, and passed the ride on his horse, *Lausbub*, to Klimke, who rode him to win a team silver medal at the 1957 European Three Day Event Championships. Two years later, Klimke won team gold at these championships on *Fortunat*.

Reiner Klimke schooling a young horse in medium canter. Photograph from Klimke's *Basic Training of the Young Horse*.

By this time, Klimke was also achieving considerable success in dressage, and his career as a lawyer was under way. With the demands of his profession to consider, he decided that he could more readily combine this with his equestrian activities if he concentrated on dressage rather than eventing. This decision saw the start of a long and immensely successful period of international competition revolving mainly, but not exclusively, around the great horses *Dux*, *Mehmed* and *Ahlerich*. During a period spanning three decades, Klimke, as an individual, won an Olympic gold medal (in 1984, on *Ahlerich*), two World Championships (1974 and 1982) and four European Championships, and was a member of teams that won Germany gold medals at six Olympics, six World Championships and thirteen European Championships. He also wrote the highly successful books, *Basic Training of the Young Horse* and *Cavalletti*.

**Knopfhart, Alfred**   Born in Vienna in 1927, Knopfhart studied economics and business administration, graduating in these subjects in 1951. Having begun riding in Austria at the age of nineteen, he then went to Germany to continue his equestrian studies. In 1962 he became a certified teacher of riding, and was awarded the German silver medal for riders. Since that time, he has worked continually as a trainer of horses and riders at all levels up to Grand Prix and, since 1989, has given annual clinics at several dressage centres in the USA.

In 1964 Knopfhart became a certified judge for dressage, showjumping and eventing; in 1968 an official of the Austrian Horse Show Association; and in 1970 an international FEI dressage judge. From 1986 to 1996, he headed the official body of Austrian show judges.

In addition to lecturing at the University of Veterinary Medicine, Vienna, Knopfhart has written three books and many articles on equestrian issues.

**Kottas-Heldenberg, Arthur** Born in 1945 in Vienna to parents who owned a well-known riding school, Kottas-Heldenberg joined the Spanish Riding School as a pupil in 1960. Apart from a brief period of service (1966–1967) in the Austrian army, he made his career at the Spanish Riding School, working up to the rank of Chief Rider (at an unusually young age for the post) in 1981 and, in 1995, he was appointed First Chief Rider, a post he held until his retirement in 2003. An instructor of the highest standard, he has travelled widely, giving lectures and clinics (he is, for example, a regular visitor to England's Training the Teachers of Tomorrow Trust) and has trained horses and riders to Olympic standard. He has two daughters who are successful dressage riders.

Arthur Kottas-Heldenberg at the Spanish Riding School. Photograph by Elizabeth Furth.

**kür** A German term meaning free programme. See **freestyle**.

**Kyrklund, Kyra** Born in 1951 in Helsinki, Finland, Kyrklund began her competitive career as a showjumper, but rapidly diversified. In 1969 she became Finnish Junior Champion at dressage, and also finished 2nd and 4th respectively in the junior eventing and showjumping championships. Having initially intended to train as a vet, she in fact became a pupil at the

Photograph of Kyra Kyrklund by Bob Langrish.

Strömsholm Riding Academy and by 1976 she had set up her own training centre in Helsinki. In the late 1970s, she trained in Germany with Herbert Rehbein and in 1979 she won the Scandinavian Dressage Championship. The following year, she took part in her first Olympics, coming 5th individually on *Piccolo*; she also competed in the Olympics in 1984, 1988 and 1992, with another 5th place in 1988 on the Danish stallion, *Matador*. This horse later made a remarkable recovery from a life-threatening condition and went on to take the silver medal at the 1990 World Equestrian Games in Stockholm and win the World Cup in Paris the following year.

In 1991, Kyrklund also moved to Sweden to be chief trainer at Flyinge, the Swedish National Stud and Training Centre. In recent years, she has been domiciled in England, but spends a lot of time in Finland and Sweden, and gives clinics and lectures worldwide. She has introduced a number of horses to international Grand Prix level, having notable success with hot-bred stallions and, besides her many international victories, she has won the Finnish Dressage Championships ten times.

**L**

**lacing**   See **plaiting**.

**lacking**   A judge's comment preceding desirable qualities such as bend, engagement, impulsion, etc. Usually denotes an inadequacy in the level of the specific quality, rather than its total absence.

**lameness**   Physical injury or disease that affects the correct movement of a limb, or limbs, thus causing gait irregularity. Attempting to school a lame horse will always prove counter-productive and obvious lameness during a dressage test will result in elimination. In cases where a very minor degree of unsoundness is suspected, but it is intermittent or barely apparent, the horse will be allowed to complete the test, but any unevenness of movement will be penalized.

**late**   Prefixing 'to', as in 'late to trot', signifies that a movement or action in a dressage test has begun after the appropriate marker; prefixing 'in front' or 'behind', signifies that a flying change has not been performed cleanly or correctly.

**lateral**   Pertaining to a side, or involving a degree of sideward movement.

**lateral aids**   Aids applied in combination to the same side of the horse; for example, the lateral aids for right canter involve a feeling on the right rein and a forward-driving effect from the rider's right leg.

**lateral balance**   A quality evident in a horse whose body remains upright when in movement, even, or especially, on turns and circles. Good lateral balance is reliant upon a number of factors, such as basic conformation, longitudinal balance (a horse hurrying or on the forehand will struggle to stay laterally upright when turning), more or less equal suppleness on both sides, and a rider whose posture and aids enhance, rather than disturb, the horse's balance.

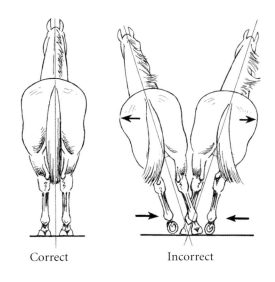

Correct                    Incorrect

Drawings and caption relating to lateral balance when lungeing, from Charles Harris's *Fundamentals of Riding.*

135

**lateral flexion**  Flexion of the horse, or part of the horse, to one side; when such flexion involves the whole length of the horse, it is also referred to as bend.

**lateral movements**  Dressage exercises that entail some form and degree of lateral flexion in the horse include shoulder-in, shoulder-fore, half-pass, renvers and travers. Leg-yielding, which may entail a considerable angle of travel, and full pass, which involves the maximum angle of travel, are lateral movements in which there is a minimal degree of lateral flexion. Other movements, such as pirouettes, terre-à-terre and certain archaic school exercises, also involve some degree of lateral flexion.

Drawing of lateral flexion under saddle, from James Fillis's *Breaking and Riding.*

**Laus, Pia**  Born in 1971, the daughter of German and Italian parents, Laus was, for many years, based in Germany, where she trained with Uwe Schulten-Baumer senior and spent four years on the German Young Riders Team, winning four team and two individual gold medals and one individual silver medal at European Championships. In 1990, she took out Italian citizenship and went on to represent that country in three World Championships, two European Championships, four World Cup Finals and three Olympic Games (1992, 1996 and 2000). A lawyer by profession, in recent years her career and other interests have taken precedence over top-level competition.

**lazy**  A lazy horse is one who is psychologically unwilling or disinclined to work, as opposed to one who lacks the actual energy to do so. A lazy horse might be said to be lacking in instinctive impulsion. Lazy movement is commonly described as inactive; however, a horse may be inactive for reasons other than laziness.

**leading leg**  The foreleg that leads the gait in canter, striking the ground after the diagonal pair have impacted and preceding the moment of suspension; for example, the left foreleg in left canter. In the four-time gait of

136

gallop, the leading leg is, similarly, the last leg to impact and complete the stride before the moment of suspension.

**leaning in**   Said of a horse who, on a corner or circle, tilts his body inward. See also **lateral balance**.

**leaning on the bit**   Said of a horse who is out of balance longitudinally (on the forehand) and seeks support by bearing down on the rider's hands, via the bit. Compare with **boring** and **nose-diving**.

**leaning on the wall**   A form of crooked movement rooted in the fact that, in an enclosed area, a horse will tend to keep his outside shoulder and quarter equidistant from the wall. Because the quarters are usually wider than the shoulders, this results in the horse being somewhat inclined through his length towards the wall, rather than being straight on the track.

**leaning out**   Said of a horse who, on a corner or circle, tilts his body outward. See also **lateral balance**.

**leaving the arena**   The prescribed way of leaving the arena at the end of a dressage test is, following the final halt and salute, to proceed briefly straight forward up the centre line and then to turn smoothly left or right and head towards the exit at A, the whole being performed in walk on a long rein. Competitors should be aware that this constitutes a part of the final, marked, movement; under British Dressage rules, leaving the arena at the end of the test at anywhere other than A will result in the deduction of two marks.

Leaving the arena involuntarily during the execution of the test will incur certain penalties, subject to the rules under which a test is conducted and, in some circumstances, the construction of the arena. Under British Dressage rules, this applies if the horse is patently out of control or if the arena surround is nine inches or more in height. If the surround is lower than this, and is marked by boards, no marks are given for the movement in which the horse places all four feet out of the arena. Where the arena is marked only by intermittent low boards, or a line, the marks deducted are at the judge's discretion. The FEI and AHSA rules state that, if the horse leaves the arena completely with all four feet, at any time between the entry and exit at the start and completion of the test, he will be eliminated.

**l'effet d'ensemble**  A French term meaning combined or co-ordinated effect, specifically the effect of using the leg or spur simultaneously with the hand. This combination of aids was employed by various notable equestrians as a means of attaining an enhanced equilibrium and more lightness in horses already quite advanced in their schooling, or to control or calm restive horses. While it is described by Baucher in his *Méthode d'équitation,* as an action of the hand and legs, Baucher's disciple, Faverot de Kerbrech, presented it as 'a coordinated effect with the spur', enabling the rider 'to overcome all resistances, and to guide the horse as one wants, and at the speed one desires'. However, Decarpentry (whose father and grandfather had been enthusiastic pupils of Baucher), wrote in *Academic Equitation:* '...the effet d'ensemble with the spur certainly enforces obedience, but a forced obedience that is not suited to academic equitation because it can never be gracious...As regards the kind of dressage considered here, it is felt that the advantages of the effet d'ensemble do not counterbalance its advantages sufficiently to warrant recommending this procedure in all cases.'

The divergence of opinion as to the intended meaning of the term, and the employment of l'effet d'ensemble, are discussed by Michel Henriquet in his book *Gymnase et Dressage* (English edition *Henriquet on Dressage).*

**left diagonal**  In trot, the left foreleg and right hind leg as a diagonal pair.

**left lead**  In canter (or gallop) the horse's left foreleg as the leading leg in that gait.

**left rein**  Literally, the rein connected to the left bit ring (seen from the rear); generally 'on the left rein' means moving anti-clockwise around the arena.

**leg aids**  Signals sent intentionally by the rider to the horse by means of bilateral or unilateral leg pressure.

**leg-yielding**  A lateral exercise in which the horse moves forwards and sideways away from pressure of the rider's inside leg. The horse's body should be almost straight, except for a slight flexion at the poll, just sufficient for the rider to see the horse's inside eye and nostril; the horse's inside legs pass and cross in front of the outside legs. The movement can be performed at all gaits. It is very rarely required in dressage tests and is more commonly employed as a training exercise, to teach a horse to move away from the rider's leg, and to increase suppleness, especially of the limb abductor and adductor muscles. Opinion on the overall value or otherwise of leg-yielding has long been divided, some trainers arguing that teaching the horse to move in this manner bent (albeit slightly) away from the direction of movement may cause confusion when exercises such as travers, renvers and half-pass are introduced later in training. There is a median view that the exercise is useful with regard to teaching early response to the rider's leg, but that it should be employed only sparingly thereafter.

Leg-yielding off a turn. Photograph by Karl Leck from Paul Belasik's *Dressage for the 21st Century*.

**lengthened strides**   In general, this term might be understood to mean any strides that are longer than those preceding (see **lengthening**). However, it is most commonly used to signify a relatively modest increase in stride length from the working gait.

Collected, medium and extended canter. Drawings by Gisela Holstein.

139

**lengthening**   Increasing the length of the current strides; a term that can encompass both the concept of lengthening from the working gait (see **lengthened strides**) and also any increase in stride length as, for example, from a collected to an extended gait.

**length of stride**   The distance covered by a complete stride, as determined by assessing the distance travelled by a particular foot, from its initial impact with the ground to the next impact. A horse's length of stride is influenced by numerous factors, including degree of mental and physical tension, rhythm, length of legs, relative length of body, degree of suppleness (especially of the back muscles and supraspinous ligament) and angulation and articulation of the shoulders and the joints of the hind limbs. See also **conformation**.

**Lesage, Col. Xavier**   French winner of the individual bronze medal at the 1924 Olympics, riding *Plumard*, and the individual gold medal at the 1932 Olympics, riding *Taine*, when he was also a member of the French team that won gold. Lesage was Chief Instructor at the French cavalry school at Saumur, where General Decarpentry had been second-in-command until 1931, and he and *Taine* feature in Decarpentry's famous book *Academic Equitation*.

Eric Lette. Photograph by Elizabeth Furth.

**Lette, Eric**   Born in Stockholm in 1943, Lette started riding at the age of nine and, at sixteen, acquired a horse who was trained to Grand Prix level. Later, whilst studying law at the University of Stockholm he supplemented his finances by training horses. In 1975, Lette rode Grand Prix on *Aintree*, who was sold on to Switzerland and was a member of that country's silver-medal-winning team at the 1984 Olympics. Another horse, *Dukat*, who competed successfully at Grand Prix at the age of eight, went on to be part of the German team that won the World Championships in 1986. Lette's wife's horse, *Top Flight*, was a long-time member of the Swedish international team and reserve horse for the 1984 Olympics.

As a judge, Lette had presided over lower-level classes in Sweden for several years from 1970, but gave up for a while because he was competing himself and had many students who were also competing. However, in

1986, he met Wolfgang Niggli, the Chairman of the FEI Dressage Committee, who viewed him as a potential successor. In the light of this contact, Lette soon qualified as an FEI judge, presiding at numerous major international events including European and World Championships, ten World Cup finals, Pan-American and Asian Games, and the Olympics in 1992, 1996 and 2000. In 1987 he also became a member of the FEI Dressage Committee and later, from 1993 to 2001, he realized Niggli's hopes for him when he served for eight years as Chairman. During his period of office he earned international respect for his positive influence on the development of dressage, from both judging and training standpoints. In recent years he has returned to his role as a trainer of horses and riders, placing particular emphasis on developing horse and rider partnerships in his native Sweden.

**levade**   A movement belonging to the family of airs above the ground, in which the horse, taking a great deal of weight on his hindquarters, sits back on his hocks and lifts his forehand off the ground, with forelegs folded, remaining stationary. The levade is broadly similar to the pesade, the most obvious difference being the mean angle of the horse's body to the ground; if the angle is greater than about 45 degrees, the air is considered a pesade, if less, it is a levade. The crucial difference between the two airs is that the levade requires more power and greater flexion of the joints of the hind limbs. Early attempts at the levade often result in the horse performing a rudimentary mézair. See that entry.

Paul Belasik riding levade. Photograph by Karl Leck from *Dressage for the 21st Century.*

**level**   Said of a horse whose limb movement is balanced and regular.

141

**levels**   The various grades of tests produced by the organizing bodies of competition dressage. British Dressage levels are, in ascending order, Preliminary, Novice, Elementary, Medium, Advanced Medium, Advanced. AHSA tests begin with Training Level and progress from First Level through to Fifth Level. While the names of the levels (and precise contents of tests within them) vary, a broadly similar system of progression is applied by other organizing bodies.

**leverage, of bit**   Leverage is a mechanical product of the design and action of a curb bit. Educated riders do not misuse this quality to impose their will on the horse forcefully, but rather use it to achieve their desired effects with minimal effort.

**leverage, of rider**   A term used by certain authors in describing the effect available to the rider if seat and upper body posture are correct. The concept is not one of exerting overt leverage on the horse's forehand, it is, rather, a fundamentally passive ability to counter the effects of a horse attempting to lean on the hand. In this respect, the rider's position is not compromised by a horse doing this; rather the rider, having passively opposed the effect, is still in a position to give aids to rebalance the horse.

Photograph of Alexis-François L'Hotte, from Hilda Nelson's *Alexis-François L'Hotte The Quest for Lightness in Equitation*.

**L'Hotte Gen. Alexis-François**   (1825–1904) A son and grandson of French cavalrymen, L'Hotte was, from an early age, a keen student of the equestrian writings of the old French Masters – much to the detriment of his academic education. He initially attended the military academy of Saint-Cyr as a young cadet, being sent on to pursue his equestrian interests at Saumur, since the cavalry section at Saint-Cyr had been closed. Despite some youthful indiscipline, he eventually attained the rank of General, and became Commandant of the reopened cavalry section at Saint-Cyr, and subsequently of Saumur.

It is of great interest to students of equestrian history that L'Hotte was a pupil of both

142

François Baucher and the Comte D'Aure, two highly influential figures who not only practised different styles of equitation, but were considered rivals and had their own factions of supporters. L'Hotte was a great note-taker, and his anecdotes about, and comparisons of, these two figures make fascinating reading.

L'Hotte himself was considered to be one of the most outstanding écuyers of a golden age: he originated the phrase 'equestrian tact' and the famous maxim 'calm, forward and straight'. His elegantly written book *Questions Équestres*, has been translated into English by Prof. Hilda Nelson.

**lift**   The elevating aspect of the power of a horse's hind limbs; the dominant element in producing the shortened, heightened steps associated with collected work.

**light**   A desirable quality to be aimed for in the application of the aids. A horse who is familiar with the aids, understands their intended meaning and is physically capable of carrying out their requirements, should, over time, respond increasingly well to lighter signals.

**lightness**   One of the major aims of schooling, lightness derives from a combination of true submissiveness by the horse, his desire to move actively forwards and the establishment of his balance beneath the rider. The term refers to the horse retaining a light, willing contact with the bit and to the relatively light movement of the forehand, which is partially relieved of its weight-bearing function by the increased activity of the hind limbs which, with the hindquarters somewhat lowered, are engaged well forward beneath the horse's body. This active, efficient use of the propulsive forces of the hind limbs also serves to lighten the steps. Thus, the interaction of the components of lightness could be summarized as follows: the horse must be obedient to the aids in order to flex his poll and jaw and to respond to the forward-driving aids by stepping forward actively into the rein contact; in making use of the propulsive powers of the hindquarters, he improves his balance and reduces the burden on his forehand; this improved balance makes it easier yet for him to be obedient to the aids and to move efficiently. See also **active**; **balance**; **collection**; **engagement**; **obedient**; **ramener** and **rassembler**.

Ernst Lindenbauer riding passage. Photograph from Üdo Burger's *The Way to Perfect Horsemanship*.

**Lindenbauer, Ernst** Born in Austria in 1881, Lindenbauer served as a volunteer in the Imperial Army from 1900 to 1903. He joined the Spanish Riding School in 1907, rising to the rank of First Chief Rider in 1927. Following his initial 'retirement' in 1948, he was considered such an asset to the school in the post-war period that he was persuaded to prolong his service until he finally retired at the end of 1950.

**Lindgren, Maj. A.** Born in Skoevde, Sweden, Lindgren was the eldest son of a Lieutenant Colonel in the Swedish cavalry. From a young age, he worked with draught horses on his grandfather's farm and was permitted to ride and groom horses in his father's regiment. Having graduated from the Royal Swedish Officers' Academy in 1948 he attended the Army Equestrian Centre at Strömsholm from 1949 to 1952, later becoming an instructor there. He was short-listed for the Swedish three-day eventing team several times in the 1950s and, in 1959, became Scandinavian champion in that discipline. In 1958, he was also short-listed for the Swedish dressage team. When the Army Equestrian Centre closed in 1968, he was reassigned to the Royal Horse Guards at Stockholm, where he became Chief of Staff. In 1971 he became Swedish dressage champion and, until his retirement from the army in 1975, he competed with two horses, *Eko* and *Strong*, at Grand Prix level in Europe.

Following his retirement, Lindgren began teaching as a civilian, giving clinics in Scandinavia and establishing a reputation as a trainer who would seek to break down exercises into simple segments, to assist both human and equine pupils. In 1981, he was asked to accompany Col. Sommer of Denmark to America to assist with conducting the annual Violet Hopkins/USDF National Dressage Instructors' Seminars. The following year, he presented a prototype Regional Instructors' Seminar for the California Dressage Society, which was to lay the foundation for a long-running series of regional seminars conducted on behalf of the USDF. When Col. Sommer retired in 1987, Lindgren took over as chief instructor at the USDF National Instructors' Seminar and, when this was superseded in 1992 by the USDF National Dressage Symposium, he conducted this in partnership with Eric Lette. In 1995 the two men returned in the same role, accompanied by Kyra Kyrklund, a former pupil of Lindgren's.

**Linsenhoff, Ann-Kathrin**  Born in Germany in 1961, the daughter of the world-renowned Lieselott Linsenhoff, Ann-Kathrin started riding when she was three and a half. Having competed for several years at national level in her teenage years, she went to Paris to work for Cartier. However, it was not long before she realized that horses were her main interest and in 1979 she returned to Germany and began veterinary studies. Having started to compete again, she was a member

Ann-Kathrin Linsenhoff riding *Courage*. Photograph by Elizabeth Furth.

of the German team that won the gold medal at the 1981 Young Riders European Championship, also taking individual bronze. Her senior international career took off in 1986 when she finished 4th at the World Cup Finals at 's Hertogenbosch; the following year she took the silver medal in the European Championships at Goodwood and went on to represent Germany at the Seoul Olympics (1988), finishing 6th individually and winning a team gold medal. She was also a member of the teams that won gold at the World Championships in Stockholm (1990) and Jerez (2002) and was reserve for the 2004 Olympic team.

**Linsenhoff, Lieselott**  (1927–1999) A German rider who competed at the highest level over a long period with great success; she first competed in the Olympic Games in 1956 (Melbourne), riding *Adular,* winning an individual bronze medal and team silver. Twelve years later, riding *Piaff* in Mexico, she made history as the first woman to win a gold medal in an equestrian event when she was a member of the winning German team. At the 1972 Munich Olympics, riding the same horse, she won the gold medal in the individual event, again becoming the first woman to do so, and she also won silver in the team event. Her daughter, Ann-Kathrin Linsenhoff, is now a highly successful international competitor.

**Ljungquist, Col. Bengt** (1912–1979)   A pupil of top trainers in his native Sweden, and a former Olympic rider, Ljungquist was invited to America in 1969 to teach at a three-week course at the Virginia Combined Training Center. Participants and onlookers were so impressed by his methods that he was soon giving several clinics a year in the US and, in 1974, he was appointed coach to the American team for that year's World Championships. Following a 5th place in that event, the team took team gold and individual silver and bronze medals at the 1975 Pan-American Games and, in 1976, team bronze at the Olympic Games. This Olympic success fired enthusiasm for dressage throughout America, and Ljungquist continued to have a great influence on many leading riders of the time. In 1976, his influential book *Practical Dressage Manual* was published and, during this time, he helped to establish a system of training judges that continues to the present day.

In 1979, however, he resigned as US team coach to concentrate on coaching students individually; apparently, he was uncomfortable with the political aspects of team coaching and wanted more freedom to visit Sweden when he and his wife wished to do so. It was later that year whilst on holiday in Sweden that he died of heart failure.

In 1998, he was inducted posthumously into the USDF's Hall of Fame, in recognition of his leadership in pursuit of excellence in dressage.

**Loch, Sylvia**   A Scottish-born rider, trainer and author with a long-standing interest in classical equitation and in the older Iberian breeds closely associated with its development. In 1969, whilst studying equitation in Portugal, Sylvia met Henry, Lord Loch, a former English cavalry officer, who had studied at both Saumur and the Spanish Riding School and had retired from his London-based business to pursue his passion for riding full time. Following their marriage, the Lochs ran a dressage yard in the Algarve, specializing in working with Lusitano horses, before returning to Suffolk in England to set up a broadly similar establishment. In 1982, the year in which Sylvia co-founded The Lusitano Breed Society, Lord Loch suffered a stroke and died. In the aftermath, Sylvia had to relinquish the Suffolk yard, but continued to teach and began to write equestrian books – *The Royal Horse of*

*Europe, The Classical Seat, Dressage, The Art of Classical Riding, The Classical Rider, Dressage in Lightness* and *Invisible Riding* – and to produce teaching videos. Following remarriage in 1985, she relocated to her country of birth, but travels widely to teach and give seminars. She also works as guest trainer at D. Francisco de Braganca's Classical Dressage School at Quinta do Archino, near Lisbon. In 1995, she founded the Classical Riding Club, an international organization based at her home. Detailed information about her activities can be obtained at www.classical-dressage.net.

Sylvia Loch riding passage. Photograph from *Dressage in Lightness.*

**locomotion**   Movement from place to place.

**long and low**   A carriage of the horse in which the head and neck are stretched forward and down, with the angle between jaw and neck fairly open and the nose close to the ground. This carriage is achieved by allowing the horse to gently 'chew' the bit and rein contact through the rider's hands following a period of demanding work (especially in collection) and can thus be viewed as a reward, in the form of relative relaxation, for the horse's efforts. However, it has an additional value in that it allows the musculature and major ligaments of the topline to stretch following a period of hard work and gives the horse the opportunity to stretch the head-on-neck flexor muscles under the jaw.

**longeing**   Derived from *longe*, the French word for halter (and, by extension in that language, the device generally known as a cavesson); working the horse from the ground on a line attached by a cavesson or other means to the horse's head. The term is more commonly rendered in current English as **lungeing** (which see for further explanation).

Longeing. Photograph by Karl Leck from Paul Belasik's *Dressage for the 21st Century.*

147

**longitudinal**   Lengthwise, as opposed to sideways (see **lateral**). For example, a horse working in collection, or low and round, will show longitudinal flexion of the body.

**long rein (on a)**   Riding with the reins significantly longer than when working a horse fully on the aids is usually done to encourage mental relaxation and a stretching of the topline muscles and ligaments. As such, it is often done before or after main periods of work, or when hacking out for the purpose of gentle exercise. This form of rein contact is also associated with the free walk required in many dressage tests. While the reins are long, a light contact is retained.

Sylvia Stanier long-reining a horse in extended trot at the Horse of the Year Show. Photograph from *The Art of Long Reining.*

**long-reining**   A means of working the horse from the ground, via long reins that are attached to the bit (occasionally to a cavesson) and, according to the actual method used, run through rings on a pad/roller, or through a collar and roller or, more rarely, through the stirrup irons on a saddle. The Spanish Riding School uses a method involving shorter than usual 'long reins', which run directly from the bit to the hands of the operator, who is positioned much nearer to the horse than practitioners of the other methods. Those skilled in using long reins can train and work horses in a wide variety of movements in this fashion.

**loose**   A term often used in the English language intended to convey more or less the equivalent meaning of the German losgelassenheit. The meaning of the latter might be better conveyed by the terms absence of, or freedom from, tension. Although looseness signifies absence of tension, it can also convey the idea of incipient, or actual, disconnection – a quality that would not be desirable in the ridden horse. See **connected**.

**loose rein**  To ride on a loose rein is to ride without any rein contact.

**loose seat**  A seat in the saddle that is not established and under the rider's control. Related to various forms of faulty posture, a loose seat will compromise both the rider's security and the balance of the horse/rider unit, will send to the horse various random and confusing weight aids, and will interfere with the application of the other aids.

Walk on a loose rein. Photograph from Reiner Klimke's *Basic Training of the Young Horse.*

**Loriston-Clarke, Jennie**  Born in England in 1943, the daughter of Anne Bullen, a talented artist and horsewoman. Early in her equestrian career, Jennie rode in many disciplines, including point-to-pointing. Her brother Michael rode in the 1960 Olympic three-day event and her sister Jane was the 1968 Olympic silver medallist in the same discipline.

In the 1970s Jennie began to specialize in dressage and, riding *Kadett*, was a member of the British team for the 1972 and 1976 Olympics. By 1977, she had begun a partnership with the stallion, *Dutch Courage* and, in 1978, she won the bronze medal at the World Equestrian Championships at Goodwood with that horse. Two years later, at the same venue, this partnership came 6th in the individual 'Alternative Olympics'. At the following 'true' Olympics (Los Angeles, 1984) Jennie, riding *Prince Consort,* was a member of the British team alongside Christopher Bartle and his sister, Jane Bartle-Wilson.

In addition to his achievements in the arena, *Dutch Courage* became a great success at the family's Catherston Stud, his progeny including two of Jennie's most successful partners, *Dutch Gold* and *Catherston Dazzler.* During a period of some six years, the former gave many notable performances at national and international level, including wins in European Championship Freestyle events in 1987 and 1989. In 1988 the partnership represented Britain at the Seoul Olympics and in 1988/9 they won the Nashua European points table for the World Cup – the only British combination to have achieved this honour. In 1990 *Dutch Gold* was Nominee Assurance Dressage Horse of the Year at Wembley and he and Jennie were 4th in the World Cup Final in 1989 and 5th in 1990, 1991 and 1992. *Catherston Dazzler* had a highly successful national and international career in the 1990s, with victories that included the 1995 Addington National Championship Grand Prix.

Loriston-Clarke retired from international competition after winning her tenth National Championship title at Grand Prix level in 1995 and now focuses her attention on judging, being an FEI International judge. Also heavily involved with encouraging young people in dressage, she has been chef d'équipe for many Under 21s teams and has helped British teams to achieve consistent success at Pony, Junior and Young Rider European Championships.

Otto Lörke riding piaffe. Image from General Decarpentry's *Academic Equitation*.

**Lörke, Otto** (1879–1957) German rider and trainer who did his early military service at the imperial stables, where an appreciation of his equestrian talents led to him being appointed to Emperor Wilhelm II's personal guard, with responsibility for training the imperial horses. Following the First World War, he did office work for a short time, but soon gave that up and, in 1920, he founded a yard in Berlin, which produced a number of highly successful horses and an impeccable display team. In 1936, he started work at the cavalry riding school in Berlin, were he trained First-Lt. Pollay and Major Gerhard, individual gold and silver medallists and members of Germany's gold-medal-winning team at the 1936 Berlin Olympics. During this period, he also contributed to the development of Felix Bürkner's school quadrille.

In 1945 Lörke was able to rescue his horses from the chaos of war, taking them to the farm of Clemens Freiherr von Nagel in North Rhine-Westphalia. He continued to work as a trainer and, when Germany won the silver medal at the 1956 Olympics with a team of three lady riders, two had been trained by Lörke and the third by his pupil, Willi Schultheis.

Lörke had the reputation of being an upright and straightforward character who refused to accept equestrian compromises and became distinctly unimpressed by any lack of concentration on his pupils' part. Some commentators suggested that, while his own riding technique was less elegant than contemporaries such as Stensbeck, or Schultheis, he knew how to produce pictures of effortless elegance and supreme control in his pupils. Any lack of elegance on his own part was nullified by instinctive feeling and tremendous diligence. Gustav Rau wrote of Lörke's horses, 'We can only admire all his horses because they are absolutely obedient…they are extremely powerful during high collection and their free paces are full of impulsion. It seems that the horses move-off with seven-league boots.'

**losgelassenheit**  A German expression that signifies absence of tension in the horse. Although this quality is manifest in the horse's physical movement, it denotes an underlying willingness on the horse's part to co-operate with the rider and move forward freely.

**loss of**  A judge's remark, preceding reference to a desirable quality such as balance, bend, rhythm, etc., denoting that the specific quality became diminished.

**low airs**  An old term for formalized movements, other than the simple execution of the basic gaits, performed effectively on the ground (as opposed to airs above the ground); the term thus covers a wide range of movements such as piaffe, pirouettes, voltes, etc.

**low and round**  A form of deep work which has some similarities with the long

Some of the low airs as illustrated in de la Guérinière's *Ecole de Cavalerie*.

and low outline, in that the horse is moving in a long frame, stretching down to the ground. However, rather than being used primarily as relaxation/reward, this form of work is employed for more active gymnastic purposes, to assist in the development of self-carriage and to develop and strengthen the topline. In order to achieve this, the horse is asked for more flexion at the poll, so that the consequent cresting of the neck and stretching of the nuchal/supraspinous ligament system and the associated musculature produce an upward-arching effect on the topline. As a consequence of the flexion at the poll combined with the lowered position of the neck, the horse's face may be a little behind the vertical but, in this position, this does not, of itself, constitute being behind the bit (if the hindquarters were to engage to the degree that produces collection, the forehand would raise the head and neck to a poll-high posture in which the nose would not be behind the vertical). However, it is important that the increased flexion at the poll is produced and maintained by light aids: first, because the horse must not be encouraged to lean on the rider's hands and go on the forehand and second, because if the horse is forced into overbending or overflexing, muscular stiffness or even tissue damage may result.

**Lundblad, Capt. Janne**    The Swedish winner of the individual gold medal at the 1920 Olympic Games in Antwerp, riding *Uno*.

**lungeing**    The Anglicized form of longeing; working the horse from the ground on a long line, normally on a circle around the trainer. The trainer communicates with the horse via the line (attached to the horse's head by a cavesson or similar device, or sometimes to the snaffle on a bridle), with a long whip (which signals mainly by pointing at, rather than striking, the horse), by the voice and, to some extent, by his own positioning and posture. The basic equipment is often supplemented, as appropriate, by side reins and auxiliary reins such as the Chambon and de Gogue.

Correct work on the lunge contributes to the training process in a number of ways. These include familiarizing the horse with the aids for forward movement and upward and downward transitions, establishing longitudinal balance and regularity in the gaits (especially, for the young horse, without the burden of a rider's weight) and improving lateral suppleness and balance. Lungeing is a useful means of exercising the horse at any time when ridden work is not appropriate (e.g. for therapeutic/remedial

152

work) or as a warming up/calming down preparation for riding, and it provides a means of observing (and improving upon) aspects of the horse's movement that can be felt but not seen from the saddle. Mounted lessons and exercises on the lunge can be of great value in helping the rider to establish good posture.

# M

**made mouth**   An old term signifying a horse whose training is at a level at which he willing accepts the bit and responds obediently to the rein aids.

**Mairinger, Franz**   (1915–1978) Born in Vienna, Austria, Mairinger entered the Austrian cavalry in 1935 and was soon selected to train at the prestigious Cavalry School of Hanover, Germany. Although dressage was part of the curriculum, the school was chiefly noted for its successes in showjumping and eventing and these, together with steeplechasing, were Mairinger's first loves. A real enthusiasm for dressage was first kindled when he attended the International Horse Show in Hanover, where the Spanish Riding School gave a number of guest appearances. Fortuitously, their horses were stabled at the Cavalry School and their Director, Col. Podhajsky, having seen Mairinger riding, asked him to ride one of the Spanish School's stallions and subsequently offered him a position at the Spanish Riding School. After six years at the school, he was appointed a bereiter, a position he held for over twelve years before spending some time in Switzerland as a private instructor. In 1951, following the suggestion of a former pupil, Maj. Sandford, Mairinger moved to Australia, where he soon made his mark, being appointed the first trainer of an Australian Olympic Equestrian Team in 1955. The following year, the Australian eventing team took 4th place at the Stockholm Olympics and in 1960 they won the gold medal in Rome. These successes demonstrated to Australian riders in all disciplines what could be achieved through training with a classical basis, and Mairinger's achievements did not go unnoticed back in Austria. On several occasions Col. Handler, by then

Franz Mairinger, from a greetings card sent from Mairinger to Charles Harris.

Director of the Spanish Riding School, approached him with requests to return to Vienna. However, family ties and an ambition to establish a National Riding Academy kept Mairinger in Australia, where he trained a total of six teams (eventing, showjumping and dressage) for the Olympics and was training a seventh at the time of his death.

In addition to his primary training role, he gave numerous clinics throughout Australia, emphasizing his gentle philosophy of classical riding. His book, *Horses are Made to be Horses* based on his notes, lectures and demonstrations, was published internationally and is considered one of the most important influences on the development of Australian equitation.

**manège**   Historically, an open or covered place of exercise, generally about 12 yds wide by 36 yds long (11 m x 33 m), the term often being broadened to include the exercises themselves. The term continues in current use, as a synonym for arena or school, describing an area that is usually larger than of old (i.e. commonly a standard-sized arena).

**markers**   The letters placed at predetermined points around the arena, which guide the rider in performance of the test. While the letters around the perimeter markers exist in fact, those 'on the centre line' are normally imaginary points, located with reference to those around the perimeter (for example, the imaginary maker G is on the centre line 6 m from C, midway between M and H).

**Markham, Gervase**   (1568–1637) The leading authority on horses in Elizabethan England, Markham taught many of the queen's courtiers the art of riding, was renowned as a breeder and was possibly the first Englishman to import an Arab stallion into the country. He wrote several books on breeding, training and horsemastership and his work *The Compleat Horseman* suggests an equestrian understanding, humanity and overall affection for the horse which place him at least on a level with his more famous European contemporaries.

**marks, dressage test**   The scale of marks applied in all FEI tests and in all tests run by affiliated bodies is standardized as follows: 10 excellent, 9 very good, 8 good, 7 fairly good, 6 satisfactory, 5 sufficient; 4 insufficient, 3 fairly bad, 2 bad, 1 very bad, 0 not executed (not executed implies that the horse has somehow travelled from the marker designating the start of the movement to the marker designating its end, but without performing any of the specific work required). One mark is awarded globally for each designated (numbered) movement, regardless of whether that movement comprises one requirement (e.g. enter at working trot and proceed down centre line without halting) or several (e.g. between C & M working canter right; B circle right 20 metres diameter; BAE working canter). In some higher-level tests, a coefficient is applied to certain movements, in order to emphasize their impact on the overall test, i.e. although the movement will be marked out of 10, if a coefficient of 2 pertains, that movement will effectively be worth 20 marks.

In addition to the marks for each movement, each test will also have several collective marks, which relate to overall performance of the test. These relate to qualities such as freedom and regularity of movement, impulsion, submission, rider's seat and use of the aids. In many tests, these marks are also subject to a coefficient, usually of 2.

For freestyle to music tests, the marking system is somewhat different; technical marks are given for certain designated movements that must be included in the test, and artistic marks are given for qualities such as rhythm, energy and elasticity, harmony, choreography, degree of difficulty and choice and interpretation of music, these being given relatively high coefficients. Time penalties are also applicable if the performance lasts longer or is markedly shorter than a designated time.

**martingale**   See **auxiliary reins**.

**McDonald, Debbie**   Born in Idaho, USA, in 1954, McDonald began her career as a showjumper and only ventured into competitive dressage at the age of thirty-seven. She represented the USA at the World Cup in Gothenburg in 1998 and won both team and individual gold medals at the Pan-American Games in 1999, when she was AHSA and USOC Equestrian of the Year. In 2002, riding *Brentina*, she finished first at the USET Festival of Champions and took a team silver medal at the World Equestrian Games. The following year, the partnership was 2nd in the World Cup and, in 2004, they were members of the American team that won Olympic bronze, being placed 4th individually.

**Medium**   Under British Dressage rules, the fourth level of tests, between Elementary and Advanced Medium.

Waldemar Seunig's drawing of turn to the left in medium canter from *The Essence of Horsemanship*.

**medium**   This term does not signify the median stride length within a gait (i.e. the middle of the working range), but rather a significant degree of lengthening beyond the working gait, getting fairly close to, but distinctly short of, the extended form. A correct medium gait is indicated by increased use, not only of the limbs, but also of the horse's back.

**memorizing**   While, under some competition rules, it is permissible for certain tests to be commanded, the majority are ridden from memory. Different individuals use a variety of techniques for committing a test to memory, the aim being to attain an 'automatic recall', which enables the competitor to concentrate upon the process of riding, rather than remembering what to do next.

**mézair**   One of the airs above the ground, derived from working towards the levade and linked to the courbette (described by de la Guérinière as a demi-courbette). In the early stages of attempting the levade, the horse may rise up a little on his haunches, jump forward off them, and then try the levade again. When these low, ground-gaining jumps are performed intentionally and successively, this is the mézair.

**mise en main**  A French term, literally 'putting in the hand'; to effect a yielding of the jaw in association with flexion at the poll; contributes to putting the horse in the position of the ramener.

**moment of suspension**  The brief period during the stride pattern when all four of the horse's feet are off the ground; occurs at trot, canter and gallop, but not at walk. See also **suspension**.

**Moser, Hans**  Swiss winner of the individual gold medal at the 1948 Olympic Games in London, riding *Hummer*.

The moment of suspension, captured in a photograph by Elizabeth Furth.

**mouthing**  The process of getting a young horse used to the presence of a bit in his mouth. Trainers have their own preferred methods of achieving this; the important point (with a view to later training) being that the horse becomes happy to accept the bit, but does not play with it excessively, or learn evasions such as getting his tongue over it.

**mouth open**  When a horse is accepting the bit, he will usually keep his mouth more or less shut; an open mouth, especially if accompanied by boring or leaning on the hand, is indicative of resistance, which may in turn be rooted in discomfort (caused by an ill-fitting or damaged bit, mouth problems or bad riding), or plain intractability.

**move away from the leg**  The reaction to a unilateral leg aid, whereby the horse moves to some degree laterally away from the leg pressure. For example, in leg-yielding to the left, the horse is responding to pressure of the rider's right leg.

**move off the leg**  A general term signifying positive response to the leg aid or aids (compare to **move away from the leg**).

157

**movement**   Simple evidence of locomotion aside, this means an element of a dressage test for which a mark is ascribed. A movement can consist of one simple element ('At C, track right'), or it may contain several more complex ones ('G Proceed in passage. Transitions from collected walk to passage and from piaffe to passage.')

Wilhelm Müseler. Photograph from *Riding Logic*.

**Müseler, Wilhelm**   (1887–1952) Born in Berlin, Müseler was, in his youth, a fine athlete – he held the German record for the 100 m sprint. Following a grammar school education, he embarked upon a career as a cavalry officer. During the years preceding the First World War, he competed with great success at dressage and showjumping, and was a member of the German Olympic equestrian team; however, upon being told by his commanding officer that he should make his career 'with his intellect rather than his backside', he intensified his commitment to his primary role as an officer. His military abilities are evidenced by the fact that, by 1918, he had become the youngest Major on the German General Staff. Later in life, when recalled to the General Staff at the onset of the Second World War, he was to attain the rank of General.

Leaving the army after the end of the First World War, Müseler again committed himself to equitation, becoming Director of Tattersall Beermann, then the largest equestrian centre in Berlin. In this role, his emphasis shifted away from active competition and towards training horses and riders and organizing equestrian events. He also became Master of the Berlin Hunting Society and President of the German Association of Hunting Clubs.

In 1931, health problems compelled him to cease his riding activities. His book *Riding Logic*, written by way of a conclusion, was originally intended for the academic equestrian societies he had founded. Once published, however, the book became a bestseller, appearing in many editions and many languages. From 1932 onward, Müseler also wrote books on the history of art, one of which sold over a million copies – he considered these books the most important work of his life.

**music**   There is a considerable history of dressage being ridden to music; it is thought that the sixteenth-century trainer Fiaschi used it to promote rhythm and it has been used for instructional and aesthetic purposes ever since. In recent times, it has been introduced to competitive dressage in the form of freestyle to music.

# N

**napping**   A serious form of resistance to, or dismissing of, the rider's aids, typified by the horse engaging in crab-like sideways movement, or even backing up. When napping occurs in a test, it will be considered a serious disobedience and, in certain circumstances, where it is protracted or involves leaving the arena, it can be a cause of elimination. However, while napping can, in some cases, be nothing other than defiance of the rider's commands, it is often exhibited by young, insecure horses who are seeking the companionship of others or the comfort and security of their stable or horsebox. With horses of the latter type it is good practice to accustom them gradually to showground environments before attempting to compete in dressage tests or other competitive disciplines.

**National Equestrian Federation**   The national governing body of equestrian sport in a country, affiliated to the FEI.

**natural aids**   See **aids, natural**.

**natural gaits**   The gaits of an untrained horse at liberty.

**Neapolitan School**   The name given to the school of riding developed in the area of Naples in the Renaissance period, by trainers including Grisone, Fiaschi and Pignatelli. It represented a significant advance upon the riding style of the medieval era and laid the early foundations for the development of classical equitation.

**nearside**    refers to the left side of the horse (as viewed from the rear).

Josef Neckermann. Photograph from Wilhelm Müseler's *Riding Logic.*

**Neckermann, Josef**    Born in 1913, Neckermann was a pre-eminent German rider and trainer whose impressive international record included individual bronze at the 1960 Olympics, team gold in 1964, team gold and individual silver in 1968 and team silver and individual bronze in 1972. He was also World Champion in 1966.

Neckermann's yard was, for many years, a meeting point for leading exponents of dressage such as Harry Boldt and Reiner Klimke and it was a meeting with Neckermann, and the inspiration provided by his yard, that gave impetus to Conrad Schumacher's career. When Schumacher's own yard became established, Neckermann decided to base his own horses there, bringing with him Ellen Bontje, who later became Schumacher's stable manager. Neckermann died in 1992, aged seventy-nine.

**neck-rein**    To give a directional aid to the horse through the use of rein pressure on the neck; the horse moves/turns away from that pressure. An aid used extensively in Western riding, the rein effect being augmented by the rider's weight aids. This rein aid is not normally employed in the same form in dressage riding when, while the indirect rein lies on the horse's neck, there is an effect on the horse's mouth via the rein contact, which does not occur in the Western style.

**Nelson, Professor Hilda**    Born in Germany and raised in Alexandria, Egypt, where her multi-lingual father worked in the foreign section of a bank, Hilda attended both French and English schools. Having absorbed many aspects of the French language and culture, she went on to study French and Comparative Literature at the University of Winsconsin, receiving her Ph.D in 1968 and later attaining the status of Emeritus Professor of French Civilization and Literature at San Diego State University.

Her father, who rode for pleasure, had a great love of horses, which Hilda inherited. Much travelled, she took lessons in England from two instructors, Minette Rice-Edwards and Danny Pevsner, both of whom had trained with Nuno Oliveira and at the Spanish Riding School. During visits to France, she befriended Michel Henriquet, making numerous visits to his establishment near Paris where, by watching training sessions, she learnt a great deal about the techniques of classical equitation.

For many years, Nelson has combined her academic skills and knowledge with her love of riding. The author of several books on her wider field of study, she has brought great benefit to equestrian scholars by translating into English Antoine de Pluvinel's *Le Maneige Royal* and producing her own two works, *François Baucher the Man and his Method,* and *Alexis-François L'Hotte The Quest For Lightness In Equitation,* which contain translations of Baucher's *New Method of Horsemanship* and L'Hotte's *Questions Équestres* respectively. In addition to dealing directly with the key subject matter, these works offer a fascinating and detailed insight into many aspects of equestrian history – a virtue that is shared by another work *The Ecuyere of the Nineteenth Century in the Circus* and her magazine articles on the development of French equitation.

In addition to these historical works, she has also translated her friend Henriquet's *Gymnase et Dressage* into English, as *Henriquet on Dressage*.

**nervousness**   A characteristic, related to their historical status as a prey species and evident to some extent in all horses, that must be taken into account throughout the training process.

Horses are instinctively nervous of unfamiliar objects and erratic movement. Photograph by Bob Langrish from Ulrik Schramm's *The Undisciplined Horse*.

**Newcastle, Duke of**   See **Duke of Newcastle**.

**Niggli, Wolfgang M.**   Born in Zurich in 1922, Niggli began riding at the age of twelve. As a teenager, he competed successfully in dressage, showjumping and eventing. Whilst studying to complete his qualifications as an engineer, he became an officer in the Swiss cavalry and subsequently a riding instructor at the Swiss Army Officer Schools. In 1947, he was seconded to the French Military Riding School in Fontainbleau which, at that time, had replaced Saumur as the main military school. Whilst there, in addition to competing in dressage and jumping competitions, he rode in major steeplechases.

From 1949 to 1952, Niggli lived in America, working as an engineer and riding only occasionally at local shows. On his return to Switzerland, he worked for the North-Eastern Swiss Power Company, of which he was later appointed Vice-President (Construction). Once re-established in Switzerland, he started to compete again in all the major disciplines and in cross-country races, and resumed a part-time role as an army riding instructor.

In 1957, he became a Swiss National Dressage Judge and he was a member of the Dressage Committee of the Swiss National Equestrian Federation from 1961 to 1986, being Chairman from 1964 to 1973. During this period he acted as the Swiss chef d'équipe at many international events, including the 1972 Olympics. In 1964 he was promoted to FEI International Dressage Judge and served on the FEI Dressage Committee from 1973 to 1976 and from 1979 to 1981; from 1981 to 1993 he was Chairman of this committee and thus a member of the FEI Bureau. Between 1964 and his retirement from the FEI Dressage Committee in 1993, he judged at numerous international competitions, including three Olympic Games.

For many years, Niggli has worked tirelessly to improve the consistency and standards of judging, and has held seminars worldwide to that end. Recently, he has spent an increased proportion of his time helping riders. His book, *Dressage a Guideline for Riders and Judges*, is a distillation of these twin aims.

**nodding**   A distinctive movement of the head, atypical of the normal gait, that suggests that the horse is unsound.

**noseband**   A strap or more complex device, usually of leather, that fits around the horse's nose and forms part of the bridle. There are a number of patterns of noseband, with various intended functions. Under most competition rules, it is obligatory to use a noseband, but there are differences between organizing bodies as to the patterns permitted, and further variations under individual rules depending on the level and type of competition. The cavesson noseband, the only pattern permitted for use with a double bridle, is universally acceptable, but other patterns should only be fitted after close perusal of the specific rules that pertain to the competition in question.

**nose-diving**   The action of a horse who raises his head somewhat above the bit then drives it down violently in an attempt to wrench the reins from the rider's hands. As with boring on the bit, this may conceivably be a response to harsh constraint on the rider's part, or to marked pain in the mouth, but it may also be an extreme act of insubordination – discerning which it is is essential to effecting a cure.

**not enough**   A judge's comment that may pertain to a specific component of a test movement, for example 'not enough lengthening'; 'not enough difference' (as between working and medium gaits, or other gait variants). The term has an obvious grammatical relationship with insufficient, but the latter is often applied to the overall performance of a movement, rather than to a particular part of it.

**Novice**   Under British Dressage rules, the second level of tests, above Preliminary.

**novice**   Generally, an inexperienced horse or rider. The term may have more specific meanings under certain competition rules, with reference, for example, to points or prize money won.

**nuchal apparatus**   The ligamentous structure that runs from the horse's poll, over the back, to the tail; a connection that plays a crucial role in the horse's movement. The front part of this apparatus, the nuchal ligament, is attached to the cervical spine by fascia, and allows free movement of the head and neck; further back, spanning the thoracic and lumbar regions, is the supraspinous ligament, which stabilizes the vertebrae and prevents unwanted movement.

**numnah**   See **saddle cloth**.

# O

**Oatley-Nist, Kristy**   See under married name of **Staczek**.

**obedient**   Describes a horse who is willingly compliant to the rider's aids. It is difficult for even a willing horse to be fully obedient to aids that he does not understand, to aids that contradict each other, or to aids that ask him to do things of which he is physically incapable.

**objection**   A formalized complaint against an apparent scoring error, or a decision by a judge or other relevant official at a competition. Usually, an objection can only be made by the horse's owner (or his designated agent) or by the rider; this must be done in writing and sent, within a certain timescale, to the competition secretary and accompanied by a financial deposit (which is forfeit if the objection is not upheld, unless it is deemed that there were reasonable grounds for lodging the objection).

**offside**   The right side of the horse, as viewed from the rear.

**Oliveira, Nuno**   (1925–1989) One of the pre-eminent equestrians of his era, this great Portuguese rider began his career as a pupil of Joaquin Gonçalves de Miranda, former Master of the Horse to the Portuguese royal family. After Miranda's death, Oliveira trained horses first for cavalry officers and a dealer, then for one of Miranda's pupils, Senõr Chefalenez. Subsequently, a friend and student, Manuel de Barros, asked him to train at his brother-in-law's stud. There, in addition to having many good horses to ride, he also had at his disposal a large equestrian library, of which he made good use. During this period, he met Alois Podhajsky when they both rode at an exhibition in the Campo Grande and the pair became firm friends.

From the late 1950s onward, Oliveira started to attract a number of highly talented pupils, and opened his riding school at Quinta do Chafaris. One of his first foreign pupils was Michel Henriquet, who was to become a lifelong friend and was instrumental in promoting Oliveira's work in France. During this period, Oliveira also began to write articles (and subsequently, books) on equitation, while a pupil organized a weekly television programme showing his lessons.

In 1961 Oliveira gave his first full-scale exhibition abroad, in Switzerland, and the following year he rode in the Winter Circus in Paris, where he met and established a lasting relationship with Capt. Durand, later to be Commandant of the Cadre Noir. From this period onward, he continued to impress the equestrian world with his tireless pursuit of absolutely correct, yet light

Nuno Oliveira in levade. Photograph from *Reflections on Equestrian Art*.

and elegant work and by his intellectual ability to meld the best elements of equitation from various classical sources. The succeeding years saw a continuing influx of pupils, many from abroad, and numerous clinics and exhibitions throughout Europe, North and South America and Australia, which continued up to the time of his death in the last-mentioned country.

**one-sided** Said of a horse who, through deficiencies of conformation, lack of correct training or overtly incorrect training, has uneven lateral development, to the extent that he has marked difficulty in bending or moving in a particular direction. See also **crookedness**.

**one-time changes** A series of flying changes, one change being performed every stride; the ultimate form of tempi changes. These are a relatively recent development in the history of dressage; multiple flying changes (tempi changes) do not seem to be mentioned in equestrian literature until well into the nineteenth century and it seems to have been Baucher who first brought the one-time changes to popular attention. For around half a century afterwards, controversy raged as to whether this movement belonged to the field of classical equitation, or was fundamentally a 'circus trick'. Alois Podhajsky, in *The Complete Training of Horse and Rider*, wrote: 'Many arguments took place at the Spanish Riding School, without ever coming to a satisfactory conclusion.' However, the FEI having decided in favour of them, they were, in time, incorporated into Olympic-level tests.

**on his toes**   Said of a horse who is full of energy; exuberant – possibly to a degree at which he is not wholly submissive to the rider's aids.

**on the aids**   Said of a horse who is positively attentive to the rider's seat, legs and rein aids. See also **between leg and hand**.

**on the bit**   Said of a horse who is demonstrating a willing acceptance of the bit, i.e. is taking a light but positive contact with it, with no attempt to evade its action, and is flexing at the jaw and poll; given the connection of the horse from back to front, it also implies the presence of attributes such as active forward movement and good balance.

Horse falling onto the forehand in canter. Picture by Maggie Raynor.

**on the forehand**   Said of a horse who is carrying a greater amount of weight on his front limbs than is commensurate with good balance in the gait performed; there is insufficient engagement of the hind limbs and the horse will feel relatively heavy in the rider's hands.

**on the left/right rein**   Convenient phrases that do no more than convey the general direction of travel round the arena. On the left rein means proceeding in an anticlockwise direction; on the right rein means proceeding in a clockwise direction.

**open(ing) rein**   See **direct rein**.

**opposite rein**   The rein (or direction) other than that being ridden on.

**Otto-Crepin, Margit**   Born in Germany in 1943, she married into a French family and, at the time of her most memorable successes, was working long hours as a bookkeeper in the family clothing business in Paris to make time for her horses, based in Dusseldorf. On *Corlandus*, she was individual silver medallist at the 1988 Olympics; she was also European Champion in 1987, runner-up in 1989 and placed third in 1991, and she won the World Cup in 1989. She has also been active in the administrative side of dressage, her roles including Chief Manager for Dressage in France and membership of the FEI board.

Margit Otto-Crepin riding *Lucky Lord*. Photograph by Elizabeth Furth.

**outline**   Effectively, the basic shape a horse would make in silhouette at any given time. When evaluating outline, emphasis is usually placed mainly on the horse's topline, but the actions of the abdominal muscles and the placement of the feet are also influential.

**out of balance**   A term sometimes used to describe a rider whose posture is such that it compromises, or actively interferes with, the horse's movement.

**outside**   Generally, the outside leg/rein/hand etc. is that further from the centre of the arena. However, (as with inside) in some particular cases, the reference may be to the horse's bend, rather than to arena location. For example, in counter-canter, where the horse is likely to have some slight incurvation away from the direction of travel, the 'outside' rein may be that towards the inside of the arena. Similarly, in a half-pass which has travelled beyond the centre line, the 'outside rein', with reference to the horse's bend, may in fact be nearer to the centre of the arena than the 'inside' rein.

167

**outside assistance**   Any assistance given by another party to a competitor by voice, signs, etc., that is intended to help improve the competitor's performance. Where identified, it will entail elimination.

**outside track**   A term used to designate the practical boundary of the internal perimeter of an arena; the widest course that horse and rider can take whilst remaining in the arena. See also **go large**.

An overbent horse. Drawing by Klaus Philip from Alfred Knopfhart's *Fundamentals of Dressage*.

**overbent**   Describes a horse whose head is carried significantly behind the vertical, either because the rider's rein aids are too restrictive, or because the horse is seeking to avoid proper contact with the bit for other reasons. A horse whose head is set on particularly high, and who has an abnormal amount of flexion at the poll, may have a natural capacity to be (or appear to be) slightly overbent. However, overbending, typically, is not a consequence of extra flexion of the poll but of excessive flexion of the cervical vertebrae further back (often known as 'false flexion' or 'broken neck'). Horses in such a posture cannot be truly 'through' – they often exhibit a hollow just in front of the withers.

A horse who is working in a low and round frame may have his head behind the vertical, but if he is otherwise moving correctly he will not be considered overbent because, in this case, the angle of the head to the ground is a product of the low carriage of the whole neck.

**overcollected**   This term does not describe 'too much' true collection but incorrect attempts to *impose* collection, typically by the rider driving the horse into an over-restrictive rein contact. Faults engendered by riding in this way include lack of true engagement of the hindquarters, irregular, dragging and probably crooked steps with little elevation, overbending and/or resistances in the mouth, a cramped neck, which may appear 'shortened' and tightness in the back.

**overtracking** Said of a horse when his hind feet step beyond the prints made by his forefeet; may be seen to a modest degree when horses of certain conformation are moving at the working gaits, but should definitely be one characteristic of the medium and extended gaits.

# P

**pace** A word that can have several meanings which might be used in an equestrian context, including 'step' and 'speed' and also describing a two-beat lateral gait with a period of suspension. The word is also commonly used in English dressage terminology (although not generally in the USA) to refer to the distinct modes of equine movement, as in 'the pace of trot', and thus the 'paces – walk, trot and canter'. Since there is a term – gait – that can define the modes of movement without the possibility of ambiguity, the use of 'pace' in this context does not seem the most appropriate choice. There may be a certain justification for relating 'pace(s)' to speed, in so far as the horse, at liberty, will tend to employ walk, trot, canter or gallop depending on how fast he wishes to travel, but such distinction becomes muddied in the trained horse under saddle when, for example, he may move significantly faster in extended trot than at collected canter.

**pacing** A term sometimes used to describe a faulty walk that is tending towards two-time movement; in dressage terminology, does not normally imply that the horse is actually performing the pace gait.

**parade** This, and the associated half-parade, are terms used by European riders that are sometimes considered to be synonymous with half-halt. However, while there are similarities between the terms in so far as they are concerned with preparation and rebalancing, they are not exactly the same. In her Note in Ulrik Schramm's *The Undisciplined Horse*, trainer and translator Nicole Bartle comments that parade is a technical word for which there is no precise equivalent in English and adds: 'A Parade or partial Parade is not a "half-halt" but an interplay of all the aids…to ask the horse to flex its hocks in preparation for any variation or change of gait.'

A pas de deux. Photograph by Bob Langrish.

**pas de deux**   A freestyle dressage programme performed by two riders.

**passade**   A turning exercise which, over the centuries, has been described in slightly different terms by eminent authorities, perhaps because they have found ways of using it to suit various training purposes. De la Guérinière, writing early in the eighteenth century, describes it as being primarily a combat figure and 'a straight line on which the horse travels and returns, performing at each end…a change of hand or a demi-volte. The line of the passade should be…five times the length of the horse, and the demi-voltes should measure only one length of the horse.' (*Ecole de Cavalerie.*) Thus, in de la Guérinière's passade, at each end of the line, the horse is performing a very tight demi-volte and must 'change leg without becoming disunited while closing the demi-voltes'.

Having discussed the combat form of the exercise, de la Guérinière goes on to write: 'Passades with demi-voltes which are as large as those of ordinary demi-voltes are also done in the manège…This is a figure of the School, not of war…' It seems that, as time went by, increasing emphasis was placed on the gymnastic value of the turns in passade as an aid to introducing other exercises, rather than on its value in mounted attack. For example, in *The Complete Training of Horse and Rider*, Alois Podhajsky writes 'As a rule, the renvers is begun after a *passade* to make things easier for the horse. A passade is a very small turn in a half volte, the hindquarters describing a smaller circle than the forehand. Executed in the walk or the canter it would be a

170

preparation for the half pirouette.' Echoing de la Guérinière's reference to the 'school passade', he adds 'It is first taught on the large circle...', but makes no reference to the straight dash between the demi-voltes of the old combat figure.

Another definition and further uses for the passade are provided by the modern classical authority Paul Belasik in *Dressage for the 21st Century*: 'Faults in the pirouette are difficult to correct, so the movement must be taught carefully and slowly. Probably the easiest method is to go down the long wall in travers...Near the corner, the horse is collected a little, and while keeping the haunches in, the rider asks the horse to step into a small circle...The haunches are held in around the half-circle and, after the half-circle, either the horse returns to the wall in a half-pass position, or on a straight diagonal, or continues straight once more on the quarter line. This turning pattern is called the passade...'

Points of interest that can be drawn from such varying descriptions are that equestrian terminology is subject to change over the years, and that the gymnastic benefits that can be derived from certain exercises are perhaps of greater importance than how the exercises are named.

**passage**   A powerful, highly collected and very elevated development of trot, with a prolonged period of suspension and thus, despite the energy of the movement, short steps in terms of forward travel; as an indicator of the degree of elevation expected, competition rules suggest that the toe of the raised foreleg should reach approximately to the level of the middle of the cannon of the other foreleg (as in piaffe); for reasons of engagement and its consequent effects (again, as in piaffe), the hind feet will not be raised quite so high as the forefeet, but there must be equal elevation of both hind feet and both forefeet.

Some of the highest-level tests contain movements that require transitions between extended trot and passage, and piaffe and passage; these indicate the rider's control over impulsion in its different manifestations and the horse's balance and ability to show (and move between) high levels of true collection and extension.

While, for purposes of current competitive dressage, passage is seen as a single form of movement, historically many authorities (particularly those of the French school) identified two main forms – doux passage and grand passage. In essence, while 'doux' translates as 'soft', this was not a 'weak' form

An extravagant passage performed by General Wattel, Chief Instructor at Saumur, on *Rempart*. Photograph from General Decarpentry's *Academic Equitation*.

of the movement, but one that placed great emphasis on the flexibility of the joints and elevation, being closely associated with piaffe. The 'grand' form placed more emphasis on a degree of extension; while it could be obtained by increasing, but retaining, the energy of the trot, authorities such as L'Hotte state that it is better integrated into the overall schooling process when it is allowed to develop or 'flow' out of the doux variant.

In his book *Academic Equitation*, another authority, the highly analytical Decarpentry, made a point about passage similar to that made by other authorities about other gaits and gait variants: 'The form of the passage can vary infinitely, and so can the height of the steps proportionately to their length. One form will be more natural to a horse than another, depending upon his conformation. He can be taught other forms which with practice will become familiar to him, but they will never reach the degree of perfection that can be attained by the original one.' This last remark is of particular interest, since it shows that the author relates 'perfection' to what can be attained by an individual horse, rather than by an abstraction.

**passagé**   A term that should be viewed with caution and in context when examining the works of eminent French authorities. It commonly conveys the same meaning as the Anglicised form 'passagey'; for example, *Michel* Henriquet (*Henriquet on Dressage*) writes: 'One often sees horses involved in competition, even at a high level, execute a totally perverted form of the *rassemblé* trot: This is the "*passagé*" trot with a "false hovering".' However, in *Academic Equitation*, Decarpentry writes: 'In the form of the "Trot-Passagé", the greater energy delivered by the hind legs enables the horse to heighten his steps without shortening them (and even to lengthen them).' He then goes on to relate this movement to both the doux passage and the 'passage proper' and is clearly giving it a different meaning from that conveyed by passagey trot.

172

**passagey trot**   Known alternatively as the hovering trot. The horse springs in a stilted fashion from one diagonal to the other, with a prolonged period of suspension but little genuine forward propulsion; it is these last two characteristics that invite the term 'passagey', but the engagement and flexion of the hind limbs, and the impulsion and lightness of true passage are absent; the movement is thus stiff and tense.

**passive hand**   A hand that is quietly maintaining a light contact on the rein, i.e. not sending any overt signal to the horse other than 'maintain the status quo'. See **acting hand**.

**Pawlenko, Mykola**   (1922–1992) The son of a Ukranian nobleman and general, who had been a pupil of James Fillis at the St Petersburg Imperial Cavalry School, was a graduate of Saumur and kept a large number of Grand Prix horses at all times. In keeping with his family's philosophy, Pawlenko received an excellent education in many subjects, including equitation, which he studied, and was to continue studying, under a number of eminent figures such as Gustav Rau, Felix Bürkner, Richard Wätjen and Alois Podhajsky. He was also, throughout his life, a great student of classical equestrian literature, and habitually carried Steinbrecht's *The Gymnasium of the Horse* in his pocket.

At the time Pawlenko attained adulthood, the political situation in the Ukraine meant that he was unable to pursue an equestrian career there and, during the Second World War, whilst fighting as a Captain in the German cavalry (aspiring to help free his country), he was seriously wounded. After the war, things took a turn for the better when he was engaged to train horses for the American army in Germany, and the equestrian career he had longed for began. In the immediate post-war period, he organized major shows and competed in dressage, eventing, showjumping and driving, as well as riding in steeplechases. He also established a reputation for working horses in-hand, and for his skills in farriery and leg care. In 1950, he was awarded the German silver medal in recognition of his competition success but, with that country awash with political unrest and a young family to consider, he emigrated to America and settled in Chicago. There, for around fourteen years, he concentrated mainly on showjumping. Since his horses were very well schooled on the flat, he had great success with them, his horse *Isgilda* being Horse of the Year no less than seven times at Madison Square Gardens.

In the mid-1960s, Pawlenko took his two daughters to Europe, where they were invited to ride some advanced dressage horses. Upon returning to America, the family decided to concentrate more upon this discipline and was a major influence in popularizing dressage in the Chicago area.

With his wide-ranging equestrian skills, Pawlenko was able to achieve great success with a variety of horses: he was one of the first people to import Warmbloods into America and also had great success in reschooling horses purchased out of racing. He died in 1992, as the result of a boating accident.

**PDAP**    See **positive diagonal advance placement**.

**Peilicke, Siegfried**    Born in Germany in 1932, Peilicke began his equestrian career by working as a groom/handyman for a farmer in Westphalia. The farmer's horses earned their keep working in the fields but, when circumstances allowed, they were used for dressage and showjumping. Peilicke's own interest in dressage began when he attended a clinic given by Paul Stenken, through whom he met the American rider, Jessica Rancehausen. He worked for her until she returned to America, after which he went to work for the Linsenhoff family, where he remained based for eighteen years. It was there that his riding interest and skills developed further, with Liselot Linsenhoff and Willi Schultheis being major inspirations. After a while he began training and proved so successful in this role that he went on to become German Young Rider and Junior Team Coach, which post he held for twenty-eight years before retiring to his small private yard. He also travelled widely as a trainer and was responsible for the development of some notable horses, including *Dynasty*, on whom Canadian rider Cynthia Ishoy was 2nd in the 1988 World Cup and 4th individual in the 1988 Olympics, and *Wall Street*, Kristy Oatley-Nist's (now Kristy Staczek) ride in the Sydney Olympics. In 2002, shortly after his seventieth birthday, Peilicke was awarded the title 'Reitmeister' in honour of his achievements.

**penalties**    Prescribed numbers of marks deducted for various infringements during the execution of a test, such as errors of course, errors of test, use of voice.

**percentage**    In competition, a competitor's score is expressed as hundredths of the total score available; for example, 150 good marks out of a total available of 200, gives a percentage of 75 per cent.

**perched**   Describes a rider's posture when there is some forward curvature or angulation of the upper body, with little weight in the saddle, or depth of seat; such weight as is in the saddle being placed forward towards the fork and/or taken on the thighs.

**perpendicular**   See **vertical**.

Pesade. Photograph by Karl Leck from Paul Belasik's *Dressage for the 21st Century*.

**pesade**   From the family of airs above the ground, the pesade is very similar to the levade, but requires rather less strength and flexion of the hindquarters than that movement. The horse, taking a good deal of weight on his hindquarters, sits back on his hocks and lifts his forehand off the ground, with forelegs folded, remaining stationary. The most obvious visual difference between the pesade and levade is the mean angle of the horse's body to the ground; if the angle is greater than about 45 degrees, the air is considered a pesade, if less, it is a levade.

**petit galop**   A term sometimes used in French to distinguish the gait of canter from that of gallop, since the French galop often serves for both.

**Petushkova, Yelena**   Born in Russia in 1940, Petushkova started riding, aged nine, at a newly opened riding school in Sokolniki Park. She gradually became more interested in the sport and in 1958, the year in which she passed her entrance exams to the Biological Faculty of Moscow University, she acquired her own horse. She subsequently met Sergey Filatov, the Russian gold medallist at the 1960 Olympics, who insisted that she take over the ride on an experienced schoolmaster, who carried her to success at Grand Prix level. In the light of this, the leading Russian trainer, Grigory Anastasev, insisted that she join the Soviet dressage team and be given *Pepel* to ride, marking the beginning of a sixteen-year partnership.

In 1965, Petushkova and *Pepel* were selected for the first time to compete at the European Championships. In 1967 they were 6th at the European Championships, the best performance of that time by a woman rider. In 1970, Petushkova won the individual World Championship and two years later, at the Munich Olympics, she won individual silver, with the Soviet Union taking team silver behind Germany. At the next World Championships (Copenhagen, 1974) Petushkova finished in 3rd place behind Reiner Klimke and Liselott Linsenhoff. By 1976 *Pepel* was twenty and, having gone lame prior to the Montreal Olympics, he was retired to the Kirov Stud where he had been born. Regrettably, the horse chosen as a replacement died suddenly during preparation for the Moscow Olympics.

Aside from her equestrian career, Petushkova became a distinguished biochemist and a Senior Research Fellow at Moscow University. She visited Australia in 1987 as part of a Soviet Peace Delegation, as a guest of the Campaign for International Cooperation and Disarmament. She also wrote *My Life and My Horses,* a fascinating account of the development of dressage in the Soviet Union.

**phenylbutazone**   See **bute**.

Richard Wätjen riding piaffe. Photograph from *Dressage Riding.*

**piaffe** Historically, used widely as preparation for the airs above the ground and today seen as evidence of advanced collection in top-level tests, piaffe is a highly collected, elevated, diagonal movement of the limbs in two-time, more or less on the spot, closely associated with the collected trot and passage. It is sometimes referred to as a highly collected trot on the spot and can be seen as evolving from that gait but (apart from the lack of forward movement) there is a difference from the trot in that, in piaffe, the forelimbs show greater elevation than the hind limbs. The limb movement is generally considered correct for competition purposes when the height of the toe of the raised foreleg is level with the middle of the cannon of the other foreleg while, in the hind legs, the raised toe is just above the level of the fetlock joint of the other hind. This differential is a result of the increased engagement of the hind limbs under the horse's centre of balance and the relative elevation, lightness and freedom of the forehand. Thus piaffe can only be performed correctly by a horse who has been well prepared, with good musculature of the hindquarters and trained to work in true collection.

While significant engagement of the hindquarters is essential for the piaffe, over-zealous attempts by the rider to drive the hind legs excessively far underneath the horse can contribute to a cramping effect and the fault known as triangulation. In order to avoid this problem, and provoking various other faults and evasions, many trainers believe in working gradually towards the finished form of piaffe on the spot and allowing a little forward movement in the early stages, and judges much prefer to see this as opposed to any backward inclination or unbalanced, irregular steps, these preferences being supported by the FEI rules relating to the movement.

**Pignatelli, Giambattista**   (sometimes rendered as Giovanni). Italian pupil of Cesar Fiaschi, born c. 1525 and active during the sixteenth century; widely considered to be the most influential figure of the Neapolitan School, and credited with the invention of the double bridle. Pupils from various European countries including England, France, Austria, Denmark, Germany and Spain took his ideas back to their homelands, two of his most illustrious pupils being the Frenchmen Salomon de la Broue and Antoine de Pluvinel.

**pillars**   Vertical structures, generally of wood or metal, used from the Renaissance period onward in the training of horses whilst not under saddle. Although there is some evidence that the Greek cavalry of Alexander the Great employed a crude method of exercising horses held in place, the first use of pillars in training is generally ascribed to Antoine de Pluvinel, who used both single and double pillars extensively, and describes a variety of exercises

Work at the pillars. An engraving from de Pluvinel's *Le Maneige Royal.*

based upon the pillars in his book *Le Maneige Royal*. Pillars have been used subsequently by various classical schools of equitation, especially those historically related to, or influenced by, the School of Versailles, in developing the rassembler and training for movements such as piaffe and levade.

Monica Theodorescu riding a canter pirouette. Photograph by Elizabeth Furth.

**pirouette** A movement in which the horse turns through 360 degrees, almost in place, i.e. a very small circle performed by pivoting around the inside hind leg. While this leg 'marks time' being raised and lowered virtually on the spot in the rhythm of the gait, the other (outside) hind foot describes a very small circle, with a circumference of 1½–3 ft (0.45–0.9 m) or so, around it; the forehand describes a second circle with a circumference of about 25 ft (7.5 m); the radius of the outer circle being approximately equivalent to the length of the horse. The whole turn is completed in 6–8 strides. To be performed correctly, pirouettes require a considerable degree of genuine collection. They can be ridden in collected walk, collected canter and piaffe. They are introduced into tests at British Dressage Elementary level (or the equivalent), usually in the form of a half-pirouette (i.e. the movement through just 180 degrees) in walk.

**pivot** To turn around a single point, as in a pirouette.

**plaiting** (1) A faulty form of movement (called lacing in the USA), in which either the forelimbs, the hind limbs or both swing inward as the feet are being grounded, so that the horse moves on very narrow tracks or tends to move nearly on a single track. This movement, which is often rooted in poor conformation but may be exacerbated by muscular weakness (especially, where it is more prevalent behind, of weak hindquarters), will severely affect the horse's ability to work effectively, especially in exercises requiring carrying power and in the lateral movements. (2) The second meaning (which also represents the 'interweaving' of steps of the first meaning) refers to the preparation of the horse's mane (and, often, tail) and is also known as braiding, a procedure generally carried out by competitors in the belief that it helps to show off the outline of the horse's neck.

**Podhajsky, Alois** (1899–1973) The son of an Austro-Hungarian cavalry officer, Podhajsky joined a dragoon regiment aged seventeen and received regular lessons from Capt. Count Telekei, whom he described as an excellent instructor.

Although in a cavalry regiment, Podhajsky spent much of the First World War on foot. After the war, following the demise of the Austro-Hungarian Empire, he was admitted to the new Federal Army, and riding once again became part of his career. Having achieved considerable success in showjumping, he was encouraged by his colonel to study dressage, which he found further improved his horse's jumping. Transferred to advanced training at the cavalry school at Schlosshof, he began to achieve international success in dressage, showjumping and three-day events.

Alois Podhajsky riding *Maestoso Alea* at the Spanish Riding School.

In 1933, he was sent to the Spanish Riding School, where he studied under luminaries such as Polak, Zrust and Lindenbauer. Their influence helped him to train his own horses to Grand Prix level and to win a bronze medal for dressage at the 1936 Olympics.

From 1934 to 1938 he worked as a cavalry instructor, first in Austria and then in Germany. In 1938 Austria was annexed by Germany, and the Spanish Riding School was placed under the command of the German Army. When, in 1939, Podhajsky became Director of the Spanish Riding School, he managed to convince senior German officers, who were experienced horsemen, of the value of the School. By this action, and others in that period, Podhajsky was instrumental in protecting the School for posterity.

In the post-war years, Podhajsky competed abroad both with his own horses and the School's Lipizzaners. He also took the Spanish Riding School on a number of foreign tours, including a major tour of the USA shortly before his retirement in 1964. He wrote two major books on equitation; *My Horses, My Teachers* and *The Complete Training of Horse and Rider*.

Gottlieb Polak riding levade. Photograph from Podhajsky's *My Horses, My Teachers*.

**Polak, Gottlieb** (1883–1942) Born in Bohemia, the son of an employee at the Imperial Court Stud of Kladrub, Polak was an accomplished young musician, who attended the academy of music at Prague. Horses were, however, his main passion and in 1900 he started work at Kladrub. Two years later, wishing to increase his experience, he requested a transfer to the Court Stables of Vienna where, despite working primarily with carriage horses, he had the opportunity to undergo further training in riding.

Following a three-year tour of duty with the Imperial Army (which he concluded with the rank of sergeant major), Polak returned briefly to his work with carriage horses before being sent to serve at the manège of the Archduke Ferdinand where, by 1912, he had risen to the position of First Class Court Horseman. It was in 1916 that he joined the Spanish Riding School, initially as a rider (bereiter) rising, by 1941 – the year before his death – to the post of first chief rider (erster oberbereiter). It was during these years at the Spanish Riding School that Polak had his main impact on the equestrian world; he was not only an outstanding trainer of horses, but also a major influence on figures such as Franz Rochowansky and Alois Podhajsky, the latter making frequent reference to Polak in his own writings.

**poll** The 'top', of the horse's head, represented skeletally by the occipital bone. When a horse is moving correctly on the aids (as distinct from exercises in which he is encouraged to lower his head and stretch his neck), the poll should be his highest point; as a result of being ridden correctly into the rein contact, he should flex at the poll rather than showing false flexion of the neck, as in the 'broken neck' posture.

**Pollay, First Lieut. H.**   German winner of the individual gold medal at the 1936 Olympic Games in Berlin, and also a member of the winning German team, riding *Kronos*.

**ponies**   Ponies are not necessarily debarred by organizing bodies from competing against horses; for example British Dressage rules allow ponies to be registered according to their grade and to compete on equal terms with horses in affiliated competitions. However, it is sometimes the case (especially but not exclusively) with competitions involving young riders or junior riders that the rules specify that animals must either exceed 14.2 hh or, in other cases, be less than that size.

**port**   The portion of the mouthpiece of a bit that curves upward in the centre, under which the horse's tongue fits; the shape is a factor in the action of the bit; normally a feature of curb bits but a modified form is occasionally a feature of certain snaffles, e.g. the Fillis snaffle, named after James Fillis.

**position**   (1) A term used synonymously for (rider's) posture. (2) A term used to describe a slight degree of lateral flexion of the horse. This is often used in early schooling to address the fact that an untrained horse will tend to 'hug the wall', aligning both outside hip and shoulder with the wall of the manège which (since the hips are wider than the shoulders), puts him in a crooked position (that is, while hips and shoulders are aligned to the wall, a line bisecting the horse along his spine will be pointing slightly to the outside). This positioning allows the inside hind leg to step somewhat to the inside, rather than stepping underneath and doing its share of carrying and propelling the load. A very slight lateral flexion inward, sufficient to rectify this alignment, is

Waldemar Seunig's drawing illustrating his discussion of 'position' from *The Essence of Horsemanship*.

181

therefore applied by the rider. In addition to its initial straightening function, this adjustment has roles in enhancing suppleness and obedience to the aids and it may be employed in a preparatory or corrective way as, for example, to correct crooked deployment of the haunches in canter.

Many writers view the term 'position' as synonymous with 'shoulder-fore', although the latter is sometimes employed in a looser sense (see that entry); some other academic writers sub-divide the term according to the level of training being addresse and the precise effect that is to be achieved.

**positive diagonal advance placement**   The trot is generally considered to be a two-time gait, in which the diagonal pairs of feet touch down at the same time; assessment of the gait by competition ruling bodies, and thus judges, remains based upon this assumption. However, it is rarely the case that *absolutely simultaneous* touching down occurs and slow-motion photographic analysis of the trot has shown that, in the case of many horses successful in high-level competition, the hind feet of the diagonal pairs touch down *fractionally* before the forefeet. This phenomenon, known as positive diagonal advance placement (PDAP) appears to be a natural consequence of conformation; it does not seem that it can be produced through training and, given the prescribed criteria for the trot, there would seem to be no purpose in attempting to do so.

**posting**   See **rising trot**.

Good posture of horse and rider. Painting by Maggie Raynor.

**posture**   Meaning attitude of the body, or the relative positions of the parts of the body, the term can be applied to both horse and rider, but is used more commonly with reference to the latter. Correct posture is of the utmost importance to the rider, since it has a significant influence on security, balance and the ability to apply the aids with minimum effort to optimum effect. Postural errors on the rider's part will always have some detrimental effect upon the horse, since he is obliged to balance himself beneath the rider.

**Preliminary**   The most basic level of tests produced by British Dressage.

**preparatory aid**   A small signal given by the rider to 'set the horse up' just before commencement of a new movement. The most common example is a half-halt, given to enhance balance and obtain extra attention from the horse. Many trainers make the point that the rider should not 'surprise the horse' with the aids, and astute riders will almost subconsciously learn the preparatory aids that assist individual horses in various situations.

**Prix Caprilli**   A type of competition formerly popular at club level in Britain, in which a test broadly similar to a Preliminary level dressage test, but usually including two small jumps was performed, with marks being awarded to the rider, rather than the horse. The object was to encourage correct riding technique and the competition particularly suited groups of riders who, not being horse owners, competed on horses hired from riding centres.

**Prix St Georges**   The first (lowest) level of international tests produced by the FEI.

**progressive transition**   A transition that involves an incremental change through the gaits, e.g. in a progressive change from canter to walk, the horse moves from canter, via a few strides of trot, into walk. Progressive transitions (especially downward) are easier for novice horses and riders than direct transitions, and thus tend to appear in the more basic-level tests.

**prohibited substances**   See **forbidden substances**.

**proppy**   A term used to describe a horse who moves with rather short, stilted strides; although such movement can be a consequence of over-restraint by the rider, the term is usually applied to horses in whom it is a consequence of poor conformation (e.g. straight shoulders, upright pasterns, poor knee action).

**punishment**   A deliberate action by the rider with the intention of conveying displeasure/admonishing the horse. Punishment in any form is only appropriate if it is evident that the horse understands what was required of him, is capable of complying and does not do so, or if the horse unilaterally performs an action that cannot be condoned. It should therefore be considered distinct from correction, as of a genuinely misinterpreted aid.

In order that the horse can associate it with his behaviour, punishment, when given, must be immediate. It must also be commensurate with the horse's actions – it is unjust (and will probably prove counter-productive) to punish a minor misdemeanour harshly, but too lenient a response to a major act of disobedience is likely to prove ineffective.

If there is good rapport between horse and rider, punishment (certainly in its more major forms) should rarely be necessary and severe punishment (e.g. excessive use of whip or spur) is proscribed in the rules of all competitive bodies.

**quadrille**  An orchestrated ride to music performed by four riders, or groups of four, often wearing historical costume or fancy dress to reflect a theme; derived from the formal dance of the same name.

**qualifier**  A competition in which a certain level of success qualifies a competitor to enter a related competition that is, in terms of reward, status, etc., of greater importance.

**qualify**  To be, or become, eligible for a competition.

**quarters**  A truncated version of hindquarters, often used for convenience on judges' score sheets, etc.

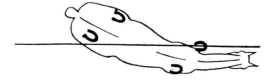

**quarters in**  The hindquarters to the inside, as compared to the forepart of the horse's body.

Diagram of quarters in at canter, from General Decarpentry's *Academic Equitation.*

184

**quarters leading**   A faulty form of half-pass. Correct, fluid and efficient execution of half-pass requires that the forehand is slightly leading the movement: rider preoccupation with the lateral element of the movement, at the expense of the forward element, may result in the horse's quarters being pushed over in advance of the forehand, compromising the fluidity and regularity of the movement.

**quarters not engaged**   A comment signifying that the horse is not using his hindquarters to produce sufficient propulsion, thus the work being performed will be relatively inactive.

**quarters out**   The hindquarters to the outside, as compared to the forepart of the horse's body.

**quarters trailing**   Generally, a comment similar in meaning to quarters not engaged, although trailing quarters may also relate to poor conformation of the hind limbs.

# R

**raddopio**   See **redopp, volte.**

**Rambla, Ignacio**   Born in 1964 in Jerez, Spain, Rambla started training at the Real Escuela Andaluza del Arte Ecuestre (Royal School of Andalusian Equestrian Art) in Jerez at the age of thirteen and was later to become its Director when Alvaro Domecq, who established the school, left in 1996. Rambla, who has been National Champion of Spain four times, represented his country at the Atlanta Olympics in 1996 and the World Cup in 1998. He missed the 2000 Olympics because of injury to his horse, but returned to the Olympic squad to win team silver in 2004.

Ramener in-hand. Drawing from General Decarpentry's *Academic Equitation.*

**ramener**  A French term describing the flexing of the horse's head at the poll (which must be associated with a yielding of the jaw), completed when the nose is pretty much perpendicular to the ground. Equestrian students should, in this instance, be wary of literal translations of ramener, which include 'to bring back'; 'pull down', since these may have connotations of backward-pulling effects of the rein. While, in its equestrian context, ramener means fundamentally the flexed outline of the head, it is axiomatic that, under saddle, this is achieved by the horse being encouraged *forwards* into the hands.

**Ramseier, Daniel**  Swiss rider born in 1963. A stalwart of the Swiss national team, he won team silver at the 1988 Olympic Games in Seoul and was a member of the 2000 and 2004 Olympic teams. He has competed at four World Championships, winning two team bronze medals, at four European Championships, winning a team silver and a team bronze medal, and he was 6th in the 1998 World Cup at 's Hertongenbosch. He was Swiss National Champion in 2000.

**rassembler**  *A* French term meaning, literally, to gather together, for which the approximate translation in English terminology is collection. Various authorities have commented on the extent to which the two terms are synonymous, and there is a line of reasoning that suggests they can have the same meaning, provided that the concept of collection is expanded a little beyond what it is commonly perceived to mean. Certainly, in years past, it seems likely that the popular conception of collection amongst English-speaking riders was narrower than may be the case today. In his book *Dressage A Study of the Finer Points of Riding* (1952), the England-based authority Henry Wynmalen (who was seeking to promote greater interest in high-school dressage) wrote: 'The literal translation of the French word *rassembler,* is the English word "collection": unfortunately, the true implication of the two expressions is so vastly different that one just cannot use the one as a legitimate translation of the other. The word "collection" as understood in English, has a strictly limited meaning; it describes the "attitude" or "bearing" as assumed by the horse in certain of his exercises. The word *rassembler*, used in its academic sense, has a far wider meaning; it embraces the entire demeanour of the horse in all his actions, the suppleness of his body, of his limbs and joints, the ease and generosity of his movements and, in particular, their rhythm and cadence; it embraces also the horse's absolute lightness…' This passage serves both to highlight the rather limited meaning that has often been ascribed to collection, and to give a good indication of what is implied by rassembler.

While rassembler, and its derivative rassemblé, meaning gathered together, are used most frequently in French equitation to refer to a horse in a state of 'high-school collection', the term can (as touched upon by Wynmalen) have a wider meaning: 'gathered together in a state of preparation'. This point is illustrated by Decarpentry in his book *Academic Equitation*: 'The rassembler is the disposition of the horse's body which affects all of its parts and places each one in the best position to ensure the most efficient use of the energy produced by the efforts of the hind legs. These efforts can have an immediate or special purpose, or can be a preparation for many eventual purposes. The race horse before the start, the show jumper before going over an obstacle, the dressage horse before performing a courbette all collect themselves, but the disposition of their body…is different in each case, and so is the direction in which their energy is spent ultimately.'

It is perhaps an awareness of this expanded meaning that has led certain authorities to promote an understanding of 'collection' along the same lines, examples being 'Collection is just a state of preparedness, of readiness to react rapidly in any direction that suits the rider…' (Alfred Knopfhart, *Fundamentals of Dressage*) and 'If *collection* is defined not merely as a bodily state in which the horse is best and most easily able to comply with the schooling requirements of the rider, it signifies, *when applied to all branches of horsemanship, increased*

Old classical rassembler. Drawing from General Decarpentry's *Academic Equitation*.

*attentiveness and a readiness of execution that best corresponds to the particular object in view.'* (Waldemar Seunig *Horsemanship.*) It is perhaps when 'collection' is used in such contexts, implying 'energy under full control' that it comes pretty much synonymous with rassembler.

**Rau, Gustav** (1880–1954). Born in Paris, the son of a Wüttemberg officer, Rau spent his first five years at school in Zurich. In 1901, he started work as a journalist on *SportWelt* and attended agricultural and veterinary lectures at Berlin University. Subsequently, he went to work for the Prussian Horse Breeding Commission and in 1933, he was appointed Prussian State Master of the Horse, a post he resigned during Hitler's ascendancy. Whilst involved with the State Stud he published a series of books on breeding horses and, during the 1920s, he established the German rural riding associations.

In 1913, he was called upon by the German Emperor to become Director of the German Olympic Committee for Equestrian Sport (DOKR) and in 1936, when the Olympic Games were held in Berlin, organized the equestrian events. After the Second World War, Rau was instrumental in shaping the future of Germany's horse breeding and equestrian sport. He organized and co-ordinated the reconstruction of the equestrian world from the rubble left by the war and led German equitation back into the international community. He discovered and encouraged a number of talented riders, one of whom was Reiner Klimke. Rau died in December 1954 at his desk at the DOKR in Warendorf.

Riders' responses to rearing. Drawings from Ulrik Schramm's *The Undisciplined Horse.*

**rearing** An extreme action by the horse in which he stands up high on his hind legs, possibly to the extent of risking overbalancing backwards, especially if a rider reacts too slowly or inappropriately. Rearing can be a panic reaction, or it can be an extreme example of insubordination (albeit perhaps under provocation) to the rider's aids. If it occurs during a dressage test, rearing will be considered to be a major resistance unless (or probably even if) it is a consequence of some exceptional external occurrence.

**recovered well**   Said of a rider when the horse/rider combination has made some error in the execution of a movement, but the rider's prompt and astute reactions have minimized the effect of the error.

**redopp**   Also rendered redoppe and redoppo; an old school movement described by Waldemar Seunig (*Horsemanship*) as 'A close volte in sharp *travers* position, the horse "rocking" with the forelegs and hindleg pairs alighting as units.' i.e., and as illustrated by Ridinger, in terre-à-terre. De la Guérinière (*Ecole de Cavalerie*) reports that the Italian word for what the French called a volte was radoppio.

**regular**   Refers to the even nature of footfalls in a gait. See also **irregular**.

**Rehbein, Herbert**   (1946–1997) Born in the north of Hessen, Germany, into a non-equestrian family, Rehbein nevertheless had a huge enthusiasm for horses from an early age. After finding an early mentor in a retired army major, he left school at fifteen and took up an apprenticeship with Karl Diehl. Although Diehl ran a predominantly dressage stable, Rehbein at first competed in jumping events. Once qualified as a bereiter, he continued his training with Walter Günther in Hamburg-Flottbeck, where he met Karin, who was to become his wife and business partner. He soon established himself as a rider and trainer, setting up stables at Grönwoldhof, which became the home of the famous stallions *Pik Bube*, *Donnerwetter* and *Donnerhall*, and a dressage centre for pupils from all over

Karin, wife of the late Herbert Rehbein, competing on the stallion *Donnerhall*. Photograph by Elizabeth Furth.

the world, including Kyra Kyrklund. As a rider, Rehbein won the German Professionals' Championships seven times and the German Dressage Derby nine times. He was voted Trainer of the Year by the International

Trainers' Club in both 1991 and 1994 and the German Federation conferred on him the title of Reitmeister. His wife, Karin, struck up a formidable partnership with *Donnerhall*, their major successes including team gold and individual silver medals at the 1994 World Equestrian Games, and team gold and individual bronze medals at the 1997 European Championships; the latter event taking place just months after her husband's untimely death.

**rein**    The piece of tack that effects communication between the rider's hand and the horse's mouth, via the bit. With reference to its fundamental directional application (see **direct rein**), it is used to denote the direction of movement, thus 'on the left rein' signifies going left-handed (anticlockwise) and 'on the right rein' signifies going right-handed (clockwise). See also **change the rein; reins, holding of.**

**rein aids**    Intentional signals from the rider's hands conveyed to the horse's mouth via the action of the reins and bit.

**rein-back**    A movement in which the horse is required to step backwards in a smooth even and unhurried two-time gait of diagonal pairs. It is inadvisable to introduce this movement until the horse has a good understanding and acceptance of the forward-driving aids and the rein contact, can halt squarely, with hind legs well engaged, and is relatively straight in his movement.

The rein-back. Drawings from Reiner Klimke's *Basic Training of the Young Horse.*

**rein contact**   The connection between the rider's hands and the horse's mouth, via the reins and bit, that occurs when there is sufficient tension in the reins for the rider to feel the horse's mouth and the horse to feel the rider's hands.

**rein effects**   Actions of the rider's hand(s) and rein(s), with specific intended effects, which are usually categorized as direct rein (or open rein), direct rein of opposition, indirect rein and indirect rein of opposition. These effects are normally employed in conjunction with other aids, according to the rider's requirements.

**reins, holding of**   There is a general requirement under most sets of dressage rules that, during the riding of a test, the reins should be held in both hands. There are, however, certain exceptions to this. In a few of the older, lower-level tests used in Britain, there was a specific requirement to perform a movement with the reins in one hand. In such cases, the convention was to hold the reins (and whip, if carried) in the outside hand, the inside arm being held down by the rider's side. During the salute, the convention is to take the reins in the left hand, while the right hand removes the hat, or is dropped down by the rider's side. In freestyle tests ridden under FEI rules, it is permitted to ride with the reins in one hand and this convention is extended under various rules to the final movement of leaving the arena at walk on a long rein.

When riding in a double bridle, various methods of separating the reins between the fingers are used, depending on the rider's school of thought, which may be influenced by traditional national practice. In one method employed by a number of the old masters, known as 'three in one', the right hand held the right bradoon rein, while the left hand held the other three; however it is more common nowadays for each hand to hold its respective bradoon and curb reins in the manner of the rider's preference.

**relative elevation**   Describes the posture of the forehand that occurs as a consequence of the horse lowering his haunches in true collection; because the hindquarters are well engaged and thus lowered, the forehand by comparison either appears to be raised above its 'normal' height or may in fact be so – the latter being likely in correctly performed movements such as piaffe, and self-evident in airs such as levade. Compare with **direct elevation**.

**relaxed**   A term that is often used imprecisely in equestrian circles. For example, a horse cannot really be 'relaxed' when doing things such as collected work. In fact, since any form of work places additional demands upon heart, respiration and musculature, a truly (physically) relaxed horse can do very little. Thus, such relaxation as may be evident in a working horse will be primarily mental – that is not to say that he should be 'switched off' mentally, but that there should be a calm mental state and an absence of the mental tension associated with excitement, discomfort, fear, uncertainty, resistance, etc. Such mental tension would be inextricably linked to the physical tension that manifests itself in tightness of the muscles, whereas its absence allows for effective respiration and the elastic tonicity of muscles necessary for effective movement. Thus, of a horse working actively, the term 'calm' (as in L'Hotte's maxim 'calm, forward and straight') might be more appropriate than 'relaxed'. There is, however, justification for speaking of periods of relaxation (as at free walk) between work periods, since there is a lessening of both the mental and physical demands being made of the horse and, with regard to the latter, a relative but genuine relaxation of the muscles.

**release of the rein**   See **uberstreichen**.

**remonte des dents**   The French equivalent term for insterburger.

**renvers**   Also known as croup to the wall or haunches out. A lateral movement or exercise that is essentially a mirror image of travers (see that entry); in renvers it is the hindquarters that remain on the track (or line of

Views of renvers, drawn by Gisela Holstein.

192

reference), while the forehand is displaced to the inside. Some trainers stress that, amongst its other benefits, renvers is a useful remedial exercise for dealing with horses who tend to disengage their inside hind legs and displace their quarters to the inside of the arena.

**resistance**   Unwillingness on the horse's part to do something that the rider requires of him, manifested by various physical actions, ranging from setting the jaw to rearing or napping. Resistance can result simply from overt disobedience on the horse's part, but may also be engendered or increased by factors such as fear (for example, not wanting to pass noisy machinery) or discomfort (for example, from ill-fitting tack or aching muscles). A horse who does not comply with his rider's requirements when he simply does not understand them cannot properly be described as resistant – this is simply confusion or lack of understanding.

In the context of a dressage competition, resistance can have a narrower, more specific meaning, i.e. to refuse to enter the arena within a set period (under British Dressage rules, 60 seconds after the bell has sounded – see also **entrance**) or to refuse to continue the test (under British Dressage rules, for a period of 20 consecutive seconds), for both of which the penalty is elimination.

A moment of resistance. Photograph by Bob Langrish.

**resistant**   The process of demonstrating resistance.

**responsiveness**   Although it is possible for a horse to respond either positively or negatively to his rider, in equestrian terms responsiveness is generally assumed to be a positive quality – the degree of prompt compliance by the horse to the rider's aids. Factors which have an influence upon a horse's responsiveness are temperament, intelligence, physiology of the nervous system, health, fitness and suppleness, exterior environment, level of training and expertise of the rider.

**restraining aids**  Judicious use of restraining aids (the hands and, as appropriate, the seat/lower back) is part and parcel of such actions as downward transitions and collecting the horse. However, the horse is more likely to perform such actions well if the rider thinks of the 'restraint' in accordance with its dictionary definitions of 'moderating' and 'controlling' (the forward movement) rather than in terms of 'holding back'.

**reversed pirouette**  A pirouette figure in which, rather than the forehand describing a larger circle around the hindquarters, the hindquarters describe the larger circle around the forehand. This exercise, which seems to have derived from the school of Baucher, is described in General Decarpentry's *Academic Equitation* in three forms. The first, mentioned in passing as

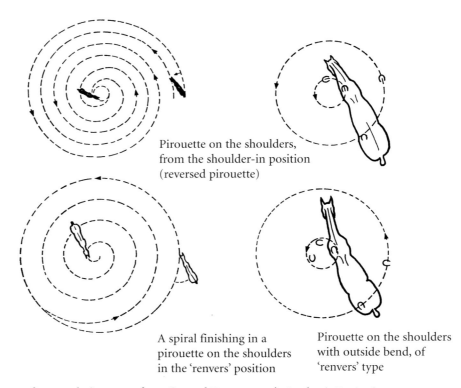

Pirouette on the shoulders, from the shoulder-in position (reversed pirouette)

A spiral finishing in a pirouette on the shoulders in the 'renvers' position

Pirouette on the shoulders with outside bend, of 'renvers' type

Forms of reversed pirouettes, from General Decarpentry's *Academic Equitation.*

194

'without inflexion', seems, in effect, to be a turn on the forehand; the other forms, described respectively as 'with inward flexion (of shoulder-in type)' and 'with outward flexion (of renvers type)' are arrived at by spiralling inward in their respective positions. Reversed pirouettes have not been widely practised, there being a common concern that they place too much emphasis on the horse's shoulders, and they are not a component of dressage tests. However, some authorities believe that introduced, at an appropriate time, and ridden correctly, they assist with the suppling of the loin muscles and the sensitive mobilization of the haunches, and may be of value in riding half-pass to the horse's more difficult side.

**reversed volte**   A volte of the two-track type, in which the forehand, rather than the haunches, is innermost.

**reward**   A signal to the horse that he has done something perceived by the rider as correct. Depending upon circumstances, the reward may be an overt action such as giving a titbit, verbal praise or patting. It may also be a temporary cessation of demands upon the horse, for example walking on a long rein after a period of concentrated work. The concept behind rewards is that of positive reinforcement; the horse learns to associate acceding to the rider's demands with a pleasant aftermath. It should be borne in mind that repeatedly failing to correct unwarranted behaviour, which is in the horse's interest, but not that of the rider, can also be interpreted by the horse as a reward.

**rhythm**   A term used to denote patterns of sound, which may be made up of longer or shorter, stronger or weaker beats, as in the rhythm of a beating heart. In equestrian terms, it is possible for a horse to move in a consistent rhythm without that rhythm being correct for the gait concerned. For example, a lame horse may walk in a consistent 1, 2, 3, hop rhythm (three regular beats and one shorter/weaker beat), as opposed to the correct 1, 2, 3, 4 sequence of a sound horse. Alternatively, a rhythm may be composed of regular beats which is, nonetheless, too fast (hurried) or too slow (laboured) to represent good movement in the gait. Unwarranted changes in rhythm, or rhythm not being established, suggest lack of balance and that the horse is not attentive to the rider's aids, or that these are being applied inappropriately.

**ride in**   A term more or less synonymous with work in; to prepare a horse, mentally and physically, prior to performing a dressage test. The time spent on riding in, and the work done, will vary from horse to horse and, to some extent, according to the requirements of the test; most experienced competitors believe that the riding-in period is absolutely crucial to the execution of the test.

Engraving by Johann Ridinger.

**Ridinger, Johann Elias** (1698–1767) A German artist who produced hundreds of detailed engravings (many of which were collected into book form) depicting the schooling of horse and rider, which provide valuable insight into the methods, exercises and equipment of his era.

**Riding Instructors' Institute of Vienna**   An institution that, from 1875 to 1914, succeeded the Central Cavalry School of Vienna. One of the European schools of its era that placed a good deal of emphasis upon 'field' (cross-country) equitation and development of spirited, impulsive, elastic gaits. One of its foremost instructors was Sigmund von Josipovich, and Waldemar Seunig was one of its most eminent pupils.

**right diagonal**   In trot, the right foreleg and left hind leg as a diagonal pair.

**right lead**   In canter (or gallop) the horse's right foreleg as the leading leg in that gait.

**right rein**   Literally, the rein connected to the right bit ring (seen from the rear); generally 'on the right rein' means moving clockwise around the arena.

**ring steward**   See **steward**.

196

**rising trot**   (also known as posting) A method of riding at the trot in which the rider eases the seat from the saddle on alternate diagonals. It originated to enhance the comfort of horse and rider when travelling over long distances on rough ground and is still employed for similar reasons when horses are being exercised out of the arena. Also used when working in the arena, especially with young horses, those being retrained and/or those with back problems or gait irregularities, to reduce the overall burden on the horse's back and to encourage free movement of the back and hind limbs.

When riding in the open for protracted periods, the diagonal on which the rider sits should be changed periodically to prevent uneven demands upon the horse's physique, which could induce one-sidedness and provoke or increase crookedness. In the arena, the standard convention is to sit as the horse's inside forefoot and outside hind foot touch the ground, the idea being that the inside leg can then support the weight better, especially on turns; this requires that the rider 'changes diagonal' at each change of rein. In some situations, expert trainers may flout this convention when addressing specific problems in individual horses.

In recognition of the desirability of encouraging free forward movement in partially trained horses, some basic-level dressage tests permit trot work to be ridden rising, but this should be confirmed by competitors with respect to the specific test to be performed. Where rising trot is permitted, adherence to the standard convention regarding diagonals will normally be expected, and non-compliance is likely to be marked down.

**Rochowansky, Franz**   Born in 1911, the son of a baker, Rochowansky joined the Austrian cavalry in 1928 and rapidly made a name for himself as a rider and trainer. In the period leading up to the 1936 Olympics, he was involved in helping Alois Podhajsky to prepare for the Games and he subsequently worked with Podhajsky at the Spanish Riding School for

Franz Rochowansky in later years, training a young horse in piaffe.

197

some nineteen years. During the Second World War, he was closely involved in organizing the evacuation of the School from Vienna; he rose to the rank of Chief Rider and was awarded a gold medal for his long-reining displays with the stallion *Neapolitano Schollo;* his likeness was used by the Austrian Government to represent the levade on the Austrian schilling and he also helped Podhajsky to compile notes for the book *The Complete Training of Horse and Rider.*

After retiring from the Spanish Riding School in 1955, Rochowansky devoted the rest of his life to teaching dressage. Based first in Holland, and latterly in England, he also travelled extensively throughout the USA. During his long career, he trained literally hundreds of international competitors – including a number of Olympic riders – maintaining his commitment to dressage up to the time of his death in 2001.

**rocking and rolling**   A fault sometimes seen in passage and piaffe, perhaps more prevalent in the former. Whereas the balancé form of these movements is most evident in the action of the forehand, rocking and rolling is seen in the whole horse; the limbs of the feet (both fore and hind) that are about to be set down swing out around the grounded diagonal then twist inward, so that the feet are grounded more or less directly beneath the horse's spine,

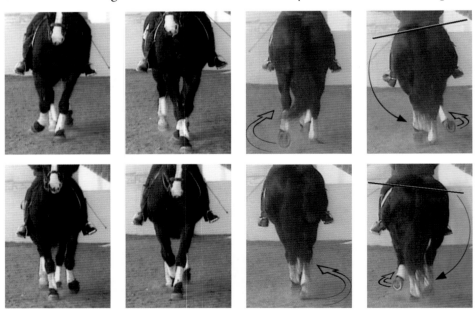

Rolling passage. Photographs from Paul Belasik's *Dressage for the 21st Century.*

marking something that approximates to a single track (in very bad cases, the feet may even cross). This faulty movement suggests insufficient impulsion and probably a lack of strength; the horse stiffens his back muscles and limbs and obtains a kind of false suspension by recoiling off the stiffened limbs, which he tries to align beneath his midline, the rocking and rolling being the product of axial twist as the horse tries to 'step around himself'.

**Rothenberger, Sven**   German-born in 1966, Rothenberger began riding as a child and, for a while, shared a horse with his elder sister, combining jumping and flatwork. During this time he met Emile Konrad, who had trained for two years with Josef Neckermann. Konrad fired Rothenberger with an enthusiasm for dressage and, having been bought two dressage horses in his early teens, he became Junior Champion of the State of Hessen at the age of fifteen. At nineteen he began training with Conrad Schumacher, at whose yard Neckermann kept his horses. When one of the other leading young riders trained by Schumacher gave up competing, Schumacher was instrumental in helping Rothenberger purchase his horse. In 1987 Rothenberger was a member of the German team that won gold at the European Young Riders Championships, and he took individual silver behind Nicole Uphoff and *Rembrandt*. In 1988, his family purchased the highly successful *Ideaal* on his behalf, and then acquired *Andiamo*, who had been a mainstay of the Swiss team, from Otto Hofer. Early Grand Prix success with *Ideaal* saw Rothenberger short-listed for the German team but, that horse having developed an infection, Rothenberger, assisted by Hofer, began to work closely with *Andiamo*, rapidly developing a successful partnership. In 1990, Rothenberger became the first German, and first male, winner of the World Cup Freestyle and was a member of the German team that won the World Championships in Stockholm. The following year, when the Kür was first introduced as a European championship event, he won the inaugural gold medal.

In 1992, the year in which he took a silver medal at the World Cup in Gothenbrg, Rothenberger married the Dutch rider Gonnelien Gordijn. Two years later, whilst still living in Germany, Rothenberger decided to adopt his wife's nationality and subsequently (amidst some controversy) rode for The Netherlands. His debut for his new team resulted in team silver and individual bronze at the 1995 European Championships and he subsequently won team silver at the 1996 Olympics, finishing 4th individually on *Weyden* and was again a member of the Dutch team that took 4th place at the 2004 Olympics.

**Rothenberger-Gordijn, Gonnelien**   Born in 1968, the Dutch rider Gonnelien Gordijn met Sven Rothenberger when training with Conrad Schumacher and married him in 1992 (Rothenberger subsequently taking his wife's nationality). Husband and wife were both members of the Dutch team that won silver at the 1996 Olympic Games. Gonnelien subsequently competed at the 1998 and 2002 World Championships, winning team silver on the former occasion.

**rounded/rounding**   Terms used to describe convex outlines of the horse's topline.

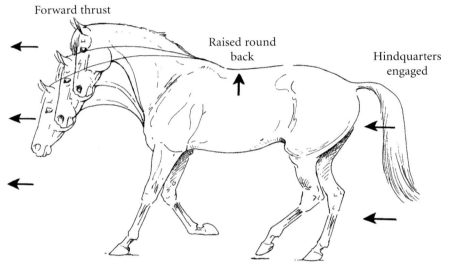

Series of convex arcs – neck and back. Efficiency in locomotion. Correctly trained horse moving efficiently.
Drawing of desirable outlines, from Charles Harris's *Fundamentals of Riding.*

**rowel**   A component part of some types of spur; a small wheel, often with radiating points. Organizing bodies that permit the wearing of rowelled spurs usually have stipulations about their pattern – typically, that the points must have rounded ends and that the rowels are free to rotate.

**running**   A horse is said to be 'running' (especially in trot) if he takes short, hurried strides. Running suggests tension and/or lack of balance, and the running horse does not give himself time to take the measured, elastic, ground-covering strides that typify correct movement. The running horse's back is usually tight and there is a lack of true engagement of the hind limbs.

200

**running reins**    See **auxiliary reins**.

**'running through the bit'**    An evasion whereby the horse, through disobedience, fear or fright, ignores the restraining signals of hand, rein and bit and continues to travel forward in a manner contrary to the rider's wishes.

**Rutten, Jo and Bert**    Dutch father and son who have both been very successful as riders and trainers. Jo Rutten trained with Ernest von Loon. Having virtually given up riding for a time in the 1960s, his enthusiasm was rekindled by that of his then young son, Bert (born 1951), and he went on to represent Holland in the 1976 Olympics, finishing 9th individually. By the time of the 1984 Olympics, Bert had established himself as a successful international competitor, representing Holland in European and World Championships, and being on medal-winning teams. He was selected for the Olympic team but his horse went lame and father Jo, who was the reserve rider, stepped in.

Father and son have, for many years, been active in both breeding and training. Bert, who was the Dutch team manager until he was succeeded in 2005 by Sjef Janssen, currently trains international competitors from several European countries and the USA and is also active as a judge on the Dutch Stallion Performance Testing Committee.

# S

**saddle cloth**    All rules of organizing bodies permit the use of a saddle cloth, but there may be constraints relating to matters such as sponsors' logos, and the circumstances in which a saddle cloth bearing the rider's national flag may be worn.

**saddle cover**    Saddle covers are not generally permitted in competition, although British Dressage rules allow them when riding in, and these rules also permit the use during the test of a gel pad seat saver that is unobtrusive and matches the colour of the saddle.

**saddle, dressage**   The fundamental consideration for a dressage rider is that the saddle used will be eminently suitable for the purpose. Apart from the important fact that the saddle will fit the individual horse correctly, this implies that the rider will be able to sit fully on the seat bones, in the centre of the saddle, in complete balance, adopting the desired leg position with minimum effort. Typical design features of saddles made for dressage include a fairly deep seat, a long, straight-cut flap and stirrup bars mounted far enough back to permit the stirrup leathers to hang vertically more or less directly in line with the seat bones. Some modern designs accentuate the depth of seat and employ large knee rolls – features which tend to impose a set posture on the rider – but many very experienced riders prefer to dispense with these features, believing that they can restrict subtle postural changes.

For competition purposes, saddle design must conform to the rules of the organizing body. These (based on the assumption that riders will generally want to use a saddle suitable for the purpose) are sometimes worded rather imprecisely, but all permit saddles of the type just described. Other than the FEI rules, which refer to a dressage saddle, most rules are worded in ways that seem to permit various other designs (such as general purpose saddles) but exclude such as Western saddles. British Dressage rules make a point of allowing side-saddles and, in a recent addition, treeless saddles.

**saddlery**   See **tack**.

**salute**   A respectful acknowledgement of the test judge(s), traditionally performed after the entrance at the start of the test and before leaving the arena at the end, although some recent lower-level tests do not require the halt upon entry. Although the salute has its basis in military protocol,

Correct forms of salute for male and female riders. Drawing by Maggie Raynor.

nowadays the traditional military salute is correct only for riders in military uniform, otherwise, male riders salute by taking the reins (and whip, if carried) in the left hand and (if wearing an unsecured hat) removing the hat and lowering it to their side with an extended right arm. If a male rider is wearing a hat with a chin harness (an increasingly common practice and allowed under most rules), he modifies the salute by extending his empty right hand downward and inclining his head in a slight bow; the same procedure is followed by female riders and juniors. The salute is an integral part of the test and, if performed well, it conveys the impression of being in control of the halt from which it is made.

**Salzgeber, Ulla**   Born in Oberhausen, Germany, in 1958, Salzgeber started riding at the age of ten, initially being involved with vaulting before moving on to dressage, at which discipline she represented Germany with marked success as a junior. On reaching adulthood, she began to study law, but soon realized that she preferred to ride full time. After marrying, she moved to Bavaria where, from 1992 to 1995, she was trainer of the Bavarian junior team. She was also, for a while, national trainer for the Philippines, before being approached by the German Federation to train with the German team. Following this, she competed in the 1998 World Equestrian Games in Rome, winning individual bronze and team gold medals, a feat she repeated in Jerez in 2002. She had produced several Grand Prix horses before purchasing *Rusty*, her mount for the 2000 Olympics in Sydney. Here, she was involved in a memorable situation when, during her freestyle test, as a result of a technical hitch, her music faltered and stopped. Obliged to leave the arena, she returned at the end of the competition to the overwhelming support of the crowd, and still took the individual bronze medal, as well as team gold. She was National Champion of Germany in the same year. In the following Olympics at Athens in 2004, again riding *Rusty*, she took the individual silver medal and team gold. Other international successes to date include

Ulla Salzgeber riding *Rusty*. Photograph by Elizabeth Furth.

individual silver and team gold medals at the European Championships 1999, individual and team gold at the European Championships in both 2001 and 2003 and World Cup victories in 2001, 2002 and 2003.

The former *Ecole de Cavalerie* of Saumur. Photograph from Hilda Nelson's *Alexis-François L'Hotte The Quest for Lightness in Equitation.*

**Saumur** A provincial town in France that gives its name to a long-established school of equitation. A manège was first founded in Saumur in 1593, as part of an existing Huguenot stronghold, but this succumbed to the religious wars that raged in this era. In 1763, following France's defeat in the Seven Years War, a cavalry school was founded in Saumur as one of a number of new military establishments. Because of the quality of training, this Ecole de Cavalerie soon became an academy to which officers were sent annually from the other cavalry schools throughout France. By 1771, Saumur had become so successful that all but one of the other cavalry schools (the school of the *gendarmes rouges* at Lunéville) had disappeared. For some seventeen years (up to the start of the French Revolution) Saumur, which taught in the traditions of de Pluvinel, de la Guérinière and the School of Versailles, remained in the ascendancy and entertained foreign visitors such as Joseph II of Austria and the future Tsar Paul I of Russia. However, the revolution and the Napoleonic era that followed saw a period of decline that was only reversed following the restoration of the monarchy in 1815. At this time, Saumur's mission was crystallized into a twofold aim: to provide academic instruction to officers whose equestrian aims were both military and academic, and to furnish instructors whose role was simply to provide training for the cavalry. It was the former who, with their black uniforms, became known as the Cadre Noir.

During the nineteenth century Saumur (which, for a while, employed civilian as well as military instructors) was deeply involved in the evolutionary process that saw the increasing development of 'exterior' riding. Many of the leading figures of French equitation of the time had connections with Saumur and a certain tension existed between those whose chief interest was in the preservation of the high-school tenets, and those who were more, or also, interested in adapting these to encompass a newer style of equitation. These tensions may, in fact, have helped both to preserve the academic emphasis and to promote new developments. The era was certainly notable for the number of famous écuyers associated with the school in this era, and the influence of Saumur continued well into the twentieth century through figures such as General Decarpentry, author of *Academic Equitation* and a leading figure in the development of the FEI. However, in 1946, in the aftermath of the Second World War, the Ecole de Cavalerie at Saumur became the Ecole d'Application de l'Arme Blindée et de la Cavalerie and the Cadre Noir was later incorporated in the Ecole Nationale d'Equitation, which relocated to Terrefort, a few kilometres from Saumur. In common with many old cavalry institutions, the horses at Saumur were subsequently replaced by tanks.

**schaukel**   Also known as seesaw; a German dressage movement developed from the rein-back; a prescribed sequence of backward and forward steps performed without an intervening halt; the rein-back steps are performed as usual in two-time and the forward steps in four-time.

**Schmezer, Holger**   Born in 1947 near Heidelberg in Germany, Schmezer discovered his passion for riding when in his teens. Initially, his main interests were showjumping and eventing but, while working for Willi Schultheis his interest in dressage developed. At the age of nineteen he began his apprenticeship as a professional riding instructor and, at twenty-five, he was awarded the German gold rider's badge. In 1979, having spent some time working for a private training yard, he set up his own yard in Verden and soon developed a reputation as a popular and successful trainer. In 1996 he succeeded Siegfried Peilicke as National Coach for Germany's Junior and Young Riders teams and, under his coaching, they won a total of twenty-five medals, including thirteen gold, at European Championships. In 2001, Schmezer succeeded Klaus Balkenhol as Chief National Coach. In addition to his coaching role, Schmezer is a Grand Prix dressage judge and a member of the German examination committee for professional riding instructors.

**school**   Of a horse, see **schooling**; otherwise, an alternative term for arena or manège.

**school figures and movements**   In general terms, those exercises carried out in a school for training purposes; more traditionally, the advanced exercises associated with school horses, i.e. haute école work.

**school horse**   An archaic term that implied not a horse used in a riding school, or a schoolmaster, but a horse who had been trained (schooled) to the highest levels.

**schooling**   A general term for training and educating a horse.

**schoolmaster**   A horse, trained to a high level, used in the instruction of relatively inexperienced riders; often a horse semi-retired from competition, but still capable of producing sound work. It is common practice for riders to be taught the aids for, and feel of, certain movements on such a horse, before attempting to ride them on other horses.

**School of Versailles**   In 1680, Louis XIV of France moved his court to Versailles and, two years later, the court's horses were moved into new stables there. In all, there were over 4,000 horses, used for a variety of purposes, and some 1,100 people were employed to look after them. In charge of the operation was the Grand Ecuyer, a very high-ranking official, one of whose jobs was to license riding academies. Because the school had a great influence on the development of equitation, the term 'School of Versailles' became synonymous with the practitioners of French classical equitation of the period. The school remained highly influential through the eighteenth century, up to the time of the French Revolution.

**Schramm, Ulrik**   (1912–1995) A vastly experienced German horseman and equestrian author, who was dedicated to the proper education of horses for all disciplines. His philosophy is expounded in his own words: 'Seat is obviously an essential element in mastery of the horse, but the rider's head is surely as important as his seat…'; 'Riding is not truly a sport if unity of mind does not exist between rider and horse.' A talented artist, Schramm used his own mild caricatures of horses and riders to emphasize the points made in his writing.

**Schulten-Baumer, Uwe (senior and junior)**
German father and son of the same name who have achieved great success despite both having demanding professional lives and viewing dressage as 'a hobby'. Born in Germany in 1926, Schulten-Baumer senior developed an interest in horses from an early age. Behind his school was a riding school and, from the age of eight, he would get up at 5 a.m. to muck out and groom in return for rides. His first horse was given to him by a local farmer. This was a jumper and not an easy horse, but he managed to win the riding school's best rider competition.

While he retained his interest in horses into adulthood, Schulten-Baumer senior found that there were other, more pressing, demands on his time. The first of these was work (he was later to head a steel conglomerate); the second was the onset of the Second World War. Indeed, it was not

Dr Uwe Schulten-Baumer. Photograph by Elizabeth Furth.

until some years after the war that his passion for and commitment to dressage really had time to develop, and these were sparked off by his second horse, originally an eventer. After the German Federation asked whether he would lend this horse to Fritz Ligges to ride in the 1964 Olympics, the horse was found to have a wind problem, so Schulten-Baumer senior took him home and started to concentrate on dressage.

Studying the methods of many different riders and trainers, he took different elements from many sources and blended them into his own system. He also drew on his professional management skills, placing great emphasis on teamwork and the value of mutual respect between rider, horse and trainer. Within a few years he, himself, began to achieve acclaim as a trainer, coming to prominence initially through the successes of his daughter, Alexa, and son, Uwe junior. Alexa, a very talented rider, competed at international level and won the Goodwood Grand Prix in 1981. Uwe junior, who made his career in medicine, had major successes in the late 1970s and early 1980s: in addition to being German National Champion in 1979, 1980 and 1982 he won silver medals at the 1978 World Championship and the 'alternative' Olympics in 1980, and was European Champion in 1981. His best horses were *Slibowitz* and *Madras*.

Following this period of success, both Alexa and Uwe junior began to focus on other areas of life – Alexa on motherhood and family life and Uwe junior on his medical career. In the aftermath, Schulten-Baumer senior continued to train other riders, including Margit Otto-Crepin, Nicole Uphoff, Pia Laus and multiple Olympic medallist Isabell Werth, whom he initially spotted at a local riding club and who worked with him for a number of years until 2002.

Willi Schultheis. Photograph from Wilhelm Müseler's *Riding Logic.*

**Schultheis, Willi** (1922–1995) German rider and trainer. Regarded as one of the masters of the twentieth century, he won thirteen national titles and won the German Dressage Derby eight times. He was the German National Dressage Coach from 1974 to 1979, mentor to riders such as Harry Boldt, Reiner Klimke, Josef Neckermann and Uwe Schulten-Baumer, and an early influence on German National Dressage Coach Holger Schmezer. He died of a heart attack in Warendorf, aged seventy-three.

**Schumacher, Conrad** A world-renowned German trainer, born in 1946 and brought up on a farm near Frankfurt, Schumacher started riding at the age of six, encouraged by his cavalry officer father. In his early years, his equestrian interests were broad-based, including showjumping, eventing and carriage driving. His fascination with dressage, which began to develop during his period of military service, was heightened when he met Josef Neckermann and eminent riders such as Harry Boldt and Reiner Klimke who rode at Neckermann's yard. With money at a premium, Schumacher began buying inexperienced horses and training them himself. He produced several to Grand Prix level and competed both nationally and internationally when so requested by the German Federation.

However, when his father insisted that the family's mineral water business should take precedence, Schumacher abandoned his own riding ambitions and decided to act as a trainer in his 'spare time'. While he was never to become a full-time professional trainer, he became a hugely successful trainer of young riders and a major influence on the dressage world. When he built an indoor school at the family farm, Neckermann decided to base his horses there, bringing with him Ellen Bontje, whom Schumacher helped to find sponsors and good horses: she subsequently became his stable manager. Another notable pair who came to be trained by Schumacher was Sven Rothenberger and the Dutch rider Gonnelien Gordijn who subsequently married. Over the years, Schumacher has trained German and Dutch pupils to win numerous medals at international level and has also exhibited a great enthusiasm for working with riders and horses from other nations. In particular, a number of top competitors from Britain and the USA have trained with him in recent years.

Conrad Schumacher. Photograph by Elizabeth Furth.

**schwung**   Described in the Official Handbook of the German National Equestrian Federation as '...the transmission of the energetic impulse created by the hind legs, into the forward movement of the entire horse. An elastically swinging back is the necessary pre-condition.'

**score sheet**   The document used by a dressage judge to record the marks and comments for an individual rider's test.

**scoring**   See **marks, dressage test.**

**scribe**   See **judge's writer.**

**seat**   In dressage, the term used to describe the rider's entire posture, rather than specifically the positioning of the backside.

**seat aids**   Those aids transmitted to the horse through the contact of the rider's backside with the saddle; these do not necessarily originate entirely in the rider's seat bones, buttocks or upper thighs but may also include influences from the lower back and abdomen.

**seat saver**   See **saddle cover.**

209

**Seefried, Mary**    Born in 1946, Australia's pre-eminent dressage judge began her riding career whilst a university student and, after showjumping and eventing for a while, developed an interest in dressage, competing successfully at national level for a number of years. Whilst she was a student in Europe in the 1970s, she attended FEI clinics run by Col. Nyblaeus. On her return to Australia, demands of family and career began to curtail her ambitions to compete and she began to concentrate more upon administration and judging, becoming an International Judge in 1983. In 1996, she became the first Australian member of the FEI Dressage Committee and in 1998 she became Australia's first 'O' Level Judge – a direct appointment by the FEI Dressage Committee which carries the responsibility of qualifying riders from other nations for World Championships and Olympic Games. Her first assignment at this level was at the 1999 World Cup Final at Dortmund, since when she has judged worldwide, including at the 2000 Sydney Olympics and the 2002 Asian Games. She is a long-standing Board Member of the Equestrian Federation of Australia and was Chair of the Dressage Committee when the first national dressage rules were formulated and the foundations were laid for the system of training and accrediting judges. Currently Chair of the Australian Dressage Judges Committee, she gives judging clinics throughout Australia and New Zealand, and is also a Board Member of the International Dressage Judges Club for the Asia-Pacific region.

**Seeger, Louis**    (d. 1865) One of the most influential trainers of the nineteenth century; a pupil of Maximillian von Weyrother and the teacher of Gustav Steinbrecht. Seeger based his own methods on those of de la Guérinière and was a vociferous opponent of François Baucher.

**seesaw**    See **schaukel**.

**Seidel, Günther**    Born in 1960 in the countryside of Bavaria, Germany, Seidel grew up surrounded by horses and later trained as a bereiter. In 1985, he moved to the USA, where he took out American citizenship and subsequently became a member of the American teams that won bronze at the 1996, 2000 and 2004 Olympic Games. He has also competed at the 1998 and 2002 World Championships, winning team silver on the latter occasion. He is trained by Klaus Balkenhol.

**Seidler, E.F.** (1798–1865) Master of the Horse of the Berlin and Schwedt Military Riding Schools for forty years. His major written works were *The Dressage of Difficult Horses and the Correction of Ruined Horses* and *The Systematic Dressage of the Field and General-utility Horse.* He was described by Seunig as 'one of the modern masters'.

**self-carriage**   The state in which the horse carries himself and the rider in optimum balance. By implication, the horse is making sufficient use of the carrying power of his hind limbs so that he remains light on his forehand and does not 'lean' on the bit.

**serpentine**   A figure consisting of a series of like-sized half-circles, curved alternately in different directions, connected by straight lines. When ridden in an arena, the size of the half-circles dictates the length of the intervening lines. The gymnastic value of the figure lies in its promoting bend and

Self-carriage evidenced in a highly animated passage. Photograph from Alois Podhajsky's *The Complete Training of Horse and Rider.*

suppleness on both reins. When ridden informally, the figure is sometimes modified by continuing each element beyond a strict half-circle into a loop, then changing the bend almost immediately into a mirror-image loop, with virtually no straight connection between them.

**setting the jaw**   A form of resistance in which, rather than relaxing the lower jaw and accepting the bit, the horse retains tension in the jaw and resists the action of the bit. This is often all part of some more general resistance (for whatever reason) to the rider's aids, in which case it will be accompanied by significant tension in other areas; in cases where the core of the resistance seems to be in the jaw, it is likely that some form of discomfort in the mouth, and/or lack of confidence in the rein aids, is implicated.

**Seunig, Waldemar**  (1887–1976) Born in the then Duchy of Krain, Seunig was educated at a military academy in Austria and entered the cavalry. He subsequently attended the Riding Instructors' Institute in Vienna, where he became a pupil of the famous Josipovich. Then, in the political upheaval of the times, he was more or less repatriated (to what was by that time Slovenia, in Yugoslavia).

Since, by then, he had established a considerable reputation, he was offered the post of Master of the Horse at the Yugoslavian Royal Court. This he accepted, on condition that he first spent a year at the French Cavalry School at Saumur, and six months at the Royal Mews in London (to learn protocol). Subsequently, he was also granted a year at the Spanish Riding School, back in Vienna.

Following a decline of royal interest in riding, Seunig became Chief Riding Master of the Yugoslavian Cavalry School in 1930. However, when offered promotion to General, he retired instead, since this would have entailed active military service for a country for which he had no patriotic feelings.

After this retirement he kept riding and, an Olympic competitor himself, also coached the German team that was successful in the Berlin Olympics. When, during the Second World War, Slovenian partisans destroyed his home, he moved to Germany where he gained high office as an equestrian instructor in the army.

After the war, he travelled extensively and became renowned as a rider, teacher and international judge. His major equestrian textbook was published in its English edition under the title *Horsemanship*; a second book, published as *The Essence of Horsemanship* includes a number of his own drawings.

**shankmover**  A term of German origin, used by authorities such as Ulrik Schramm to describe horses who throw their forelegs out stiffly from the elbow in extended trot and hover in the collected trot. This is a consequence of excessive tension of the muscle groups of the spine and trunk and thus of insufficient attention to attaining calm, absence of tension and throughness during training.

**shoeing**  While it is normal practice for horses competing at dressage to be shod, there is no specific requirement for this in the rules of the main organizing bodies. However, appropriate shoeing and attention to foot care will minimize the likelihood of irregular or uneven movement. As with shoes, there are no specific rules relating to the use of studs.

**shortened neck**   A term used to convey the impression created by overuse of the rein aids. The horse's head is pulled tightly into his neck, the muscles of which are compressed. Since the muscles and ligaments of the horse's neck and back are intimately connected, this posture tightens the whole back, blocks the activity of the back and hindquarters and both compromises the development of impulsion and prevents such energy as is developed from being transferred freely from back to front. The errors of aiding that most commonly produce this effect are those associated with the rider trying to 'pull' the horse into a semblance of 'collection' from the front. However, when they arise from a misconception that the horse is thus on the bit, they will also impede any attempts to produce lengthened strides since, in addition to interfering with the production of activity from behind, they also restrict the activity of the shoulders.

Horse with a shortened neck. Drawing by Gisela Holstein.

**shortening**   A reduction in length of stride; can signify a marked reduction from one gait variant to another, or a more subtle reduction within a gait variant as, for example, a slight shortening within the working gait. While shortening means nothing more than taking shorter strides, this might encompass a dropping off of activity, as through laziness or fatigue. In equestrian terms, shortening is correct only when the level of activity remains constant, so that what is lost in length of stride is gained in elevation.

**short side**   Either of the geometrically short sides of a standard rectangular dressage arena.

**shoulder-fore**   An exercise that might be described as 'a touch of shoulder-in', since it involves the same basic characteristics of that exercise, but a much slighter angle of the horse's body. In the 'classical' form (which equates to the first position as described by Seunig and others) seen from the front, the movement is such that the horse's inside hind foot tracks between his two forelegs. More loosely, 'shoulder-fore' is sometimes used to describe a modified version of shoulder-in (i.e. performed at a significantly lesser angle), as might sometimes be used to introduce a horse to the 'idea' of that movement. This introductory role aside, shoulder-fore is of value in realigning the horse's shoulders and haunches, assisting with the overall straightening process and preparing for exercises such as half-passes and pirouettes.

Shoulder-in. An engraving from de la Guérinière's *Ecole de Cavalerie*.

**shoulder-in**   Regarded by many authorities as the most important of the lateral exercises, shoulder-in was developed by de la Guérinière, whose work on the matter made reference to earlier exercises used by Salomon de la Broue and the Duke of Newcastle. De la Guérinière wrote (in *Ecole de Cavalerie*): 'This exercise has so many benefits that I regard it as the alpha and omega of all exercises of the horse which are intended to develop complete suppleness and perfect agility in all its parts.' The chief benefits of a correctly-performed shoulder-in are that it improves engagement (especially of the inside hind), thus having a collecting effect, lightens the forehand, frees the shoulders, supples the hindquarters and the whole horse laterally and promotes obedience to the aids.

The form of the exercise is that the horse, bent throughout his body around the rider's inside leg, moves at a mean angle of about 30 degrees to the direction of travel; his head is flexed away from the direction of movement; his inside hind steps forward and under his body, in advance of, but not across, his outside hind; his inside foreleg passes and crosses in front of the outer, requiring a little extra lifting of the knee. Usually (and as required in competition), shoulder-in is performed on three tracks, that is, the outside hind follows one track, the inside hind and outside fore follow a second and the inside fore follows a third. However, very supple and highly schooled horses may be able to perform the exercise on four tracks (i.e. distinct tracks are made by all four feet) and this version of the exercise is performed in various classical schools around the world. In this form, the mean angle of the horse's body will be somewhat greater than in the three-track version, but it is essential that it is performed with a correct degree of lateral bend, otherwise it degenerates into a sort of leg-yielding and the gymnastic benefits are lost.

Shoulder-in can be ridden at walk, trot and canter. It is most commonly performed in trot, the gait which lends itself most readily to the biomechanical benefits of the exercise. Walk can be used to introduce the 'idea' of shoulder-in to a young horse (and it can be performed correctly in this gait) but some trainers have concerns that the relative lack of impulsion in this gait limits the benefits of the exercise and that, in the shoulder-in posture, the horse may lose the necessary desire to go truly forward in walk. While shoulder-fore is used extensively to prepare for, and provide adjustments in, canter, many trainers are wary of performing the full shoulder-in too frequently in this gait, because of concerns that the horse may become too used to not being straight and that, in this gait, the exercise may tend to put the horse too much on his outside shoulder.

**shoulder-out**  An exercise in the form of shoulder-in, but performed on the opposite rein; i.e. the bend and other criteria of left shoulder-in performed whilst on the right rein, or vice versa.

**shying**  Essentially, a natural reflex action of the horse in response to some sight or sudden sound that alarms him.; the horse will start, or actually jump, away from the direction of the perceived threat.  Punishing a horse for what is a genuine fear reaction will only reinforce the level of fear; building up the horse's confidence in himself and his environment, and habituating him to various sights and sounds should, over time, lessen the frequency and (generally) the intensity of shying. Horses who are a little 'fresh' or full of themselves may sometimes make a game of shying, looking for things of which they are not genuinely fearful to 'spook' at. An experienced rider should be able to differentiate between this behaviour and genuine fear or surprise reactions.

A shying horse. Drawing from Ulrik Schramm's *The Undisciplined Horse.*

215

**side reins**   Reins used when lungeing the horse; usually connected to the snaffle and either a roller or the saddle girth; provide a 'point of reference' for the horse's front end and (when adjusted in an appropriate manner and employed in conjunction with lungeing skills) can assist in modifying the horse's movement and outline. Side reins are the one form of auxiliary rein that can generally be used when warming up the horse on the lunge prior to a test.

Blanche Allarty of the *cirque Molier* performing an extravagant capriole side-saddle. Photograph in Hilda Nelson's *Alexis-François L'Hotte The Quest for Lightness in Equitation.*

**side-saddle**   A form of saddle that is permitted for competition use under the rules of British Dressage, but may not be so under the rules of other organizing bodies; competitors wishing to ride in this style are advised to check the rules of the organizer concerned.

**simple change**   A change of canter lead effected through walk. When this change is required at the lower levels of competition (Elementary and below under British Dressage rules), the downward transition from canter to walk can be progressive but the upward transition to the new lead should be direct; at higher levels of competition, the transitions to and from walk should both be direct.

**sitting trot**   Riding at trot with the seat remaining in contact with the saddle; the form employed when the rider requires to exercise maximum control of the gait; also, with the exception of a few basic-level tests under some rules, the form usually required in dressage competitions.

**size (of horse)**   The physical size of the horse has a bearing on the horse's capacity for various movements and in some cases on the manner in which they are ridden in an arena. For example, the canter zigzags in some higher-

216

level tests require a defined number of strides in half-pass to be fitted into the distance between the D and G markers. In order to perform this figure evenly, starting and finishing at the prescribed points, the rider of a big, long-striding horse may need to ride with a relative degree of collection, and quite a lot of angle in the half-pass, while the rider of a smaller, short-striding horse may need to ride in a relatively lengthened frame, with less angle in the half-pass. See also **conformation**.

Ann Croft's coloured Shire-cross gelding *Samson* in the process of winning an Elementary level dressage competition.

**slack** Lacking tonicity of muscles.

**snaffle** Mouthpiece used for riding horses who are not yet sufficiently educated to benefit from a double bridle, or in circumstances in which a double bridle is not required. Archetypal snaffles consist of a single bar or single-jointed mouthpiece, with rings at each end to which the reins and cheekpieces are attached. However, the family of snaffles is ever-expanding, and some designs have features of mechanical operation which tend to mimic aspects of some curb bits, while others are made of a combination of different materials. Snaffles in their more basic patterns are generally prescribed for use in the lower-level competitions, and may be permitted at somewhat more advanced levels. However, the specific types and models allowed in tests are governed by the rules of the organizing body which are subject to periodical revision so, if in any doubt about what is permitted, competitors are advised to check the relevant (current) rules.

**Soto, Rafael** Born in 1957 into an equestrian family in Spain, both his father and grandfather being professional riders, Soto trained initially under Alvaro Domecq and became a leading light of the Royal School of

Andalusian Equestrian Art in Jerez. He fulfilled a personal goal when he represented Spain at the 1996 Olympics on a horse (the Andalusian, *Invasor*) bred and trained in Spain and went on to represent his country again at Sydney in 2000 and Athens in 2004. He was also a member of the Spanish team that won a bronze medal at the World Equestrian Games in 1998, and competed in that event at Jerez in 2002 and in the European Championships in 1995, 1997, 1999 and 2001.

**sour**   Describes a horse who has been worked too hard or too frequently, or with a lack of variety, especially if demands have been made of him that are at or beyond the limits of his physical and mental capabilities. Signs of sourness include lack of willingness/co-operation, resistances, inactivity/lack of impulsion and, sometimes, outright defiance or panic.

**Spanish Riding School**   Commonly referred to by this name, but its full title is Imperial Spanish Riding School of Vienna.  Charles I of Spain (1516–1556) was also Emperor Charles V of what was still then known as the 'Roman Empire'; his family dynasty resided predominantly in Vienna, and Austria

Full evening dress performance at the Spanish Riding School.

was part of his empire. Charles was regarded as one of the best riders of his age, and he had immense influence on the development of equitation in both Spain and Austria. His brother, Ferdinand I, was the first to import Andalusian stallions and mares of Spanish-Barb origin to Vienna and Prague in around 1530, and later, from around 1560, to the stud at Kladrub in Bohemia. Ferdinand's son, the Archduke Charles, was interested in the Spanish breeds and moved part of the herd to Lipizza, a village near Trieste, in what is now Slovenia. It was from these horses, crossed with Northern Italian and Neapolitan stock, with a certain admixture of other breeds, that the famous Lipizzaner horse developed.

It was these Spanish connections, coupled with the spreading influence upon European equitation of the Neapolitan School, that led to the founding, in 1572, of the Imperial Spanish Riding School of Vienna. The initial aim of this school was to instruct nobility in the equestrian arts. It was originally a wooden construction adjacent to the Imperial Palace; the present location, the Winter Riding Hall, was built for Emperor Charles VI and completed in 1735. During his reign, and for many years thereafter, the School was (along with other Imperial Schools of those times) closely associated with the military. However, at the Spanish Riding School, there was always an unchanging emphasis on true classical equitation. Through the centuries, the school has produced many figures who have become pre-eminent in the equestrian world, and others, who have not been direct products of the school, have interacted closely with the school and its representatives. One of the Directors most influential in promoting the school and its teachings was Alois Podhajsky who, during the final stages of the Second World War, was instrumental in evacuating the horses and riders from Vienna and also in ensuring the protection of the Lipizzaner stud. The school remains to this day a world-famous home of classical equitation.

**Spanish trot**   A variation of the trot gait, rarely mentioned in equestrian works and practised mainly by adherents to Iberian equitation; in this gait, in a manner similar to that of Spanish walk, the forelegs are raised unusually high; although, in a still photograph, the gait may look superficially similar to extended trot it is very much distinct from that variant; it is not required in competition.

**Spanish walk**   A variation of the walk gait, in which, while the hind legs move as in collection, the forelegs are almost straightened as they are elevated nearly to chest height, so that the horse appears to be pointing at some object in front of him. The Spanish walk is most commonly practised by riders from Iberia (or those influenced by Iberian equitation), usually on breeds from that region. It is not required in competition.

Sylvia Loch riding Spanish walk on *Espada*. Photograph courtesy of Sylvia Loch.

219

**speed**   Distance travelled in a given period.

**spinning**   A term used to describe a horse throwing himself round in a pirouette in an uncontrolled fashion, as opposed to retaining the regular, rhythmic beat of canter.

**spooking**   Describes a horse shying or propping in response to some unexpected or unfamiliar sight or sound.

**spurs**   Devices attached to the heels of a rider's boots, intended to heighten the effects of the leg aids. If they are designed and worn correctly, they will contact the horse's sides only when the rider so desires. Used with discretion by a skilled rider, they can send refined signals to the horse; used indiscreetly, they can provoke undesired reactions. Excessive use of spurs in competition is forbidden, however most organizing bodies *permit* them to be worn from the lower levels of competition onward, and it is *compulsory* to wear them at the higher levels (under British Dressage rules, from Advanced level; under AHSA rules, above Fourth level). It is a general requirement that spurs be made of metal, but there are some differences pertaining to details of design, so competitors are advised to consult the rules of the relevant organizing body.

Square halt – John Winnett on *Greystoke*.
Photograph from *Dressage as Art in Competition*.

**square halt**   A posture of the horse at halt, whereby both lateral pairs of feet, and the fore and hind feet respectively, are parallel. This is considered the correct positioning of the feet at halt, provided that there is a reasonable degree of engagement of the hind limbs (i.e. they are not trailing).

**Staczek, Kristy**   Born Oatley-Nist in New South Wales, Australia, in 1978, and married in 2004, she holds joint nationality, having an Australian mother and a German father. Her early training was in Australia with the well-known FEI rider and coach Rozzie Ryan; she subsequently trained in Germany, first under the late Herbert Rehbein and latterly under Karin Rehbein. She won the European Young Rider Championship in 1995 and 1997 and was a member of the German teams that won gold medals in the European Championships in 1996 and 1997. She also won the Neumuster Grand Prix in 1998

Kristy Staczek. Photograph by Elizabeth Furth.

and competed for Australia at the World Equestrian Games in 1998 and the Sydney Olympics in 2000, where she became the first Australian ever to finish in the top ten.

**Staeck, August** (1880–1942) Born to a farming family in the Brandenburg area of Germany, Staeck joined the army around the turn of the century. Already a skilful rider, he was soon in demand as a trainer of officers' horses and, while he possessed other military virtues, it seems that his success in this field was a factor in his promotion through the ranks.

In 1911, when his military service ended, Staeck started work as head groom and riding instructor at the Berlin Tattersall, at about the same time that Käthe Cobau (later Franke) started her training there. Following the First World War, the show stable was rebuilt as a theatre and a new show and training stable, the Stall Westen, was constructed. From this venue Staeck was a major contributor to the resurrection of German equitation, and organized numerous post-war competitions. His most important supporters in these endeavours were Käthe Franke and Hertha Kayser – later the wife of Gustav Rau.

Despite possessing outstanding skills, Staeck was aware that all riders live and learn, and he was always willing to study with, and learn from, other experts. In this respect he led his employees and pupils by example. He won the German dressage championship twelve times and the record of Käthe Franke in the same era was phenomenal. Another of his star pupils was the legendary perfectionist Fritz Stecken. It says something for Staeck's character that, having trained the gelding *Draufgänger* to the highest level, he gave the horse to Freiherr von Langen who shortly afterwards rode him to win the 1928 Olympic gold medal in Amsterdam.

Although the years preceding the Second World War were problematical and prompted a change of location, Staeck continued to train numerous horses and riders with great success, until he succumbed to the illness that caused his death in 1942.

**St Cyr, Col. Henri**   Swedish winner of two successive individual gold medals at the Olympic Games: Helsinki 1952, riding *Master Rufus* and Melbourne, riding *Juli*. On both occasions, he was also a member of the Swedish teams that won gold medals.

**Stanier, Sylvia, LVO**   British rider and trainer who began riding at an early stage with a hunting and showing background; one of her first teachers being the eminent producer of show hunters, Sam Marsh. After the 1948 Olympic Games, held in the UK, she went to Ireland to study under Col. Joe Dudgeon who had trained the British team. Later she trained with the eminent Danish trainer, Einar Schmit Jensen and also with Nuno Oliveira. She has worked and competed at a high level with many breeds and types of horses in different disciplines and reprised the classical European tradition of working with circus horses. She has also prepared horses belonging to the British royal family for events such as the Trooping of the Colour. In addition to her successes as a rider, she is acknowledged as an expert on lungeing and long-reining techniques and is the author of two books, *The Art of Lungeing* and *The Art of Long Reining*, which have been highly influential worldwide.

**Stecken, Fritz**   (1912–1987) Born into an equestrian family, Stecken was trained by August Staeck in Berlin during the period between the two World Wars, and also studied at the Spanish Riding School, rapidly becoming one of the most successful dressage riders in Europe. He developed a reputation for his painstaking insistence on absolutely correct basics, and was often accused of making slow progress, but the validity of his methods was borne out by the lightness and ease of the numerous horses he trained to Grand Prix level.

Shortly after the Second World War, the Hungarian government sent Bertalan de Nemethy (later to become coach to the American showjumping team) to Stecken for further training and, a few years later, Stecken went to

America, where he became friends with Guy Henry who persuaded him to write the highly regarded *Training of the Horse and Rider*. Stecken taught mainly in the East Coast area, and worked for a while with John Winnett, prior to Winnett's trip to Germany to study with Reiner Klimke.

**Steinbrecht, Gustav**   (1808–1885) Born in Saxony, Steinbrecht studied veterinary medicine before becoming a pupil of Louis Seeger, one of the most influential trainers of the nineteenth century, who had himself been a pupil of Maximillian von Weyrother, a celebrated figure of the Spanish Riding School.

Steinbrecht stayed with Seeger for eight years, during which time he married Seeger's niece and became an accomplished écuyer. He then took over direction of a manège in Magdeburg, where he remained for a further eight years, before rejoining Seeger.

In 1849, Steinbrecht became director of Seeger's establishment and, at about this time, began to make the notes that were to form the basis of his book *The Gymnasium of the Horse*. Seeger himself disagreed with the teachings of François Baucher – also active at this time – preferring methods and principles expounded by de la Guérinière. That Steinbrecht shared Seeger's view of Baucher is obvious from the vigorous attacks upon Baucher's method which permeate *The Gymnasium of the Horse*.

As Steinbrecht's health failed, he entrusted the completion of his book to his pupil/disciple, Paul Plinzer. Through Plinzer, and Plinzer's eminent pupil, Hans von Heydebreck, the work of Steinbrecht had a major influence on the formulation of the German [army] Riding Rules and on German equitation in general.

**Stensbeck, Oskar Maria**   (1858–1939) Born in Königsberg, East Prussia, the son of a stud farm director who also taught riding at the university in Königsberg, Stensbeck was given a pony for his seventh birthday and, by the age of fifteen, was training dressage horses. From 1886 until the early 1930s, he worked for a number of different dressage stables. During this period one of the horses he produced, *Gimpel*, represented Germany (who won team gold on both occasions) at the 1928 and 1936 Olympics – on the latter occasion *Gimpel* was seventeen years old. Stensbeck, by then regarded as one of the finest trainers of horses of his era, was then appointed by Gustav Rau to work with the cavalry riding academy in Hanover and, more or less at the same time, the Stensbeck Riding Academy was founded with the aim of training civil riding instructors. It was primarily through the influence of the latter establishment that Stensbeck also became recognized as one of the most important trainers of professional riders.

As a trainer, Stensbeck was noted for teaching by example, being sparing with words, but impressing and convincing by his work in the saddle. Many of the horses he worked with were not ideal 'dressage types', but his elegant seat and precise aiding developed their impulsion and self-carriage to the maximum. At the age of seventy-two he wrote a book, *Riding*, primarily about his life with horses, and at the age of eighty, one year before his death, he was riding a horse, *Nicolo*, whom he had trained.

**steward**    An official assisting with the running of a dressage competition; sometimes called ring steward, especially if the designated duties include ensuring that competitors are ready to enter the arena at the appointed time. Under the rules of most organizing bodies, the steward has a role in checking competitors' saddlery and equipment prior to the competition, to ensure that it complies with the rules. However, despite this, it may remain the ultimate responsibility of the *competitor* to ensure that equipment meets requirements. (Thus, if a judge spots something amiss, and the competitor is disqualified, the fact that the steward carried out a check is no defence.)

**stiffness**    An undesirable quality in the horse, usually related to musculature but sometimes to other tissue, such as ligament, or even a product of conformation if this causes certain joints to articulate less than would be considered normal. Purely physical stiffness, especially of muscular origin, can usually be alleviated to some extent in the short term by allowing the horse sufficient time to warm up, and over the longer term by appropriate and progressive suppling exercises and, if necessary, by the intervention of a qualified equine physiotherapist; in older horses, stiffness may become more prevalent, in which case more regular, rather than more intensive, suppling work may be required. Relative lateral stiffness (the horse bending more readily to one side than the other) is endemic in virtually all horses to some degree and must be alleviated so far as is possible (see **crookedness** and **straightness**).

In some cases, physical stiffness may be primarily a manifestation of mental tension (arising from discomfort or anxiety). In such cases, removing or minimizing the source of the anxiety so far as is practical is usually the first step towards reducing the physical effects. If, for example, a young horse becomes 'wound up' at his first show, it is usually good practice to spend some time at walk accustoming him to the sights and sounds of the showground and reassuring him before attempting to work him in.

**stirrups and stirrup leathers**    The point is made in both British Dressage and AHSA rules that the use of this equipment is compulsory in competition.

**straightening**    A term meaning either the protracted process of rendering the horse straight (see **straightness; crookedness**), or the more momentary correction of short-term loss of straightness, as arising from loss of balance, minor evasion or incorrect aiding, or reverting to moving straight after performing a circular exercise or a lateral movement.

**straightness**    A highly desirable but elusive quality in horses which can only exist when a horse is equally supple on both sides. While all serious dressage riders seek to obtain straightness in their horses, it is rarely if ever achieved to perfection, one reason being that horses, like humans, tend to carry some degree of physical asymmetry. In movement (whether on a straight line or a circle), 'straightness' is deemed to be evidenced by the horse's hind feet following the same tracks as the forefeet; when the horse is performing lateral movements, a quality of movement equating to straightness is evidenced by the feet moving consistently on lines that are parallel and spaced appropriately according to the exercise being performed and the angle of travel required.

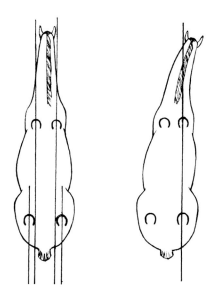

llustrations relating to straightness, from John Winnett's *Dressage as Art in Competition*.

225

**strength**   A quality required in considerable measure by horses required to perform advanced work, especially collected work in its various forms. Work designed to build up a horse's strength should always be carried out in conjunction with the development of suppleness in order that the muscles do not become stiff and tight, thus putting too much strain on the associated tendons and ligaments and impeding joint mobility.

**stretching**   Producing lengthening of muscles; part of the process of developing musculature and suppleness; riders carrying out stretching exercises should be mindful that the stretching of a muscle or muscle group is a passive process produced by the contraction of the agonist(s) – the 'opposing' muscle/group – and that the work should not be too demanding or protracted if spasm, strain and other injuries are to be avoided. Appropriate and carefully conducted stretching exercises can also be of benefit to other tissues, such as the nuchal/supraspinous ligament of the horse's topline.

**stretching the frame**   Also described as 'letting the horse take the reins out of the hands'; an exercise that has been added to some AHSA tests in recent years. As required under AHSA rules, the rider should retain a soft contact on the lengthened rein and the angle at the horse's poll should remain approximately the same as before the stretching; the horse should stretch over his back, reaching forward and down with his head and neck and maintaining his tempo. Similar in concept to descente d'encolure.

Reiner Klimke at the start of a lesson for a young horse. Rising trot on a circle with the horse's neck long, low and forward-stretched. Photograph from *Basic Training of the Young Horse.*

**stretching the topline**   Riding in a way that encourages the horse to stretch the ligaments and musculature of his topline by lowering his neck and rounding his back. See **descente d'encolure; long and low; low and round; stretching the frame.**

**stride**   One completed unit (completed cycle of footfalls) of any gait.

**strike off**   The moment of upward transition into canter.

**stroking the horse's neck**   An action sometimes asked for in dressage tests in years past; did not imply stroking the neck with a free hand, as a rider might do to reassure a horse, but an action almost identical to give and retake the reins, which has now generally superseded it as an instruction.

**stubbornness**   A considered disinclination on the horse's part to do something that is required by the rider (as opposed to a fear reaction or lack of understanding).

**Stückelberger, Christine**   (b. 1948) Swiss rider trained by Georg Wahl, who has achieved great success at the highest levels of competition over a number of years. Her most famous partner was the great *Granat*, on whom she first appeared at the Olympics in 1972. At the next Olympic Games, in 1976, Stückelberger and *Granat* won the individual gold medal and were part of the Swiss team that won silver; they did not compete at the 1980 Moscow Olympics but appeared instead at the Goodwood Festival (effectively an Olympic substitute for those who boycotted the actual Games), where they again won the individual title, and were part of the Swiss team that finished second. In addition, this partnership had great success at the European Championships, winning individual gold and team bronze in 1975, individual gold and team silver in 1977, individual silver and team bronze in 1979 and individual and team silver in 1981. They also won team silver at the World Championship in 1978 and 1982, and individual silver on the latter occasion.

Christine Stückelberger riding *Aquamarin*. Photograph by Elizabeth Furth.

Following *Granat's* retirement from competition, Stückelberger rode *Tansanit* as a member of the Swiss team that took the silver medal at the 1984 Olympics in Los Angeles. In 1988, riding *Gaugin de Lully* at the Seoul Olympics, she took the individual bronze medal and was, again, a member of the Swiss team that won silver. On the same horse, she also won the World Cup in 1987 and 1988. Stückelberger went on to compete in the 1996 and 2000 Olympics on *Aquamarin*, making a total of seven occasions on which she had represented her country at Olympic level.

**studs**   See **shoeing**.

**stumble**   To take a false step. Seen in isolation as, for example, stepping on false ground, this will usually be considered no more than a minor fault by the judge; repeated stumbling, however, may indicate a faulty way of going or lameness and will be viewed accordingly.

**submission**   As a quality desired in the horse, this is best defined as willing obedience to the rider's aids, which presupposes that he understands them and is physically capable of complying with them.

**suppleness**   The quality attained when the horse's musculature, and the associated tendons and ligaments, have developed the optimum capacity for freedom of movement, with the minimum risk of strain, tear, cramp or other damage. It is a classical precept that suppleness must be developed in tandem with *strength*, and research by modern equine physiotherapists supports this view. Suppleness without sufficient strength can lead to injuries during movements, such as piaffe and canter pirouettes, where real power and joint stability are required, while strength without suppleness (the development of strong but short, stiff muscles) can lead to repetitive stress injuries and to strain injuries when a larger range of movement (e.g. from collection to extension) is suddenly required. A lack of suppleness will always make it difficult, or impossible, for a horse to perform certain movements correctly, and uneven lateral suppleness is a major factor in the problem of crookedness.

**supporting rein**   A term used to describe the action of a rein that is supplementary to, or augments, the effect of the principle rein aid; it does not imply that the horse is being physically 'held up' by the rein.

**supraspinous ligament**   See **nuchal apparatus**.

**suspension**   The **moment of suspension** (see that entry) is the period of a stride (of trot, canter or gallop) during which none of the horse's feet are in contact with the ground. Sometimes, by extension, the degree or quality of that period is referred to in phrases such as 'showed marked suspension'. Such use normally conveys the idea that the suspension is associated with elastic, forward movement and, as such, is distinct from stilted 'hovering' or 'passagey' movement.

**sustaining hands**   Hands that retain a level of contact consistent with what is being required of the horse at that time; thus, while not overtly taking or yielding, they are still acting in so far as they are conveying a message to the horse: 'maintain the status quo'.

**swinging back**   A term that describes the muscles of the horse's back when moving freely and in co-ordination with the movement of the limbs; an essential component of losgelassenheit, schwung and throughness.

# T

**tack**   The equipment in which a horse is ridden (the term saddlery, whilst strictly more limited in application, is often employed as having more or less the same meaning). For the purposes of competition dressage, this usually consists simply of a saddle (probably with a saddle cloth) and bridle. Organizing bodies have their own specific rules about patterns and types of tack and equipment permitted in various competitions; since these are subject to periodic changes and variations, competitors should always acquaint themselves with the current, relevant rules. See also **bit; bridle; double bridle; saddle, dressage** and **snaffle**.

**tail carriage**   Since the tail is a continuation of the horse's spine, the way in which it is carried can be indicative of the freedom of movement, or lack of freedom, of the horse's back muscles. Ideally, the tail should oscillate freely at each stride, in a manner synchronous with the movement being performed. A tail carried rigidly upright is often a sign of excitement, and is likely to be associated with some degree of 'hollowness' and general tension. A clamped-down tail is indicative of the type of tension associated with anxiety or pain, the manifestation of which will not be isolated in the tail. A

The horse's tail movement synchronized with the movement of body and limbs in half-pass. Photograph from Paul Belasik's *Dressage for the 21st Century*.

tail carried crookedly to one side is likely to indicate some physical problem in the back; where such crookedness is apparent only in collected work, this may indicate that the apparent collection has been imposed by strong aids to a degree beyond the horse's current capacity – possibly on a horse who lacks straightness.

**tail swishing** Generally considered to indicate nervousness, tension or resistance on the horse's part; when occurring in a test it is likely to influence the judge(s) to mark down the movement(s) in which it is evident, and also the collective mark for submission. See also **tail carriage; teeth, grinding**.

**taking hand** The rider's hand when employed in conjunction with forward-driving aids or impulses in such a way as to increase the contact on the rein; a holding or resisting effect, rather than a pulling backwards; the opposite effect to a yielding hand.

**team competition** A competition in which the scores of team members are combined to compute the result, which may be run separately from, or in tandem with, an individual competition. In some cases, there is the facility for a 'discard' score (e.g. teams may consist of four members, but only the best three scores from each team are taken into consideration). Whether all scores are counted, or a 'discard' system is applied, it is usually the case that a prescribed number of team members have to complete the competition for the team score to be considered. For example, if the format is teams of four with one 'discard' score, and one team member is eliminated for some reason, that member's score can be 'discarded' and the other three will count. If, however, a second team member was eliminated, or had to withdraw, this would lead to the elimination of the whole team from the team section of the competition.

**teeth, grinding** Generally considered to indicate nervousness, tension or resistance on the horse's part; when occurring in a test, it is likely to influence the judge(s) to mark down the movement(s) in which it is evident, and also the collective mark for submission. See also **tail swishing**.

**temperament** Collectively, those aspects of a horse's (or human's) nature and being that control thoughts, feelings and behaviour. Taking account of an individual horse's temperament is an essential part of training and competing.

**tempi changes** Multiple flying changes, one change being performed every prescribed number of strides.

**tempo** From the Latin *tempus,* meaning time; a word brought into equitation from the field of music. In music, tempo is related to speed but in the context of the number of beats in a bar, thus the speed is relative, not absolute. In equitation, something similar should apply. For example, trot is a 'two-time' gait and, for an individual horse, his tempo, in terms of the number of strides per minute, should ideally remain the same in all its variants. However, while, in this context, the tempo of the collected and extended forms should remain constant, the horse in extended trot will travel considerably faster (in miles per hour) than when in collected trot, since, while he will take the same number of strides per period, the extended strides will cover more ground than the collected ones.

**tendon boots** A form of leg protection which, like the use of bandages, is permitted whilst warming up for a test but not permitted in the test itself.

**tension** Nervous tension in the horse may have various specific physical manifestations, including teeth grinding and tail swishing, however the most prevalent and global physical effect will be general muscular tension, which will cause some degree of stiffness and stilted movement. In a similar way, tension in the rider will inevitably compromise the overall ability to communicate with the horse to optimum effect; for example, tension in the seat will compromise the rider's ability to move with the horse and may induce stiffening of the horse's back; tension in the hands or forearms will be transmitted to the horse down the reins.

**terre-à-terre** An archaic form of movement; a kind of rocking, jumping, two-beat 'canter' on 'two tracks', formerly used in the preparation for airs such as the mézair and courbette. De la Guérinière, with reference to the Duke of Newcastle, described it as: '…a gallop in two beats, on two tracks, much shorter and more collected than an ordinary gallop, and with a different position of the legs, where the forelegs and hind legs are raised together and strike the ground together in regular succession…a series of very low jumps, the horse moving slightly forwards and to the side.'

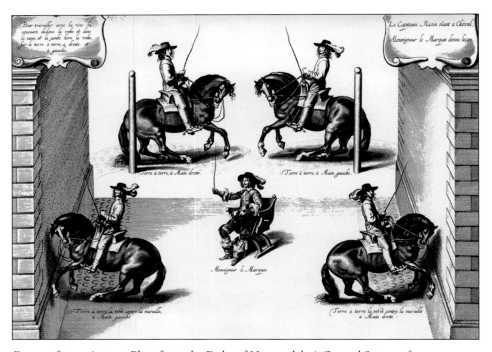

Forms of terre-à-terre. Plate from the Duke of Newcastle's *A General System of Horsemanship*.

**test** A formalized series of prescribed movements, the whole forming the basis for a dressage competition.

**Thackeray, Col. Donald W.** (1916–1995) A graduate of West Point Military Academy, Thackeray served as a US cavalry officer prior to the Second World War, during which he worked as an intelligence officer in Europe and Russia. Continuing as a serving officer after that war, he was wounded in Korea and was subsequently appointed the military attaché for Vienna and then Berne.

Whilst in Vienna, he met Alois Podhajsky, who became a great influence on his dressage training. In Berne, he became AHSA representative to the FEI.

Having concluded his military career at the Pentagon, Thackeray devoted his life to equestrian sport: he was an FEI Olympic-level judge for driving, showjumping and eventing, as well as dressage, which he judged at the Olympic Games in 1976, 1984 and 1988, as well as the 'alternative' games in 1980. He was similarly involved at the highest levels as an organizer and administrator in roles including the Chairmanship of the USET Dressage Planning Committee and long-term membership of the AHSA Dressage Committee. In 1998, he was inducted posthumously into the USDF's Hall of Fame for his outstanding contribution to equestrian sports in the United States.

**Theodorescu, Georg**  Born in Romania in 1926, Theodorescu started riding as a young boy.  His grandfather, who produced racehorses, initially gave him a horse without any tack. He told him to make friends with the horse and said that, when the horse would come to him willingly, he could have a saddle and bridle. It took Theodorescu about five days to win the horse's trust and this early experience laid the foundation for the philosophy of friendship and understanding on which his training became based. (Significantly, when Theodorescu became established as a trainer, all his retired horses remained in the boxes they had occupied during their competitive careers.)

In his formative years, alongside his passion for riding, Theodorescu developed interests in tennis, skiing and music; he also studied law and became multi-lingual. However, horses remained his main focus and, in 1956, he represented his country at the Olympic Games. The following year, he went to Aachen with the Romanian team and stayed on in Germany as a political refugee. There, he started a new life near Warendorf, renting some stables that were quickly filled with showjumpers, eventers and dressage horses owned by friends. Willi Schultheis and Walter Gunther were major supporters at this time.

With his skills as a trainer underpinned by his ability to communicate in five languages, Theodorescu was soon attracting squads of riders from a number of countries, including France, Italy and the USA. In 1991, the year in which he was voted Trainer of the Year by the International Trainers' Club, he also proved that the passing years had not diminished his skills in the saddle, when he won the Men's Derby at Hamburg. This victory was made sweeter by the fact that his daughter, Monica, herself an Olympic medallist, won the Ladies' Derby that year. In doing so, she was following in the footsteps of her mother, Inge, a former showjumper who went on to win the Hamburg Derby Ladies' Dressage four years running, and also trained the Polish Dressage Squad in 1998.

Monica Theodorescu riding *Grunox*. Photograph by Elizabeth Furth.

**Theodorescu, Monica** Born in 1964 at Sassenberg, Germany, the daughter of Georg Theodorescu, she started riding on a Shetland pony bought for her by her grandfather before she was born. Early successes included two gold medals and two individual silver medals at European Junior and Young Rider Championships and she went on to be a member of the German dressage team that won gold at the 1988 Seoul Olympics, finishing 6th individually. She was also a member of the teams that won gold at the 1992 and 1996 Olympics, finishing 4th individually on the latter occasion. She won the World Cup on *Ganimedes* in both 1993 and 1994 and narrowly missed a third successive victory the following year.

**Theuer, Elisabeth** The Austrian rider who won the individual gold medal at the 1980 Moscow Olympic Games, riding *Mon Cherie*.

**three-quarter lines** The imaginary lines halfway between the two long sides of the arena and the centre line, i.e. 5 m from both the long side and the centre line. A 5 m loop ridden from a long side should touch the nearer three-quarter line; a 15 m circle or half-circle ridden from the long side should touch the further three-quarter line.

**three-time** The correct rhythm of the canter, being the three distinct, regular footfalls of the individual hind foot, the other hind foot and diagonally opposite forefoot together, and the individual 'leading' forefoot.

First time of the canter;
near hind in support

Second time of the canter;
left diagonal in support

Third time of the canter;
off fore in support

The footfalls of the canter. Drawings from James Fillis's *Breaking and Riding*.

**three in one**   One method of holding the reins of a double bridle; practised by some of the old masters, who held the right bradoon rein in the right hand and the other three reins in the left. See also **reins, holding of**.

**through(ness)**   See **durchlässigkeit**.

**thrust**   The propulsive aspect of the power of a horse's hind limbs; the dominant element in producing length of stride.

**ticklishness**   Abnormal sensitivity of the skin that produces a reflex action when triggered. Some horses are constitutionally prone to being ticklish, sometimes in specific areas; they may, for example, react to such stimuli as the rider's coat tails touching them behind the saddle, or being hit in the belly by loose pieces of the arena surface. Mares in season may exhibit a similar response to the actions of the rider's legs, as a result of hormonally heightened sensitivity of their flanks. Riders of genuinely ticklish horses should be mindful that, even though the horse's reactions may be unwelcome, they do not constitute disobedience, being reflexes beyond the horse's control. They should, however, take all practical steps to minimize the possibility of triggering the relevant stimuli, and be particularly careful in their use of spurs and whip.

**timidity**   A characteristic (whether genetically inherited or invoked) of some horses that may render them liable to various fear reactions and a tendency to 'cling' to stablemates; it may also be evidenced in a tendency to 'curl up' beneath the rider, rather than moving boldly and freely forward. Timidity will not be resolved by harsh, demanding riding (which will only worsen the condition, or make the horse hurry his work out of fear), but by a training regime that aims to build the horse's self-confidence gradually.

**timing of aids**   It is axiomatic that, to elicit the best response from a horse, a rider should apply the aids (especially for actions such as upward transitions and flying changes) at the moment when the horse is best able to respond to them. This requires not only an acute awareness of the disposition of the limbs within the gaits, but also an appreciation of the speed of reaction of an individual horse's nervous system (since there will be a fractional delay between the giving of an aid and the horse's ability to receive and respond to it). In a slightly different but related context, timing of the aids has an impact on the accurate execution of test movements at the prescribed markers.

**tongue faults**   Resistances or evasions such as getting the tongue over the bit, or sticking it out of the side of the mouth; associated with discomfort or unease and, in some cases, invoked or exacerbated by inappropriate choice of bit or unsuitable mouthing procedures with young horses. These evasions are more readily avoided or nipped in the bud than cured once they have become habitual; when evident during a test, they will be construed as lack of submission.

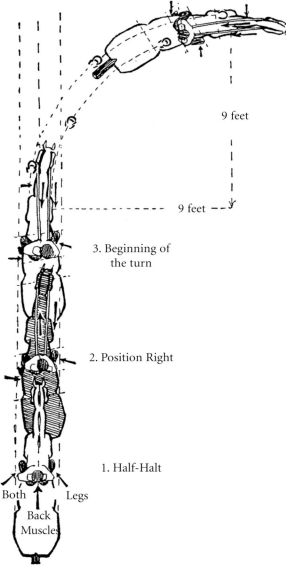

9 feet

9 feet

3. Beginning of the turn

2. Position Right

1. Half-Halt

Both    Legs

Back Muscles

Progression of aids for a turn as illustrated in Wilhelm Müseler's *Riding Logic.*

236

**tongue strap**   A device sometimes fitted in an endeavour to cure tongue faults; not permitted in competition.

**topline**   The profile of the horse's head, neck, back and haunches and, by extension, the musculature associated with these regions, together with the spinal process and associated ligaments. A well-developed, free-moving musculature of the topline, and a profile of convex arches of the neck and back, are signs that training is heading in the right direction.

**Törnblad, Anne-Grethe**   See under married name of **Jensen**.

**track**   A term used loosely to refer to the outside track. More specifically, forms part of the command 'track left' (or right); an instruction to turn in the prescribed direction upon meeting the outside track; for example, after crossing the arena from B to E, the instruction might be 'At E, track left'.

**tracking up**   Said of a horse whose hind feet are stepping into the prints made by the corresponding forefeet.

**trailing**   Said of the hind limbs/hindquarters when they are not engaged sufficiently to carry out their roles of carrying and propelling the horse effectively; trailing limbs are associated with reduced impulsion and quality of steps and compromise the horse's balance, effectively increasing the load on the forehand. Associated with actual lack of energy or the desire to use it (perhaps linked to inappropriate or ineffective riding) and, in some cases, may be linked to poor conformation.

Insufficient engagement, with trailing hind legs. Drawing by Klaus Phillip from Alfred Knopfhart's *Fundamentals of Dressage.*

**training**   The process of improving the horse's physical attributes, his understanding of the requirements of his rider and his willingness to comply with them. Also encompasses subsidiary but important matters involving an acceptance of his environment so that, for example, he can be shod, clipped and boxed without fuss, ridden, if necessary, in traffic, hacked out alone or in company and remain confident without becoming over-excited at showgrounds.

**Training the Teachers of Tomorrow (TTT)** An educational trust located at East Whipley Farm, Shamley Green, Surrey, England. Founded in 1986, the core aim of the trust is to assist aspiring trainers by promoting equestrian philosophy and practice based on sound classical principles. To this end, the trust organizes regular lectures and clinics with trainers of international repute. While many members of the trust are aspiring or qualified professional trainers, other interested parties are welcome to attend the various events as members of the audience. The trust has a website at www.ttttrust.com and an email address: secretary@ttttrust.com.

**transition** A change from one gait to another, or a change of variants within a gait (e.g. collected trot to extended trot).

**travers** Also known as head to the wall and haunches in. A lateral movement or exercise which may be performed along the outside track, on the centre line or, indeed, in relationship to other lines – however, it is usually introduced to the horse along the outside track and, for ease of definition, is usually described with reference to the outside track, or the wall of the arena.

While the movement is required in some dressage tests, its primary value is as a suppling exercise of the lateral musculature and the hind limbs, and different trainers show slight variations in how they describe and employ it. Essentially, the horse's head remains on the track, with the forehand travelling fairly close to parallel along the track while the rest of the horse's body is bent to the inside, round the rider's inside leg. The horse, looking in the direction in which he is moving, moves parallel to the wall (or line of reference) with an overall mean inclination in his body of approximately 30 degrees. In its finished form, as considered correct for competition purposes, the movement of the limbs is on four tracks (although the space between the track of the outside hind leg and that of the inside fore is likely to be relatively narrow), however, in the introductory stages, some trainers are content with a three-track form, with these two limbs moving on a single track.

**traverse** From the French word for cross, this term is used in two different ways in old equestrian terminology. The more common use is to signify some degree of side-stepping associated with crookedness, as for example when a horse disengages his inside hind leg. The other use is to signify the movement referred to more commonly as full pass.

**triangulation** A fault seen in piaffe, in which the horse's forelegs are seen to slant backwards, so that a downward pointing triangle is formed by the forelegs, hind legs and belly. This may occur when the rider pushes the hind legs so far under the horse (in search of more engagement) that they get into a cramped position and cannot lift the horse effectively, so the forelegs endeavour to help the process. It can also occur if the horse's neck is too low, thus interfering with the correct balance and the correct interaction of the back and hind limbs.

Triangulation in piaffe. Drawing by Brian Tutlo, from Paul Belasik's *Dressage for the 21st Century.*

**tride** An archaic term that was especially current in France during the eighteenth century and more or less disappeared with the nineteenth century. Essentially, a horse or his movements had tride if they were animated, elevated, and elegant.

**trot** A two-time gait in which the horse moves his legs in diagonal pairs with a brief period of suspension between the grounding of each diagonal pair. See also **positive diagonal advance placement**.

**TTT** See **Training the Teachers of Tomorrow**.

**turn** A significant change of direction usually performed by riding forwards on an arc of a circle, although it is also possible for a horse to turn within his own length by a turn on the centre, forehand or haunches.

239

**turn on the centre**   A method of turning in which the horse, in walk-time, pivots around his own centre; quite common in the horse at liberty, especially in a confined space, but rarely performed as an exercise under saddle and not required in tests.

**turn on the forehand**   A turn in which the horse pivots around his inside foreleg, which marks the time (of walk) with the movement.  Mainly used as a training exercise to teach the rider application of, and/or the horse response to, the aids; not required in tests.

**turn on the haunches**   A turn in which the horse pivots around his inside hind leg; can be performed in walk, piaffe and canter. The turn in walk is included in some tests at a relatively early stage in which case, under British Dressage rules, a few forward steps at the beginning of the turn are permitted. When performed in tests at canter or piaffe, the turn is required in the form of a pirouette or half-pirouette and judged according to the criteria required for these forms.

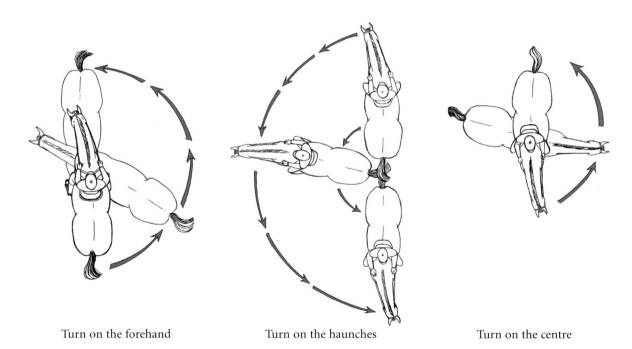

Turn on the forehand          Turn on the haunches          Turn on the centre

Turns on the forehand, haunches and centre. Diagrams by Maggie Raynor.

**Tuttle, Col. Hiram E.** (1882–1956) Born in Maine, USA, Tuttle grew up on a farm. Like many of his generation, his love of horses grew from sitting bareback on his father's plough horses. Musically gifted, he studied violin and orchestral and choral directing, and used these skills to earn money to put himself through college. Having become a lawyer, he practised in Massachusetts, filling his spare time with music, dramatics, watchmaking and equitation.

With the outbreak of the First World War imminent, Tuttle enlisted for officer training and was initially commissioned a second lieutenant, serving first as a Motor Transport Officer, then in the Quartermaster Corps. After the war he remained in the army and, following attendance at the Troop Officers' Class at Fort Riley, he was put in charge of the buying and training of remounts at Fort Robinson. It was from this time on that Tuttle's skills as a dressage rider came to the fore. In 1932, he won individual and team bronze medals at the Olympic Games on a horse called *Olympic*, who had been sold to him for one dollar by a friend whose polo ponies he had been schooling. He also competed at the 1936 Games. Whilst continuing his military career, he achieved great fame for the dressage exhibitions he gave on a number of horses, including *Vast*, who was sometimes ridden with silk thread in place of reins. In one year, the $8,000 he raised from his exhibitions was used to help finance the American Olympic team. These performances helped raise the profile of dressage in the USA and it was an exhibition by Tuttle that provided inspiration for Robert Borg, who subsequently went to work with Tuttle, the two becoming close friends.

Tuttle owned all the horses he rode, and refused to sell any of them. When he retired from the army, with the rank of Colonel, he got special permission to keep his horses at Fort Riley (at no expense to the army), since it was close to his home at Junction City, and he continued to ride daily for as long as his health permitted.

**two-time** A gait in which there are two distinct footfalls, each of a pair of legs, during a complete stride. The trot is considered a two-time gait in which the limbs are moved in diagonal pairs, and in the rein-back there is also two-time diagonal movement. The pace (most commonly associated with harness racing) is a gait in which there is two-time movement of the lateral pairs of limbs.

**two-track**   A term that has been traditionally used in many quarters to describe lateral work in its various forms, the rationale being that the forehand and the hindquarters (as two entities) follow different tracks. The first logical drawback of this term is its assumption that a horse who is not performing lateral work is moving on one track, when, in reality (assuming that he is straight), he will, in fact, be making one track with his nearside lateral pair and a second track with his offside lateral pair (i.e. two tracks). The second drawback is that, in many forms of lateral work, the horse is clearly not moving on two tracks – most definitions of the form of shoulder-in required for competition dressage actually define it as a 'three-track' movement, and in many forms of lateral movement the horse's feet will be following four distinct (albeit not necessarily equidistant) tracks. For these reasons, a number of writers dismiss the term as being both factually inaccurate and needlessly misleading.

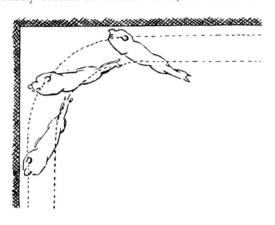

A two-track exercise. Drawing from Waldemar Seunig's *The Essence of Horsemanship*.

# U

**uberstreichen**   A German term rendered in English as 'release of the rein', this terminology being used in the AHSA rules; despite slight differences in the details of definition, it is essentially the same movement, with the same intentions, as give and retake the rein.

**unaffiliated**   A show or competition that is not run under the auspices of the national organizing body. National bodies often have rules restricting their members from taking part in such a competition if the prize money available exceeds certain low limits.

**unbalanced**   Said of a horse who lacks balance in any respect, either laterally or longitudinally. While a rider whose position is very poor/precarious may, in fact, be unbalanced, it is more usual to describe a rider as out of balance.

**uneven lateral development**   A condition in which the horse, either for inherent reasons, in the aftermath of injury, or as a consequence of inappropriate schooling, has significantly greater development on one side of his body than the other. The last is probably the most prevalent reason and it can be exacerbated by actions as basic as the rider always performing rising trot on the same diagonal or working too much on the rein the horse finds easier. See also **crookedness; one-sided**.

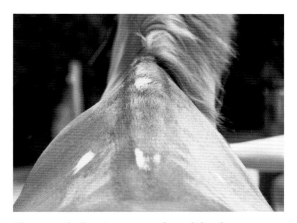

Photograph showing uneven lateral development, from Ken Lyndon-Dykes' *Practical Saddle Fitting*.

**uneven steps**   A remark sometimes made by judges in the light of perceiving a horse's steps to be unequal in length; may signify slight lameness or may be related to the relative strength and weakness of the hind limbs, which is likely to be associated with some degree of one-sidedness/crookedness.

**ungraded**   While organizing bodies such as British Dressage run most competitions under a grading system (see **grading of horses**), some classes may be designated as ungraded. This has the effect of opening up the entry to a greater number of horses. However, since these classes are ungraded, no grading points are awarded and success in such classes does not count towards qualification for various other events.

**unilateral**   One-sided, or on one side only.

**united** In respect of canter, the opposite of disunited, i.e. the horse moving in the correct sequence of footfall in true canter. Sometimes (more commonly in former days) the term is also used to convey a general picture of the whole horse moving in a harmonious, balanced fashion.

**United States Dressage Federation** (USDF) An affiliate body of the American Horse Shows Association, established for the purpose of promoting a high standard of accomplishment in dressage in the United States of America, primarily through educational programmes.

**unlevel** A term used to describe slight unevenness of movement of the horse's limbs, as in unequal height or weight-bearing, which may signify a minor degree of lameness or, as with uneven steps, may relate to uneven physical development. If, during a test, a judge perceives moments during which a horse appears unlevel (but to a degree short of outright lameness), the competitor will be allowed to complete the test, but any impact upon quality of movement will be reflected in the marks given.

**un pas un saut** An old French term, 'a step and a leap', for a movement in three parts: a short gallop (more probably, canter), a courbette and a capriole.

**unsound** A term signifying that a horse is lame. See **lameness**.

**unsteady contact** A rein contact that varies in intensity in a random fashion, without this being intentional on the rider's part. Usually a consequence of unsteady hands, which may, in turn, be a product of postural error. In cases where the immediate cause appears to be related to the horse's way of going, this still indicates a failure on the rider's part to keep the horse fully on the aids.

**unsteady halt** A halt that is not fully confirmed by the horse being square, balanced and attentive, as a consequence of which there may be a minor degree of fidgeting or rebalancing on the horse's part.

**unsteady head** A term that implies erratic movement of the horse's head as provoked by incorrect use of the reins and/or various minor resistances or evasions on the horse's part or possibly flawed balance. It does not refer to the correct, rhythmic cycle of head movement that is a natural feature of the walk and canter.

'**uphill**' A term used to describe a horse whose back appears to slope upward a little from quarters to forehand, either because this is a fact of his conformation, or, in more common usage, because his hind limbs are well engaged beneath him in movement, causing a degree of relative elevation of the forehand (i.e. the angulation that would be evident if he were, in fact, going uphill). Compare with '**downhill**'.

**Uphoff, Nicole**   Born in Germany in 1966, the daughter of a German shipping agent, Uphoff started riding at the age of nine at a riding school, before owning her first horse two years later. In her formative years she studied with German trainers Fritz Tempelmann and Klaus Balkenhol, before working for a while with Uwe Schulten-Baumer (senior) at the age of twenty. The

Photograph of Ernst Lindenbauer, exemplifying the concept of an 'uphill' canter.

following year she was based at the German Federation's headquarters at Warendorf, where she trained with Harry Boldt who was, at the time, the Chef d'Équipe of the German Dressage Team. Whilst at Warendorf, she met, and subsequently married, the showjumper, Otto Becker. In 1987 she made her mark on the highly competitive German scene by taking individual and team gold medals at the 1987 European Young Riders Championships. With *Rembrandt*, a horse she had purchased as a three-year-old, she went on to numerous international successes. In 1988, with Boldt as her personal trainer, she won both team and individual gold medals at the Seoul Olympics becoming, at twenty-one, the youngest ever Olympic dressage champion. During the following four years, she won the 1989 European and 1990 World Championships, was 2nd in the 1991 German and European Championships and won both team and individual gold medals at the 1992 Olympics.

In 1993, when *Rembrandt* was injured and had to undergo surgery, Uphoff won the European Freestyle Championship on *Grand Gilbert*. The

Nicole Uphoff and *Rembrandt*. Photograph by Elizabeth Furth.

following year, *Rembrandt* made a remarkable recovery to win a silver medal at the World Equestrian Games and, in 1996, Uphoff exercised her right as reigning Olympic Champion to ride him as an individual at the Atlanta Olympics. However, despite top-ten finishes in the initial tests, her now ageing partner was deemed insufficiently sound to take part in the final and was subsequently retired from competition. *Rembrandt's* career included twenty-one gold medals, three silvers and one bronze in major international competitions.

In 1997, following divorce, Uphoff moved to northern Germany, where she set up her own yard near Cloppenburg. In 1999 she was named Germany's Sportswoman of the Year and earned German National Honours in recognition of her contributions to her country's equestrian sport. Recent years have seen further changes in her personal life and relocations of training bases, but she remains heavily involved in dressage and has expressed her desire to produce another top horse.

**USDF**   See **United States Dressage Federation**.

# V

**van Baalen, Coby**   Born into a farming family in The Netherlands in 1957, van Baalen's riding career began when she persuaded her reluctant father to buy her a horse. From these beginnings she progressed, with her husband Ari, to running a farm in Brakel which contains a yard housing some twenty-five dressage horses.

On a visit to a stud near Arnhem, van Baalen's eye was attracted to a young stallion being trained for showjumping and she purchased him more or less on a whim. With this horse, *Olympic Ferro*, she went on to make a major impression at the 1998 World Equestrian Games in Rome when they were part of the Dutch team that won the silver medal, the partnership being placed 6th individually. Further success followed in the 1999 World Cup, where they took the silver medal behind compatriot Anky van Grunsven (with another Dutch rider, Arjen Teeuwissen, coming 3rd) and the 2000 Olympics, where van Baalen finished 5th individually and was a member of the team that won silver.

Van Baalen's daughter, Marlies, is following in her mother's footsteps. She achieved early international success when helping the Dutch Young Riders team to second place at the Young Rider European Championships in 1999 and was a member of the Dutch team that came fourth in the 2004 Olympics in Athens.

**van Grunsven, Anky**   Born in 1968 in Erp, The Netherlands, van Grunsven first turned to dressage when she discovered that her horse *Prisco* did not like jumping. With *Prisco*, she quickly progressed through the Young Riders' events to a place on the Dutch adult team, representing her country, aged twenty, at the Seoul Olympics in 1988. With another horse, *Bonfire*, she went on to compete at three Olympic Games: in 1992 at Barcelona she was 4th individually and won team silver; in 1996 at Atlanta she won

Anky van Grunsven riding *Bonfire* in extended canter. Photograph by Elizabeth Furth.

both individual and team silver and at Sydney in 2000 she won individual gold and team silver. During the same period, she competed at four World Championships (1990 Stockholm, 1994 The Hague, 1998 Rome and 2002 Jerez), winning one individual gold and one individual and two team silver medals, and at five European Championships, winning one individual gold medal, two individual and three team silver medals and one team bronze. She has also competed in eleven World Cups, first winning the Kür in 1995 at Los Angeles and going on to win the event in 1996, 1997, 1999, 2000, 2004 and

2005. Having rounded off a magnificent career, *Bonfire* was retired after the Sydney Olympics, but van Grunsven went on to win the individual gold medal again in 2004 with *Salinero*. In May 2005, she married her trainer, Sjef Janssen.

Dr van Schaik riding at his New England home. Photograph from *Misconceptions and Simple Truths in Dressage.*

**van Schaik, Dr H.L.M.** (1899–1991) Born in Holland, Dr van Schaik began his riding career as a showjumper. In this discipline, he represented his country many times with conspicuous success: in 1936 he was a member of the team that won silver at the Berlin Olympics. Gradually, however, his interest turned more and more towards dressage.

After the Second World War, he settled in the USA, where he opened a riding academy in Vermont and became highly respected as a rider, trainer and judge. Throughout the 1960s, 70s and 80s, he was one of a number of riders from the classical mould who were increasingly concerned that competition dressage was departing from classical principles. His book *Misconceptions and Simple Truths in Dressage* has its roots in articles he wrote to try to reverse that trend.

**Vendeuil, Antoine de**   Director, in the early years of the eighteenth century, of the Riding Academy of Paris, and the teacher of de la Guérinière.

**Versailles**   See **School of Versailles**.

**vertical**   Sometimes interchanged with perpendicular when referring to the angulation of the horse's face. It is considered incorrect in most circumstances for the horse's head to drop behind the vertical (see that entry) and low and round.

Vertical also describes the upper body posture of the rider that is normally desirable in the dressage rider. When riding in the light seat, or when performing rising or posting trot, the upper body may be inclined a little in front of the vertical; in some circumstances, certain seat and back aids may result in the upper body inclining slightly behind the vertical, but this posture should be temporary and not protracted.

**vice**  An undesirable ingrained activity that is likely to cause a horse harm, or to render him a danger to other horses, handlers, or riders. Stable vices such as crib-biting and wind-sucking can have a negative impact on a horse's training under saddle, since they increase the risk of digestive disorders, may cause problems with the teeth and promote inappropriate development of the neck muscles, while marked weaving and box-walking can promote excessive wear to the limbs. The vices most likely to have a direct effect upon the horse's training under saddle are bucking, rearing and napping. However, in crowded practice areas competitors riding in should also take great care if their horse has a tendency to kick out at other horses, and should also give a wide berth to any other horse who exhibits that tendency.

**voice, use of**  Although it is a natural form of communication, use of the voice (which includes sounds such as clicking with the tongue) is not permitted in tests under FEI rules or those of affiliated bodies. Slight differences in wording between the various rules allow the possibility of different interpretations in the application of penalties. For example, whereas the AHSA rules state that the penalty involves 'the deduction of at least two marks from those that would otherwise have been awarded for (each) movement where this occurred', the British Dressage rule reads 'the use of the voice will be penalised by the loss of two marks from those that would have been awarded for the movement in which this occurred'. Where more than one judge is officiating, there does not have to be unanimity in penalizing use of the voice: only the judges, or judges, hearing it will penalize it.

**volte**  A term which has had different meanings in different languages and times. As used in current international dressage rules, it means a circle of 6 m, 8 m or 10 m diameter. This modern definition is very close to the original meaning as described by de la Guérinière in *Ecole de Cavalerie*: 'The word *volte* is an Italian expression signifying *circle* or *circular track*. It should be remarked that in Italy this term designates the circle traced by a horse moving on a single track…' However, the writer goes on to explain: '…in

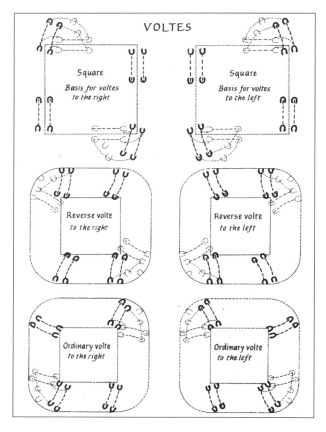

VOLTES

Square

*Basis for voltes to the right*

Square

*Basis for voltes to the left*

Reverse volte
to the right

Reverse volte
to the left

Ordinary volte
to the right

Ordinary volte
to the left

Diagrams of various voltes, from de la Guérinière's *Ecole de Cavalerie*.

France the word volte signifies a movement on two tracks, the horse forming thereby two concentric circles, or a square with rounded corners.' (He goes on to mention that the Italians call this exercise radoppio – see the terre-à-terre form of this figure under **redopp**.) Later, de la Guérinière expands on the 'French' form, explaining that it was originally a mounted combat movement (in which the circular form was used) but: '...subsequently this practice became part of the School to train the hindquarters and show the adroitness of horse and rider.' (This form being based on the square with corners rounded by virtue of quarter-turns on the haunches.)

Whether the term is being used in its original (Italian) and modern meaning, or in de la Guérinière's French form, depends largely upon which school the user subscribes to, but can usually be determined from the context. To avoid any possible confusion, those using the 'two-track' terminology will often identify the fact by using a phrase such as renvers-volte.

**von Blixen-Finecke, Baron Hans**  Born into the Swedish aristocracy in 1917, the son of the dressage bronze medallist of the 1912 Olympics, von Blixen-Finecke spent the first forty-eight years of his life in Sweden. He joined the Swedish Army as a cavalry officer in 1937 and, having achieved high honours, was Commandant of the famous Swedish Military Equestrian Centre at Stromsholm from 1959 until his retirement in 1964. His time as an officer was punctuated by numerous equestrian activities and achievements.

He was Swedish Amateur Steeplechase Champion in 1943 and 1944, Swedish National Three-Day Event Champion eight times between 1946 and 1955 and the Scandinavian Three-Day Event Champion in 1947 and 1949. He also won individual and team gold medals in eventing at the 1952 Helsinki Olympics, but was particularly proud of the fact that the horse he had trained, *Master Rufus,* also won the Olympic gold medal for dressage that year, ridden by Henri St Cyr.

His first wife having died, von Blixen-Finecke married an English lady in 1959 and, following his retirement, moved to England, where he ran establishments in Surrey and the West Country. One of his pupils at the latter establishment was Christopher Bartle who, like his teacher, achieved success in racing, eventing and dressage.

**von der Au, Pinter**   German rider, active in the seventeenth century, who was one of the first (in his book *Horse Treasury,* 1688) to advocate the rider's seat being positioned fully on the seat bones.

**von Holbein, H.E.**   Director of the Spanish Riding School from 1898 to 1901; published the *Directives* upon which the philosophy and practices of the School remain based.

**von Josipovich, Sigmund**   (1869– 1945) Austro-Hungarian cavalry general considered by his contemporaries to have had a true genius for teaching. He worked with von Heydebreck as an instructor at the Kaiserliche und Königliche Reitlehrer Institut (the Riding Instructors' Institute of Vienna) prior to 1914. After the First World War, he became chief instructor at the Hungarian military riding school. One of his most illustrious pupils was Waldemar Seunig; another notable pupil, Bertalan de Nemethy, later became Olympic coach to the American showjumping team.

Sigmund von Josipovich. Photograph from Charles de Kunffy's *Dressage Principles Illuminated.*

**von Langen, C.F.F.**   German winner of the individual gold medal at the 1928 Olympic Games in Amsterdam, riding *Draufgänger*. That same year, he was also a member of the German team that won the team gold medal in the inaugural team competition.

**von Linder, Gen. Ernst**   Swedish winner of the individual gold medal at the 1924 Olympic Games in Paris, riding *Piccolmini*.

**von Löhneysen, Baron George Engelhard**   A sixteenth-century German nobleman, originally influenced by Grisone, and a pupil of Pignatelli, Löhneysen introduced a modified form of their methods into Germany; his work *The Newly Opened Court Military and Riding School* appeared in 1588.

Egon von Neindorff. Photograph from Dr van Schaik's *Misconceptions and Simple Truths in Dressage*.

**von Neindorff, Egon**   (1923–2004) Born in Saxony, the son of a cavalry officer, von Neindorff was taught from an early age by some of the best cavalry instructors, and also rode his father's horses. After the Second World War, he studied with Oberbereiter Zeiner of the Spanish Riding School and also worked with Richard Wätjen. Imbued with the finest principles of classical equitation, von Neindorff established his own riding institute in Karlsruhe, from where, for half a century, he passed on his knowledge and philosophy to numerous pupils, including Erik Herbermann. In 1994, von Neindorff was accorded the title *Reitmeister* by the German Federation, and he was also awarded the German Golden Rider Cross.

**von Oeynhausen, Baron**   From an aristocratic German family, Oeynhausen received training at various German riding schools and was, for many years, instructor and second-in-command of the Military Equitation School in Salzburg. Between 1850 and 1869 he published several books, in one of which he stated that it had been his object to

252

collect and pass on any principles that might be useful in the training of horses. To this end, his own work quotes extensively from other writers, in particular Weyrother, which is interesting in the context of the time, since there is apparently no firm evidence that he was ever Weyrother's pupil.

**von Weyrother, Maximillian Ritter**
The most outstanding member of a family of talented riders, Weyrother arrived at the Spanish Riding School in 1813 and was made head rider in 1825. A devotee of the methods of de la Guérinière, he had a great influence on the school and his reputation spread far beyond the Austrian borders. After his death in 1833, some friends published a book containing extracts from his papers, and this contains many of

Maximillan Ritter von Weyrother, from an old engraving.

the principles upon which the Spanish Riding School has operated since his day. One of his most illustrious pupils was Louis Seeger; who was influenced by Weyrother to the extent that his own book, *System of the Art of Riding*, contains complete sentences from Weyrother's extracts.

**Wahl, Georg**   Born in 1920, Wahl joined the Spanish Riding School in 1938 and (apart from a period as a prisoner of war post-1944), worked there as a bereiter and then oberbereiter until 1951. He then moved to Switzerland, where he became an independent dressage trainer, his most notable student being World and Olympic Champion, Christine Stückelberger.

**waiting list**    A sequenced list of entries balloted out (see **balloting**) of a class or competition that is over-subscribed. Those on the list may have the chance to take the place of competitors whose initial entry was accepted, should the latter withdraw. Under British Dressage rules, it is the responsibility of those on the waiting list to check whether they have been given a place; any competitor who does not wish to be placed on a waiting list should stipulate the fact at the time of entry.

**walk**    A four-time lateral gait in which the sequence of footfall is one hind leg; the foreleg on the same side; the other hind leg; the foreleg on the same side. The individual steps should be the same length and footfalls should occur in an even 1.2.3.4 rhythm.

Medium, collected and extended walk. Drawings by Gisela Holstein.

**wandering**    Said of a horse who does not move consistently along the line required, but makes minor deviations without obvious motive. Often seen in young horses who lack strength and have not yet learned to balance themselves consistently under the rider's weight; may also be a product of bad ground, tiredness or inattention in the horse, or lack of direction or poor balance on the part of the rider.

**Warendorf**    The German National Training Centre, located in the town of that name. In 1913, following the first Olympic Equestrian Games in Stockholm,  Kaiser Wilhelm initiated the foundation of the German Equestrian Olympic Committee (DOKR), of which Gustav Rau was the first Director. Following several changes of location, the DOKR finally established its headquarters in what was the German Military Riding and Driving School at Warendorf in 1950. In 1968, along with the other German equestrian organizations, the DOKR gave up its independence to join the newly established German National Equestrian Federation. Two years later, in a project linked to preparation for the 1972 Olympic Games in Munich, the German government and the North Rhine-Westphalian state began the construction of exemplary training premises at Warendorf. The centre continues to be supported by State funding; the German Home Office finances nearly 40 per cent of the yearly budget, the National Federation is responsible for 30 per cent and the balance is derived from boarding fees for horses and riders and donations from various sources.

Since the initial construction, the training grounds have been continuously enlarged. In addition to the dressage and lungeing arenas, there are extensive facilities for showjumping, driving and vaulting, a cross-country course and over 100 stables. Members of German National teams (especially junior teams) attend Warendorf regularly for clinics with the national coach, and many top riders visit, sometimes for extensive periods, to use the training facilities. Also a major competition venue, Warendorf is used for Federal Championships.

The Olympic Committee/National Federation, now so closely associated with Warendorf, are responsible for a number of functions that lie at the heart of dressage (and other equestrian sports) at national and international levels. These include selection and training of horses and riders, training judges, the appointment of national coaches, buying, or helping to finance costs of, top-class horses, and working on equestrian scientific projects.

**warm up**    A term used more or less synonymously with ride in and work in, although, by definition, it focuses on the warming (and suppling) of the muscles and related tissues. Asking a horse for strenuous work of any kind before he has warmed up runs the significant risk of physical damage: it will also be physiologically impossible at this stage for a horse to work to his optimum level.

**warning aid**    See **preparatory aid**.

**Wätjen, Richard**    (1891– 1966) Born into a prominent family in Hamburg, backing from his parents enabled Wätjen to embark upon a career devoted entirely to equitation – and he did not squander this privileged position. After studying at Trakehen and Graditz, both German government studs, and being taught by the pre-eminent rider and trainer, Oscar Stensbeck, he

Richard Wätjen riding *Burgsdorff*.

spent six years (1910–1916) as a pupil of the Spanish Riding School, then stayed on for a further six years as a guest amateur instructor and trainer.

In 1925, he moved to Berlin and began training horses and riders on a professional basis. He was involved in the preparation of the German riders who won team and individual gold medals at the 1936 Olympics and, post-war, while he continued to work with the German squad, the American military team also sent him a number of horses and riders for training. In 1952, he worked for eight months with the British eventing team prior to their participation in the Olympics. In 1957, he went to the Sunnyfield Farm centre in New York, where he trained a number of the top American riders of the day and, in 1963, he spent a short period as trainer for the United States Equestrian Team, before returning to Germany, where he died in 1966.

As a rider, Wätjen produced many horses of various breeds to the highest standards, and achieved international success competing in both dressage and showjumping, two of his best-known horses being *Burgsdorff* and *Wotan*. Many authorities regard him as being one of the most elegant riders of his era and photos of the author in his book *Dressage Riding* bear testament to this.

**way of going**   A general term referring to the overall impression made by a horse in movement; normally used in a positive context – 'has a nice way of going' – it signifies characteristics such as fluidity and elasticity of movement, willing obedience, etc.

**weight aid**   An aid produced by an intentional change in the disposition of the rider's weight. As a function of the automatic balancing mechanism common to most creatures, horses have an instinctive tendency to respond to changes in the weight distribution of the rider. Repeated training and association can serve to refine responses to these aids, as to other aids.

**Werth, Isabell**   Born in Rheinberg, Germany, in 1969, Werth became the most famous pupil of Uwe Schulten-Baumer (senior), whose yard was nearby. Among her many international triumphs, Werth enjoyed a remarkably enduring and successful partnership with *Gigolo*. At the 1992 Olympic Games in Barcelona, they won the individual silver medal and were members of the German team that won gold. They then went on to win individual and team gold at the 1996 Olympics in Atlanta and individual silver and team gold at the 2000 Olympics in Sydney. In addition to these Olympic triumphs, other major successes by this partnership included team gold at the 1989 European Championships and both individual and team gold at the same event in 1991, 1993, 1995 and 1997 and also at the World Championships in 1994 and 1998. Werth also won international medals on other horses, including the 1992 World Cup with *Fabienne*.

Isabell Werth and *Gigolo*. Photograph by Elizabeth Furth.

Following various personal changes, Werth left Schulten-Baumer's yard in 2001 and took a job in a marketing department, but she continues to be active in the field of dressage.

**whip**   An artificial aid, the use of which is to heighten response to the rider's leg aid when necessary, the overriding aim being to keep the horse responsive to light aids and prevent him from becoming dead to the leg. Whether or not a whip can be carried in a dressage test and, if so, its type and dimensions, will depend on the rules of the organizing body relevant to the specific class in question, however, doing so is permitted in many competitions (although not international competitions under FEI rules). There is no specific penalty for appropriate and judicious use of the whip – indeed, a judge may wonder why a rider carrying one does not use it if necessary – but any obvious need to do so may be taken into account when the judge is assessing factors such as impulsion and submission. If a whip is dropped during the test, it is not usually permitted to pick it up; abuse of the whip, in the form of harsh punishment, is not permitted and, in extreme cases, may result in elimination. See also **dressage whip**.

**Wilcox, Lisa**   American-born in 1966, Wilcox began her equestrian career as an event rider, turning to dressage when she met her first husband, German Grand Prix rider and trainer Jan Ebeling. In 1994, she travelled to Germany to train with Herbert Rehbein. Following divorce, she spent some time in Denmark, then returned to Germany. During the 1997 European Dressage Championships she was offered the chance to train and compete on three stallions (*Relevant, Rohdiamant* and *Friedensfuerst*) owned by Gundula Vorwerks. She was the first non-European to enter the top ten of the BCM FEI World Dressage Rider Rankings, winning numerous CDI three-star events in Europe and competing at the World Equestrian Games in Jerez 2002 for an individual 5th place and a team silver medal. She was subsequently a member of the American team that won team bronze at the 2004 Olympics.

**Windlassing**   A term of German origin; attempting to obtain inflexion of the horse's neck, or a yielding of the poll and jaw, by pulling the head and neck from side to side through overt movements of the rider's arms. This action slackens the muscles which should stabilize the horse's neck at the withers and promotes overbending of the neck both longitudinally and laterally.

**winging**   A term sometimes used in the USA for dishing.

**Winnett, John W.**   Born in Los Angeles in 1928, Winnett was educated in Paris, where he was introduced to riding in the French classical tradition by Victor Laurent, a retired officer from Saumur who had studied under the doctrine of L'Hotte. Winnett subsequently became interested in showjumping and became French Junior National Champion in 1945.

As a young adult, Winnett 'abandoned serious riding to pursue a career' in the Indian sub-continent, Europe and subsequently New York. This 'abandonment' did not prevent him from amateur race-riding, playing polo and representing the USA in the 1952 World Showjumping Championships.

Retiring early from a successful career, he turned his full concentration upon horses and went to Germany, to study with Reiner Klimke. In Germany, he was initially surprised to discover a very free-moving style of equitation which traced back to the teachings of de la Guérinière. Much influenced by these German methods, to which

John Winnett. Photograph from *Dressage as Art in Competition.*

he added a detailed study of equine biomechanics, Winnett achieved great success in competition dressage, becoming riding captain of the American team at the 1972 Olympics and continuing to represent his country at the highest levels throughout the 1970s and 1980s. His book, *Dressage as Art in Competition* addresses the practicalities of competing at the top level with horses of various physiques and temperaments, whilst stressing the need to adhere to the artistic precepts of the classical school.

**work in**   To ride the horse in preparatory exercises designed to warm and supple the muscles and engage the horse's attention, prior to the main work of the day. See also **ride in; warm up.**

**working**   One of the gait variants officially recognized by the FEI and other bodies that organize dressage competitions; it is applied to the trot and canter. The working gait is the first form developed during the schooling of young horses – essentially, it is the horse's natural gait enhanced to assist him to balance himself under the rider and to move forward in a reasonably active manner, with even steps and a good rhythm. In order to achieve these criteria, it is self-evident that the horse should show reasonable activity of the hindquarters, the beginnings of a rounded topline and an acceptance of the leg and hand aids. Once these basic requirements have been attained, the form is refined progressively, being used for much general work and exercise, and becoming the basis from which the other gait variants are developed. In terms of stride length, the working gait lies between the collected and medium forms, but in terms of progressive training, it precedes both.

**work in-hand**    See **in-hand**.

**wrong bend**    A term used generally to describe a serious error in the execution of circles or turns, in which whatever lateral inflexion is apparent in the horse is on the opposite side to the direction of turning. Usually rooted in misapplication of the rider's aids, it may be exacerbated by chronic crookedness or lack of balance in the horse, especially in canter.

**wrong lead**    Applies to the canter; to strike off inadvertently with the incorrect leading leg; it may be caused by rider error, communication breakdown between rider and horse, lack/loss of balance or disobedience, or, especially with partly schooled and one-sided horses, chronic crookedness.

Diagrams of wrong bend, from Ulrik Schramm's *The Undisciplined Horse.*

**Wynmalen, Henry**    (1889– 1964) One of the most influential figures in mid twentieth-century British equitation, Wynmalen was Dutch by birth and spent his early life in Holland, moving to England in 1927. An engineer by profession, Wynmalen's many interests included aviation and it was a flying accident, which left a legacy of back trouble, that resulted in him subsequently adopting a somewhat individualistic riding posture, but this did not prevent him from being a consummate all-round horseman.

His early years were devoted primarily to showjumping, cross-country riding and racing, and he was, for many years, MFH to the Woodland Hunt. Always concerned with the correct schooling of horses, and renowned for his quiet, patient methods, he became increasingly interested in classical dressage. In 1948 he won the British Dressage Championship and followed this with many other successes. His displays at the Royal Windsor Show, and the ease with which his 'dressage' horses performed across country, served to ignite a greater interest in dressage in Britain – an interest he helped to promote with no reduction in his enthusiasm for the other disciplines.

A highly successful breeder and exhibitor of show horses, and a respected judge and President of the Arab Horse Society, Wynmalen also served on the Executive Council of the BHS. Largely responsible for organizing the horse trials competition at the 1948 (London) Olympics, he played a major role in instigating one-day events and,

Henry Wynmalen. Photograph from *Equitation.*

for some years, served as President of the Jury at Badminton horse trials. His wrote several books, including *Equitation* and *Dressage A Study of the Finer Points of Riding*, which reflect his ability to combine classical precepts and a gift for analysis with a down-to-earth approach to his subject.

# X

**X**   The imaginary marker letter that identifies the geometric centre of the dressage arena.

**Xenophon**   (c. 430–354 BC) A Greek historian, philosopher and military commander, Xenophon wrote one of the earliest books on riding, which is now known as *The Art of Horsemanship*. While his book would not, nowadays, be considered of particular value in terms of its overall technical content, it is nevertheless the case that Xenophon had a sound grasp of many of the technical principles of equitation. What is more remarkable about his work is his humane understanding of equine psychology, which was rarely equalled anywhere until well into the Renaissance era. It is chiefly this characteristic, so far in advance of his time, that has earned him the respect of succeeding generations of riders.

# Y

**yield**   In equestrian terminology, has the meanings: to comply, be submissive, be soft and pliable. Thus, in leg-yielding, the horse does not stiffen against the rider's leg aid, but complies with its signal; when flexing at the poll and jaw, he is yielding to the request from the rider's hand. Alternatively, the rider can yield the aids (for example, see **yielding hand**) although, in this case, this is not usually in response to the horse's request, but is, in effect, an invitation to the horse.

**yielding hand**   A hand that intentionally softens the rein contact to encourage or allow the horse to stretch his neck or move forward or lengthen in response to the driving aids; the opposite effect to a taking hand.

**Young Horse Tests**   A series of tests designed for, and restricted to, young horses of a specific age (usually, four, five and six), as provided by certain national organizing bodies.

# Z

**zigzag**   A figure based upon half-pass with counter-changes of hand at prescribed points, performed about the centre line. When ridden at trot, the figure is usually defined by the distance travelled either side of the centre line, e.g. from the prescribed starting point the figure might be 3 m, 6 m, 6 m, 3 m, so that the first strides of half-pass take the horse 3 m to one side of the centre line, there is then a counter-change of hand, the next series of strides take the horse back over the centre line and 3 m to the other side (6 m in all), there is another counter-change of hand, another progression of 6 m in the other direction, a further counter-change of hand and then half-pass over 3 m back to the centre line. The figure should be symmetrical, with the same number of strides in each sequence of 3 m and 6 m respectively, and the same distance advanced forwards (in respect of the centre line). When ridden in canter, each counter-change of hand must be preceded by a flying change; in canter, the figure is usually defined by the number of strides in each segment, e.g. 4–8–8–4.

**Zrust , Wenzel** (1882–1940) Born in Bohemia, the son of the riding master to Archduke Friedrich, Zrust began his long career with the Spanish Riding School as a sixteen-year-old stable boy. Apart from a period of military service during the First World War (when he won a medal for bravery), Zrust served at the school for the whole of his adult life, becoming a bereiter in 1906 and being First Chief Rider from 1926 until the time of his death. One of Zrust's pupils, during the latter's early years at the school, was Alois Podhajsky, who described Zrust as being a teacher of infinite patience.

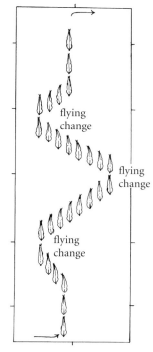

Canter zigzag 4–8–8–4

Diagram of canter zigzag, from John Winnett's *Dressage as Art in Competition.*

Wenzel Zrust riding levade. Photograph from Wilhelm Müseler's *Riding Logic.*